BUSINESS CONTINUITY AND HOMELAND SECURITY, VOLUME 1

The Homeland Security & Defense Business Council is a not-for-profit, non-partisan organization of the leading companies that bring homeland security/homeland defense solutions to the marketplace. The Council works to ensure that the perspective, innovation, expertise and capabilities of the private sector are fully utilized, recognized, respected and integrated with the public sector in our nation's security. It is the leading forum for homeland security senior executives in industry and government to substantively engage with one another.

Sponsorship of this series is part of the thought leadership initiatives of the Council and many of the authors in these volumes are representatives of the companies actively involved in the organization. This sponsorship, together with other Council programs and initiatives, including its year-long '9-10-11 Project' monograph series, serve to illustrate the role and responsibility of the private sector in working with the public sector in providing world class products, services and technology solutions for domestic and global homeland security challenges.

For more information on the Council, please visit www.homelandcouncil.org.

Business Continuity and Homeland Security, Volume 1

The Challenge of the New Age

Edited by

David H. McIntyre

Integrative Center for Homeland Security and the Bush School of Government and Public Service, Texas A&M University, USA

and

William I. Hancock

Integrative Center for Homeland Security, and the Bush School of Government and Public Service, Texas A&M University, USA

Edward Elgar
Cheltenham, UK • Northampton, MA, USA

Published by
Edward Elgar Publishing Limited
The Lypiatts
15 Lansdown Road
Cheltenham
Glos GL50 2JA
UK

Edward Elgar Publishing, Inc.
William Pratt House
9 Dewey Court
Northampton
Massachusetts 01060
USA

A catalogue record for this book
is available from the British Library

Library of Congress Control Number: 2007938020

ISBN 978 1 84720 250 5 (cased)

Typeset by Servis Filmsetting Ltd, Stockport, Cheshire
Printed and bound by MPG Books Group, UK

Contents

PART III   DISASTER STORIES WE CAN LEARN FROM

Contributors

Dean Alexander, JD, LLM, is Assistant Professor, Homeland Security and Director of the Homeland Security Research Program at Western Illinois University. His books include *Business Confronts Terrorism: Risks and Responses* (University of Wisconsin Press, 2004) and *Terrorism and Business: The Impact of September 11, 2001* (Transnational, 2002). Dean has served in executive, finance and in-counsel roles at companies in Chile, Great Britain, Israel and the United States. Dean has worked as a consultant to the State Department, World Bank, Organization of American States, homeland security firms and investment companies. He has lectured on homeland security, legal and business subjects at universities and conferences in the United States and internationally.

Fred Burton is one of the world's foremost authorities on security, terrorists and terrorist organizations. In his capacity as Vice-President for Counterterrorism and Corporate Security at Stratfor, Mr Burton oversees the terrorism intelligence service and consults with clients on security-related issues affecting their organizations or personal safety. He leads a team of terrorism experts and a global network of human intelligence sources to analyze and forecast the most significant events and trends related to terrorism and counterterrorism. Before joining Stratfor, he was a Special Agent in counterterrorism for the US Department of State, where he was instrumental in many high-profile operations. He orchestrated the arrest of Ramzi Yousef, mastermind of the first World Trade Center bombing, and investigated cases such as the assassination of Israeli Prime Minister Yitzhak Rabin, the killing of Rabbi Meir Kahane, the al Qaeda New York City bombing plots before 9/11, and the Libyan-backed terrorist attacks against diplomats in Sanaa and Khartoum. He has also served as the US liaison officer to several international security, intelligence and law enforcement agencies providing consulting on global intelligence and threat identification.

Bill Eggers is the Global Director for Deloitte Research – Public Sector, where he is responsible for research and thought leadership for Deloitte Touche Tomatsu. He is the author of an award-winning book on transforming government. He is the former Project Director of the Texas Performance Review/e-Texas initiative, and he was the Chair of the Government Reform Policy Committee for then Governor George W. Bush during his first presidential campaign. He is a former Senior Fellow at the Manhattan Institute for Policy Research, and he assisted reformers in Eastern Europe and the former Soviet Union with the transition from socialist to free-market economies while an analyst at the Heritage Foundation. Bill graduated *magna cum laude* from the University of California at San Diego.

Elin Gursky, ScD, is the Principal Deputy for Biodefense in the National Strategies Support Directorate of ANSER/Analytic Services (Arlington, VA) where she focuses on biodefense and health security issues. From 1986 to 1998, she held senior executive positions in local and state public health agencies in Maryland and New Jersey. In 1999 she accepted the position of Vice-President for Public Health for a ten-hospital acute care health system. She did a one-year fellowship at the Johns Hopkins Center for Civilian Biodefense Strategies. An epidemiologist, Dr Gursky received a Doctor of Science degree from the Johns Hopkins University Bloomberg School of Public Health. Dr Gursky has advised top officials from the Department of Homeland Security, Northern Command (NORTHCOM) and the Joint Task Force Civil Support on their interface with the civilian sector on issues pertaining to bioterrorism preparedness and response.

William I. Hancock is Adjunct Professor of Business and Homeland Security at Texas A&M University's Bush School of Government and Public Service. He has a Master of Arts degree in international relations from the University of Southern California, an Advanced Professional Certificate in international business from New York University, and a Bachelor of Science degree in engineering, national security and public affairs from the United States Military Academy at West Point. He teaches business courses at several undergraduate and MBA programs in New York and Connecticut. He is a business development consultant and has launched new technology products and services for more than 25 years.

Jason Jackson is the Director of Emergency Management for Wal-Mart Stores, Inc. This department is responsible for mitigation, preparing and planning for, and orchestration of the response and recovery efforts for all forms of business disruptions globally, to include natural and man-made disasters, security-related issues, significant epidemiological issues, and other emergencies. Prior to Wal-Mart, he was a Trooper/Special Agent for the Arkansas State Police and an Assistant Chief for the Sylvan Hills Fire Department. Jason holds an undergraduate degree in emergency administration and management from Arkansas Tech University and graduate degrees in both organizational and business security management and business administration (MBA) from Webster University, St Louis, Missouri.

Paul B. Kurtz is the Executive Director of the Cyber Security Industry Alliance. He served on the White House's National Security Council and Homeland Security Council, most recently as former Special Assistant to the President for Critical Infrastructure Protection. He contributed to President Bush's National Strategy to Secure Cyberspace, which was released in February 2003.

Peter Leitner is Chief Executive Officer and a senior Advisor to Waterford Advisors LLC, New York. His roles and responsibilities include serving public and private firms in their acquisition, alliance and other corporate development initiatives. He is a Certified Management Accountant (CMA). Peter has a Bachelor of Science degree from Ithaca College and an MBA from Lehigh University.

Kevin Lindsey is Special Counsel to the law firm of Halleland Lewis Nilan & Johnson, practicing with the Employment Law Group. Prior to joining Halleland, he worked for Target Corporation where he served as a senior counsel, providing employment counseling and litigation management. Prior to that, he was the Chief Operating Officer and General Counsel for Axis Incorporated, where he was responsible for risk management, health care, real estate, litigation and collective bargaining matters. He also served as a Commissioner for the Shakopee Mdewakanton Sioux Community Employment Commission and practiced for eight years as an attorney for Oppenheimer Wolff & Donnelly LLP in the firm's employment, product liability and business litigation groups. Vin graduated with high distinction from the University of Iowa College of Law in 1991 as President of the Law Review. He has served as an Adjunct Professor at William Mitchell College of Law and the University of Iowa College of Business.

David H. McIntyre, Director of the Integrative Center for Homeland Security at Texas A&M University and former SWOTT participant, is paving the way for the continued study of homeland security, a field of inquiry under the umbrella of security studies. His military, strategic, and academic experience have helped him apply security studies to the recent push for both an academic and a pragmatic understanding of homeland security. Dr McIntyre spent 30 years in the Army, serving in both strategic and educational capacities. Before spending six years advising the Army Chief of Staff and the Commander of US Forces in the Pacific on strategy, he served in airborne and reconnaissance units in the US and Germany. He taught English at West Point and Strategy at the National War College, where he served as Dean until 2001. In 1999 he developed the first graduate course on homeland security, and from 2001 to 2003 he served as the Deputy Director of the ANSER Institute for Homeland Security. Since then, he has taught graduate courses in strategy, terrorism and homeland security at the National Defense University, the George Washington University, the LBJ School at the University of Texas and the Bush School at Texas A&M.

Greg McNeal is Senior Fellow in Terrorism and Homeland Security and Assistant Director of the Institute for Global Security Law and Policy at the Case Western Reserve University School of Law. He helped to write a congressional bill that prohibits assistance to foreign entities and governments whose senior leadership includes members of terrorist organizations. Greg previously was a guest lecturer in the School of Public Affairs at American University. He was an officer in the US Army, and he earned a JD from the Case School of Law with honors in international law. He earned a Masters in public administration degree with distinction from American University and a degree in international relations from Lehigh University. Greg served as Executive Editor on the *Harvard Journal of Law and Public Policy*.

Michael Minor is Professor of Marketing and International Business at the University of Texas-Pan American. He is the co-author of textbooks on international business and consumer behavior, and is widely recognized for his writing on physiological influences on consumer behavior and expropriation. Michael has a PhD from Vanderbilt University and a BA from the University of North Carolina at Chapel Hill, and attended American University and Cornell University.

Greg Pellegrino serves as the Public Sectory Industry Leader for Deloitte Touche Tohmatsu. In 2002, he helped the newly created US Transportation Security Administration create an award winning e-government program for communications and information sharing. Greg currently is responsible for Deloitte's work with the US Department of Homeland Security and the firm's efforts in homeland security globally. He is the Chairman of the Board of Directors for the Washington-based Homeland Security and Defense Business Council representing the leading companies focused on helping achieve the vision for homeland security and promoting the role of the private sector in achieving the mission. He was the Co-Chair of the Privacy and Security Working Group for the national study on Homeland Security from the Citizens' Perspective sponsored by the Council for Excellence in Government.

Neal Saiff was formerly the Vice-President of Global Production Services at Lehman Brothers in New York, one of the world's largest and most successful financial services firms. In this position, he was responsible for the investment bank's complex telecommunications infrastructure headquartered in lower Manhattan, not far from the World Trade Center. Now an independent consultant, Neal is completing a degree in communications at Rutgers University.

Gad Selig is the Associate Dean, Business Development and Outreach, Graduate Studies and Research Division at the University of Bridgeport in Connecticut. He earned degrees from City, Columbia and Pace Universities in economics, engineering and business. He has authored three books and over 70 articles and conference proceedings. His best-selling book published in 2008 by Van Haren Publishing is called, *Implementing IT Governance: A Practical Guide to Global Best Practices in IT Management*. He recently co-authored his fourth book, *Implementing Strategic Sourcing: A Manager's Guide to World Class Best Practices*. published in May 2010 by Van Haren Publishing. He is a dynamic, popular and thought after speaker at industry conferences and corporate events in the US and abroad.

Dr Selig is Managing Partner and founder of GPS Group, Inc., a consulting, research and education firm that focuses on strategic marketing and growth, business and technology transformation, new product development, product management and innovation, IT strategy and governance, program/project management and strategic sourcing issues and opportunities. Select clients include Fortune 500 companies.

Dr Selig has more than years of diversified domestic/international executive, management and consulting experience with both Fortune 500 and smaller companies in the financial services, utility, telecommunications, software and high-technology, manufacturing and retail industries. His experience includes: marketing, sales, planning, operations, business development, mergers and acquisitions, general management (with full P&L responsibility), systems/network integration, strategic sourcing and outsourcing, MIS/CIO, electronic commerce, product development, project management, business process transformation, governance and entrepreneurship.

He has been a board member of Telco Research, BIS Group, Ltd and AGS. He is a member of the Academy of Management, Academy of Business Administration, and Society for Information Management (SIM), Project Management Institute (PMI), IAOP, ISACA and the Connecticut Technology Council. He holds a Top Secret Clearance with the Federal Government.

Ken Senser is Senior Vice-President, Global Security, Aviation and Travel for Wal-Mart Stores, Inc. Before joining Wal-Mart, Ken was the Assistant Director of the FBI for

Security. In this role, he established the first division at the FBI focused on security. His transformation of the FBI security program followed the espionage arrest of Special Agent Robert Hanssen. Ken also had responsibility for continuity of operations. Prior to his assignment to the FBI in 1999, Ken served for 16 years at the Central Intelligence Agency. His assignments encompassed physical, technical, protective and personnel security. While with the CIA, he received the Distinguished Career Intelligence Medal, as well as the Career Intelligence Medal, Intelligence Commendation Medal and many other awards and commendations. Ken received a Bachelor of Science degree in criminal justice from the University of Cincinnati.

Christopher Shays, in more than three decades of public service, has distinguished himself as a thoughtful and independent advocate for commonsense social and fiscal policy. He is Vice-Chairman of the Government Reform Committee, Chairman of its Subcommittee on National Security, Emerging Threats, and International Relations and is a member of the Homeland Security Committee. An expert on terrorism who has held more than 60 hearings on the terrorist threat, he devotes much of his time to improving the US nation's military, intelligence and homeland security operations through tough oversight and legislative reforms, such as implementing the 9/11 Commission recommendations.

Geoff Williams is a full-time freelance journalist based in Cincinnati, OH. He has been a frequent contributing writer to *Entrepreneur* magazine since 1998 and has also written numerous business articles for publications as diverse as the *Cincinnati Post* and *Small Business Success*, the flagship magazine for the Small Business Administration. He also has had his work published in a variety of publications, including *LIFE*, *Ladies' Home Journal*, *Entertainment Weekly*, *Writer's Digest*, *Archaeology Digest* and *National Geographic Kids*.

David Wyss is the Chief Economist at Standard & Poor's, based in New York. In this position, he is responsible for S&P's economic forecasts and publications, and co-authors the monthly *Economic Forecast* and the weekly *Financial Notes*. David joined Data Resources, Inc. in 1979 as an economist in the European Economic Service in London, which was acquired by McGraw-Hill. He came back to the USA in 1983 as Chief Financial Economist for DRI/McGraw-Hill, became Chief Economist for Standard & Poor's DRI in 1992, and Chief Economist for Standard & Poor's in 1999. Before joining DRI he was a Senior Staff Economist with the President's Council of Economic Advisers, Senior Economist at the Federal Reserve Board, and Economic Advisor to the Bank of England. David holds a BS from the Massachusetts Institute of Technology and a PhD in economics from Harvard University. David testifies regularly before Congress, is quoted regularly in the press, and has appeared on many major TV programs. He is currently on the economic advisory boards for SIMFA, FINRA and Harvard's Joint center for Housing Studies. He was named by *Treasury and Risk* magazine as one of 2009's '100 most influential people in finance'.

Foreword: the challenge of the new age
Christopher Shays

For over 70 years, freedom-loving nations were opposed by a bloc of countries whose governments prohibited individual liberty, democracy and free enterprise. The communist world became aggressive after World War II, eventually engulfing all of Eastern Europe, China, and countries like Cuba, North Korea and Vietnam. The United States led the free world in opposing the Marxist–Leninist ideology of socialist despotism, military expansion and oppression.

Today, free nations are faced with a new enemy just as determined and potentially as dangerous as the earlier communist menace. Make no mistake: terrorists do not want to change our system; they want to destroy our political and economic system, and our free way of life. The end of the communist monolith may not have been the 'end of history' as Francis Fukuyama put it, but it certainly ended a long period of relative peace, albeit terribly expensive in its consumption of human and natural resources.

The Cold War's fortunate demise opened a Pandora's box of nationalist, cultural and civilizational conflicts. Will the freedom-loving nations unite as we did in earlier decades to overcome this new danger? Will the United States assume its natural role as the moral, political and military leader of this multinational effort? For the sake of all Americans, our friends abroad, and for future generations, I believe we must take on this challenge.

Terrorism is not the only challenge in the new millennium. We began this century with frantic efforts to correct the shortsightedness of technical planners who failed to incorporate the necessities brought on by a simple change of numerical dates – the crisis we called Y2K. We did what we had to do, and we suffered little disruption to the computer and telecommunications systems that support our modern lives. Soon thereafter came the 'Tech Wreck', when the dot.com bubble burst and the 'new economy' of internet start-up companies came crashing to a near halt.

The stock market 'correction' in 2000 caused the evaporation of trillions of dollars of investment capital. However, our capitalist system again demonstrated its amazing fundamental resilience. A decade later we barely remembered the huge stock portfolio losses that at the time seemed to threaten our standard of living and the Baby Boomers' retirement prospects.

The 2000 stock market crash contributed to a worldwide recession beginning in 2001. For the first time since the end of World War II, global gross national product began to shrink. As the economy sickened, the worst enemy attack in US history occurred in our country's economic and political capitals.

On 11 September 2001, the unthinkable happened. Radical Islamist terrorists used our own technology to attack our iconic places of industry and government. Within days, President George W. Bush initiated the War on Terrorism, and we went abroad to root out their places of training and hiding. The War on Terrorism is an international effort that includes countries on every continent and people of every faith, including moderate Muslim societies who disavow the inhuman and ungodly mandates of Islamic jihadists.

Businesses today in America and abroad must help governments and their agencies at all levels to pursue the goals of homeland security. Managerial greed and fraud must give way to selflessness that complements the investor-driven goals of return-on-investment and short-term financial performance. As President Coolidge said, 'The business of America is business'. It was true then, and it is now. Without a strong economy, our country cannot be politically or militarily strong. Without strength we cannot be safe, and without safety we cannot be free.

In order to succeed in supporting our standard of living and way of life, businesses must continue to make and sell their products and services. Continuity of business operations is essential, and business continuity depends on the protection of both private assets and public infrastructure in an environment of credible and predictable homeland security. How do we do this? We must prioritize who and what we protect and how we allocate limited resources in this effort. Wherever we can, we must protect ourselves and our property from terrorism, natural disasters, catastrophic accidents and pandemics. This is a mutual responsibility – it's everyone's job. Everybody will benefit from our success, or we will all suffer from our failure.

We must be smarter than the enemy. We have to understand their motives, their capabilities, and how much they are willing to sacrifice in order to defeat us. It may sound strange to apply this logic to hurricanes and diseases, but we must use our superior analytical abilities to find creative solutions to all of the threats to business continuity and to homeland security at federal, state and local levels. This book brings together an outstanding group of expert thinkers from various fields to pool their expertise in pursuit of answers – answers to the critical problems of the new millennium. Intelligence, determination and cooperation are the keys to our success.

Preface
David H. McIntyre

Homeland security represents an unprecedented challenge to American business and the economic sinews of the Western World. Even individual businesses stand to be impacted in ways they do not expect and have never before experienced.

The problem is that while past wars and economic disturbances have affected the economic environment through trade, markets, the availability of resources and so forth, the new domestic threat could destroy the very ability of companies and economies to operate at all.

Terrorist attacks and massive natural catastrophes can disrupt or destroy production facilities, skilled workers, key leaders, capital worth, insurance support, business partners, essential suppliers, delivery systems, and even the all-important customer base. And the threat of widespread disaster can prompt burdensome government action (or over-reaction) that impacts business as much as an actual attack.

These challenges require new understanding of the new interconnected world, new ways of thinking about the business environment, and new concepts that envision security as a benefit provider, and not just a necessary cost. We must think of ways to make security pay, even as we better understand the risk of ignoring the problem, and the foolishness of thinking someone else will solve it for us.

But where do we start? The challenges seem overwhelming:

- How can an individual business mitigate the impact of a multi-billion dollar storm, or a massive earthquake?
- How can a business contribute to preventing attacks that may cascade to threaten its existence?
- How can business leaders protect their most precious assets from disruption and destruction?
- How should they respond – both as citizens and as corporate entities, with responsibilities and liabilities?
- And how can they recover as quickly as possible at the minimum cost – and maybe with additional benefits?

Well, we can start with the voice of experience. Today's American business leaders are not the first to face the danger of massive domestic disruption through natural or man-made disasters. Many global companies have been meeting this challenge for years, and have developed sophisticated systems and facilities to protect themselves. Many American business leaders dealt first hand with the challenge of the 9/11 attacks and the massive destruction of Hurricane Katrina. Some are stronger for the experience; some are not. All have lessons to learn if we will listen.

And all these experiences taken together suggest theories, backed by real-world experience, that we can use to shape our readiness and our success for the future. We can use these voices of experience to great benefit.

We ignore them at our peril.

Credits and acknowledgements

The editors wish to thank several individuals and organizations for their assistance in making this book possible. These are not in order of importance, as all of them contributed significantly to this challenge over a span of several years.

First we want to acknowledge the role of Texas A&M University's Bush School of Government and Public Service, where both of the editors teach homeland security in the graduate program. Much of the understanding of the emerging field covered in this book comes from our having also taught at the following educational institutions: the National War College, the United States Military Academy at West Point, and Monroe College. We would also like to thank our former business partners at the Anser Institute for Homeland Security and Numeria Incorporated.

Several individuals in particular made contributions without which this two-volume book would never have come into being. Dean Alexander contributed chapters based on his previous book, *Business Confronts Terrorism: Risks and Responses* (University of Wisconsin Press, 2004). Our wonderful young friend Geoff Williams in Cincinnati contributed a chapter about Neal Saiff's heroic actions on 9/11. Based on his demonstrated skills and readiness to help, we asked him to interview and write about Neal Saiff's heroic actions on 9/11. In addition, Geoff turned John Brady's briefing slides into a chapter about ConocoPhillips during Hurricane Katrina. Thank you, Geoff.

Some of the finest analysis in our book came from an earlier white paper developed by the brilliant staff at Deloitte, written by Greg Pellegrino and Bill Eggers. In addition, Bill provided us with a totally new article analyzing the need for improved networked government–private sector response during disasters like Katrina.

Ken Senser took time from his incredibly busy schedule as head of security at the world's largest corporation to write an excellent chapter for us. Jason Jackson joined Ken in creating this interesting case study. We met Ken while working with the government–private sector task force for homeland security convened by Business Executives for National Security in Washington, DC, at the request of the US Senate Majority Leader and the Speaker of the House of Representatives. Ken also allowed us to interview him on the program 'Homeland Security, Inside and Out' which is broadcast and streamed via the Internet each week by radio stations KAMU in the Southwest and WAMU in the Washington, DC area.

Fred Burton, Frank Rodman and Dr Michael Minor joined us along with others for a workshop at Texas A&M in College Station in the summer of 2005, in which we discussed many of the ideas that later we incorporated into our book. Experts who contributed previously written pieces included Kevin Lindsey and Paul Kurtz at the Cyber Security Industry Alliance. General and Chief of Staff of the US Army (Retired) Dennis Reimer, Dan Verton, Brent Woodworth at IBM Corporation, and Dr Robin Hanson.

The remainder of our book's contributors dedicated large chunks of their valuable time to create entirely new chapters for our book in areas of their special expertise. This they did with no compensation except the knowledge that others would benefit from their knowledge and seminal thinking in the field of business and homeland security. We deeply appreciate their effort which clearly was above and beyond the call of normal workplace demands.

Lest we forget those whose work must not go unsung, four people deserve special recognition for their exceptional organizational and administrative talents. Alan Sturmer at Edward Elgar Publishing first realized the potential for this book while visiting us in College Station, and he became our champion both inside and outside of his company. Heather Perkins at Edward Elgar took charge of the monumental task of editing a manuscript that grew much larger than expected and consistently ignored many of the editorial guidelines so kindly provided to us in the beginning. When the book was in danger of running aground on the authors' personal calendars, Marilyn Lewis stepped in and rescued it by completing the critical final editing process.

And finally, a gifted student at Monroe College proofread most of the book's manuscript. Germaine Mendez accomplished this thankless job with great success, after being given only the instructions, 'Please fix our formats, spelling, grammar, punctuation, and word choice. And while you're at it, correct the facts where necessary.' She did all of this and more. Thank you.

William I. Hancock
David H. McIntyre

Introduction to Volume 1

Who in business today doesn't want their firm to maintain continuity of operations? Who in modern America doesn't think that homeland security should provide the umbrella under which companies can do business safely and with the assurance of protection from harm by terrorists, natural disasters and other destructive forces? If these assumptions are commonly held, why does the controversy exist about the role of each party in the process? Why is business not sure about government's commitment to protecting the nation's critical infrastructure, the great majority of which is in private hands? Why is government often unable or unwilling to share with business leaders its assessments of threats and possible solutions to the dangers of destructive attacks, pandemics or hurricanes?

'Theory versus practice'. Is this where the answer lies to the questions asked above? As Einstein once said, 'In theory, theory and practice are the same. In practice, they are not.' We all know, however, that in practice theory and practice are often quite different. The devil's in the differences. Where you stand on an issue depends on where you sit. What is clear, from 'inside the beltway' in Washington, DC is not at all clear from a hazmat depot on I-80 in the central US. Companies have legitimate concerns about the increased cost of doing business that results from unfunded legislative mandates that put homeland security regulations into effect. The law of unintended consequences reigns supreme at federal agencies run by career government executives with little or no experience in the private sector.

What do we know for sure? First, serious threats to business continuity and homeland security are real and intertwined. Businesses have access to plenty of valuable incident data that may be relevant to terrorist plans, industrial vulnerabilities and disease outbreaks. Government agencies at all levels need this vital information in order to evaluate the nature and probability of the threats to our population, facilities and cultural monuments. In order to plan for the prevention and protection of their employees, assets and communities, businesses need to be aware of the government's threat assessments and how local, state and federal agencies plan to react to emergencies. Companies are usually prepared to help in any way possible, and this assistance in many cases could be significant. Unfortunately these offers often receive no response, due to government's failure to include companies and individual volunteers in its planning.

How do we facilitate the partnership between business and government, in order to prevent, protect against and mitigate the damage that results from a major calamity? To complete the Department of Homeland Security taxonomy, how do the two key players respond jointly to emergencies and work together to help communities recover from destruction and loss of life? The questions are large; the answers are vital to the survival of our society and our way of life.

Finally, business executives look at things differently from those in government. A business person wants to know the expected return on investment. This way of thinking actually supports the effort to invest in homeland security measures. Many of these expenditures have dual benefits, both in terms of improved security and in other ways. For instance, the cost of installing radio frequency identification (RFID) technology on shipping containers to prevent the entry of dangerous cargos into our country can be offset by the savings to shippers in avoiding the loss of merchandise due to theft and mis-routing. This demonstrates that business leaders and government managers have a great deal to learn from each other, both in culture and in practical applications.

PART I

BUSINESS IN DANGEROUS TIMES: THE NEW REALITY

CHAPTER 1   TERROR AND THE ECONOMY

David Wyss, Chief Economist at Standard & Poor's, leads off this section of the book with an overall analysis of direct and indirect impacts on the economy that result from terrorist attacks. He explains the 'four Ds': Destruction, Depression, Diversion and Deterrence. With the exception of the two World Trade Center bombings (1993 and 2001), the Pentagon attack and the Oklahoma city disaster, the US mainland has suffered few terrorist incidents. Hence, he examines other countries' histories of terrorism, which include the Basque problem in Spain, the Northern Irish separatists, and the Israel–Palestinian dispute. Terrorism moreover is not just a modern phenomenon, as his historical references illustrate. David Wyss puts dollar estimates on both the threat of terrorism and the actual costs of damages sustained.

CHAPTER 2   TERRORISM: A SHORT-TERM PHENOMENON?

Michael Minor, Professor of Marketing and International Business at the University of Texas-Pan American, takes a somewhat contrary view in discussing whether terrorism is here to stay or is merely another phase in the evolution of the global economy. He compares the current situation to earlier problems of expropriation and privatization, especially in Latin America. Many people agree with Samuel P. Huntington of Harvard who views terrorism as a long-term trend in his book *The Clash of Civilizations and the Remaking of World Order*. This view coincides with President George W. Bush's references to the multi-generational nature of the war we are now fighting. However, Michael Minor takes a more optimistic position that the war on terrorism may subside as times change. For instance, theological and cultural disagreements amongst Sunnis, Shias and Wahabis may refocus the target of Muslim extremists away from Western societies.

CHAPTER 3   BUSINESS CONTINUITY AND ENTERPRISE VALUE

Peter Leitner is the Chairman of Waterford Advisors and Chief Executive Officer (CEO) of the first organization that uses the power of marketplace pricing to determine the true value of privately owned corporations. In this chapter, he explores the relationship between business continuity and enterprise value, and he assesses the direct and indirect effects on companies of catastrophes such as pandemics, hurricanes and acts of terrorism. He provides an important insight that a business's value is not just its overall asset total, but a potentially much higher amount. However, terrorism and similar disasters can result in lowered corporate valuations and therefore reduced company capabilities to raise funds through equity and debt offerings, asset sales and business liquidations. True enterprise value is possibly the most vulnerable thing about business that is threatened by terrorism and other disasters. He analyzes the risks to a business's assets and compares them to those during the Cold War. Peter Leitner provides detailed recommendations on how business leaders can prepare their companies to endure disasters in order to maintain business continuity while preserving their assets.

CHAPTER 4   THE LEGAL IMPACT OF HOMELAND SECURITY ON BUSINESS

Greg McNeal teaches law at Case Western Reserve University and specializes in terrorism and homeland security. He explains in layman's terms the legal liabilities that businesses live with in the new age of terrorism and the impact of threats, terrorist incidents and homeland security programs on companies and our legal system. Greg McNeal encourages business to rely on government guidelines such as NFPA 1600 (the National Fire Protection Association's Disaster/Emergency Management and Business Continuity Programs) to avoid litigation. The role of federal and local government in setting standards for disaster preparedness will be covered in depth in later chapters.

CHAPTER 5   LEGAL LIABILITY WHEN BUSINESSES ARE UNPREPARED FOR DISASTERS

Kevin Lindsey is a lawyer and human resources consultant. This chapter, in its original version, first appeared as an article in the August 2006 issue of *HR Magazine* as 'Legal Trends: Crisis Alert'. It discusses the need for businesses to abide by the provisions of the Occupational Safety and Health Act (OSHA) to avoid culpability for negligence in protecting employees from physical and emotional harm. NFPA 1600 and relevant case law are also covered. Kevin Lindsay emphasizes the importance of company human resources managers taking an active leadership role in planning for and preventing workforce injuries resulting from terrorist attacks and other disasters.

CHAPTER 6   THE IMPACT OF THREATS AND CATASTROPHES ON CORPORATE GOVERNANCE

Gad Selig, Associate Dean, Business Development and Outreach, Graduate Studies and Research Division at the University of Bridgeport in Connecticut, has rendered a major service to our book's readers by explaining the impact of catastrophic occurrences on an area of new business emphasis: corporate governance. This chapter is an excellent primer about the new attention-demanding regulations that govern corporate actions. Precipitated by the accounting scandals of the late 1990s, the Financial Accounting Standards Board imposed greater transparency of corporate financial statements in order to protect investors through better information. Subsequently, the Sarbanes–Oxley Act (SOX) was passed and became the most important business legislation since the Securities Act of 1933. This new law puts the responsibility for accurate balance sheets, income statements and cash flow reports squarely on the shoulders of the CEO. 'SOX' became the new mantra for corporate leaders, similar to Y2K. When CEOs now talk about business continuity planning, they inevitably mention the impact of terrorism and other disasters on corporate governance.

1 Terror and the economy
David Wyss

We're at war . . . somebody's going to pay. (President George W. Bush, 9.45am, 11 September 2001, *9/11 Commission Report*, p. 39)

INTRODUCTION

When the President spoke these words to the Vice-President on that fateful morning, he no doubt was referring to the unknown attackers. His words, though, had another meaning. America would suffer told and untold losses from the horrific events of 9/11. Terror attacks have an impact on the overall economy as well as on individual companies and lives. Damage to property is usually far less important than damage to confidence and the increase in perceived risk. As companies concentrate on minimizing risk, they back away from investing in affected areas, moving instead to less risky locations. Consumers cut back spending on travel and entertainment; instead they concentrate on 'cocooning' with their families in the suburbs.

The costs of preventing terror also have an impact on the economy. Homeland security adds to government and private costs. The impact on gross domestic product (GDP) depends on whether the payments are by the private sector or the government, but this is an accounting issue. Someone must pay the costs.

Terrorism is an economic weapon as well as a political weapon. Attacks on critical facilities can affect bottleneck industries and thus the economy. Pure terror attacks, such as the one on the World Trade Center (WTC), will affect the economy indirectly through its effect on confidence and financial markets. Attacks on oil facilities in the Middle East have a direct impact on supplies and prices.

These factors came into play after the 11 September attacks in New York. The US economy was already near recession, but until 11 September, the decline was concentrated in the manufacturing sector, with most services remaining firm. The attack and the resulting pullback in travel spending turned a near recession into a full-fledged one – albeit still a relatively mild one. The major lesson of 9/11, however, was that the consumer recovered more quickly than many had expected after the attacks – but what if there had been another one?

Most of the evidence from other countries that have been afflicted with continuing terrorism – Spain with Basque separatists, the UK with Irish nationalists, and most dramatically Israel – suggests that advanced economies can continue to function despite significant terrorism. Only if the rule of law breaks down completely, as in some of the less-developed states, does the economy suffer severely. However, in all these cases the loss of life and property to terrorism was relatively small compared to the wealth and population of the country. Would the result be the same if the scale of the attacks becomes even greater?

Terrorism affects the economy through the 'four Ds': Destruction, Depression, Diversion and Deterrence. The destruction of physical capital is seldom a significant impact in developed nations, but it can be in developing countries, especially those dependent on material exports. Depression will affect demand, as consumers shift away from buying goods and businesses delay investing. Activity will be diverted to regions seen as safer from attack and to industries less directly affected. Deterring future attacks costs money and can reduce productivity, but is clearly cheaper than being an open target.

DESTRUCTION

The destruction of productive capacity, including human life, is the most spectacular impact of terrorism, but seldom the most economically important. In most cases, the destruction of productive capital is small, certainly relative to the economies of major industrial countries. Even 9/11, with the destruction of the two WTC towers and surrounding buildings, had only a tiny impact on the stock of capital in New York, much less the US. The disruption caused by the shutdown of the subway system in downtown New York was a temporary problem, lasting about two weeks. This caused the closure of the New York Stock Exchange (NYSE) and the American Stock Exchange (AMEX), as well as the New York Mercantile Exchange (NYMEX).

The loss of 3000 lives in the attacks was certainly a personal tragedy, but this is a tiny fraction of the US workforce. The loss of output was small relative to the US economy. The impact on those individuals not directly affected was small, and psychological more than financial.

In a smaller economy, the impact can be much greater. This is particularly true if much of the economy is tied to trade through a single port or pipeline. The vulnerability of these choke points can be critical, as has been shown by the ongoing insurrection in Iraq. If terrorists can close off these critical points, they can have a much bigger impact on the economy. This is more likely in oil states where the choke points are more critical.

DEPRESSION

Activity can be depressed by the trauma and uncertainty created by the attacks. Even though most Americans were not directly affected by the events of 9/11, the news reports caused a general fear. Spending dropped, most notably on travel because of fear of flying, but also on items such as entertainment because people felt that too much joy was somehow unseemly. The drop in spending on services turned what had already been a manufacturing downturn into an economy-wide recession.

Since I was one of the persons running out of the WTC after the attacks of 9/11, I was not surprised that people stopped spending out of fear. The attacks caused many people to change their lifestyles and perhaps convinced them that they might have more important goals than just making more money.

However, it takes money to change one's lifestyle, and the attacks did not lower spending very much. In fact, the saving rate actually dropped after the attacks (in part because of weaker income). Spending declined immediately, but the downturn did not last very long. By October, car sales were back, rising to a 20-year high, and by November, consumer spending was back to its pre-attack level. However, consumers may have been spending as much money as before, but they were spending it differently, as discussed in the following paragraphs.

The impact on investment was longer lasting. Businesses were frightened by the attacks and did not know what to do next. The result was that they did nothing. Capital spending dropped 9 percent in the year following the attacks, and did not recover to its 2000 level until 2005. Admittedly, some of the slowness was due to the collapse of the dot-com boom and the stock market scandals, but the recovery in capital spending and jobs was the slowest of any post-war expansion.

Models of the impact of 9/11 on US investment suggest that it cut capital spending by 0.2 percent of GDP (Becker and Murphy, 2001), or about 1.5 percent of investment spending. Although this impact is not large, it will cut long-term growth of productivity by about 0.1 percent, out of a 2.5 percent trend productivity growth. How permanent this impact is, remains to be seen, but recent evidence suggests that after five years the impact had largely disappeared, although investment may have been rechanneled to housing from non-residential construction.

A special issue for construction is the availability of insurance. It is impossible to get a mortgage on a building without adequate insurance in force, and in the wake of 9/11, insurance was unavailable because companies could not gauge the risk of future attacks. The government stepped in to reinsure for terrorist events, at least temporarily. The program ended in 2007, but any impact was dwarfed by the credit crisis that began that year.

DIVERSION

Terrorism can divert activity from one region or sector to another. A clear example was the sharp drop in tourism after the 9/11 attacks in the United States. Individuals were afraid to fly and cut back sharply. Restaurants suffered from a general 'cocooning' effect, as businesspersons seemed more eager to go home to the suburbs than to stay in the city. On the other hand, spending on housing and furniture rose, as people stayed at home more and focused on the home and family. The sharp drop in interest rates exacerbated this trend by encouraging home sales.

The diversion can also be regional. After 9/11, New York worried that financial firms would pull operations out of the city into the suburbs or more distant areas. In practice, that did not seem to occur, although the trend of putting backup facilities into the surrounding areas was accelerated. There was also a continuation of the trend to move to midtown instead of downtown, and to Brooklyn and Queens. Availability was part of the issue, given the loss of office space downtown, but the quest for more separation of space was also important.

One clear lesson of 9/11 was that backup facilities should not be too close to primary facilities. Several firms suffered because both primary and backup facilities were down because of the attack (including one software firm that had its backup in the other WTC tower, and one major bank whose backup computer was only a few blocks from its main computer and on the same telephone exchange). The loss of telephone service through-out lower Manhattan meant that computers were down over a wider area than had been anticipated in risk scenarios. Facilities are now being spread over a wider area, with backup facilities by preference in other states, not four blocks away. This trend has clear implications for regional development.

Consistent terrorist actions will divert investment from the affected region. This has occurred in many emerging economies, but even in industrial regions such as the Basque region of Spain and Northern Ireland, investment has fled to the rest of Spain and Great Britain. The degree of impact has varied with the severity and length of the attacks.

DETERRENCE

The deterrence of future terror attacks is also costly to an economy. Someone has to pay for the costs of extra guards and bear the costs of disruption necessitated by terror risks. Insurance requirements may make it necessary to expand security even more than a manager might think appropriate. The costs of 'hardening' new and existing buildings for terror attacks, including the giant concrete flowerpots now protecting most New York skyscrapers, have been borne by private owners. Other costs, such as stepped-up security at airports and ports, are borne by the government, and thus ultimately by taxpayers.

Government spending actually increases measured GDP. Government spending counts as output in the national economy, and thus if the guards are hired by the government, they are counted as additional output. On the other hand, if the guards are hired by a private manufacturer, they are counted as a cost of production and do not change the output of the firm. They thus reduce productivity rather than increase GDP.

Note that this distinction has nothing to do with reality. The guards are the same, and they cost the same. In the long run, the costs are paid for by the same people – the tax-payers and consumers – only the data are different.

The spending on security is a diversion of resources to protection from more produc-tive possibilities. It will thus reduce funds available for consumption and investment, which in turn reduces future growth. Government spending on homeland security is about $50 billion per year, or 0.4 percent of GDP, which comes out of consumer spend-ing and investment, depending how the spending is funded. In general, funding by increasing taxes has a larger impact on consumption, while funding through borrowing comes out of saving and affects the trade deficit and investment.

Increased government spending will increase demand and can, at least in part, pay for itself by raising the level of GDP. However, that argument only works if the economy is operating below potential. During the 2001 recession, the increased spending was not a burden on the economy, since there was plenty of potential GDP to use up because of the drop in demand. The early boost given to growth by government spending helped offset the weak private investment and drop in consumer spending, thus helping the economy out of recession. When the unemployment rate fell back under 5 percent, however, spending had to come out of other productive uses of labor.

THE TYPE OF RESOURCES MATTERS

The other issue for the economy is what resources need to be employed in the security programs. If the resources are scarce, they have a larger impact on the economy than if they are plentiful, or unemployed. Fortunately, most of the employment needs of the new programs are for relatively unskilled workers (as anyone who has gone through an airport inspection knows). Even the private employees are mostly building guards and other relatively low-skilled workers. The unemployment rate for these workers is relatively high, and thus their use for security takes less out of the production of other forms of GDP.

There are some obvious exceptions. The security of electronic communications is critical and at risk. Although so far most of the threats are more from hackers and crooks than from terrorists, maintenance of electronic security requires the use of highly skilled programmers. These people are in relatively scarce supply, and diverting them to security purposes means they are not developing the next generation of Web browsers or the newest video games.

Security is becoming more capital intensive as businesses and the government use scanners instead of people. Developing these devices requires high-tech engineers who are in short supply. The manufacturing capacity needed to produce the machines is also going to compete with other output.

As homeland security evolves into just another pork barrel for politicians to divide, it will be generic government spending and use pretty much average national resources. It will also become even less effective at protecting the country from terrorism. The recent allocation of funds by the Department of Homeland Security illustrates this, as funding was shifted from protecting obvious terror targets in New York and Washington to generic spending for new fire engines and police radios in Fort Wayne, Indiana and Memphis. The division of the spoils seems to have far more to do with ensuring that every representative (especially on the relevant committees) gets his or her share of the spending for his or her home district, rather than protecting the country, as we continue to leave our ports open to terror shipments and our borders open to terrorists. 'Political considerations played no part in the allocation process – none whatsoever', said George Foresman, Department of Homeland Security Under Secretary for Preparedness, after the announcement of the 2007 allocations (*NY Times*). I do not think the reporter believed him.

COSTS TO PRIVATE INDUSTRY

Security issues also create costs to private industry that are probably at least equal to government costs. Some of these are direct costs, such as the added costs of guards, added computer security and data backups. Others are indirect, but still monetary, such as higher insurance rates. A third set is indirect in the form of added shipping times, employee time spent waiting in lines at airports, and inconveniences to clients caused by the company's own security.

The direct costs are the easiest to analyze. Companies need more guards, they need more programmers and computers to cover electronic security needs. The costs are clear to the firm, and probably aggregate to about $20 billion per year (0.2 percent of GDP), although estimates vary widely.

The higher insurance rates and shipping fees are harder to assess, but so far, the costs do not seem high. The unchanging costs, however, may simply reflect the presence of the government reinsurance plan for commercial buildings. Although the subsidy has expired, the insurance costs have risen only modestly. Most of the recent insurance cost increases have been caused by the recent spate of hurricanes and concerns about global warming and its impact in terms of storm damage, not by terrorism. Any increase in shipping risk caused by terrorism has been overwhelmed by the enormous rise in energy prices.

The increased shipping and travel times have been a slight cost increase for firms, but not as much as we had feared in the immediate aftermath of 9/11. The airport security waits have been less than expected once the initial panic wore off, although it is still necessary to get to the airport further in advance of your flight than it was before 2001. Shipping times have not increased as much as expected, because port security has been less onerous than it was right after the attacks. In 2002, the Organization for Economic Co-operation and Development estimated that the extra trade security measures added about 2 percent to US import costs (about $10 billion). The current impact is probably even smaller in dollar terms, and much smaller as a share of trade. Our main worry is that port security is not onerous enough now.

COSTS OF NOT PREVENTING TERRORISM

Whatever the costs of combating terrorism, it is clearly cheaper than allowing future attacks. The problem, however, is that even the best security system is not absolutely impenetrable, and the US system is far from the best available. Evidence from countries that have had extended terror attacks shows that successful control of these attacks can add 0.5 to 1 percentage point to the share of investment in GDP, and raise economic growth by 0.5 to 1.25 percentage points.

The costs of security are thus significant, but the costs of not having security are far greater. Estimates of the total costs of the 9/11 attacks to the US economy exceed $300 billion, and if the military efforts in Afghanistan and Iraq are included, perhaps four times that. Security is cheap relative to the alternative.

EVIDENCE FROM THE PAST

Terrorism is not new. Terror has been a part of warfare since ancient times, and a part of normal existence perhaps forever. Violence against civilians goes back to the earliest days of history, including the Roman destruction of Carthage, the obliteration of entire cites by Genghis Khan and Tamurlane, atrocities by Germans and Japanese during World War II, and the alleged gifts of smallpox-infested blankets to the American Indians in the Western US.

In modern times, most of the violence against civilians has occurred during wartime, some of it sanctioned by the military and some carried out by individual soldiers in disregard of orders. However, there has also been the use of violence by revolutionary groups against authority, and by groups within society against other groups. The actions of the Red Brigades in Europe, the Irish nationalists in the UK, and the Ku Klux Klan in the United States are only a few examples. In most of these cases, however, the violence has been directed against a specific group within the society, and by persons who are members of the society. The political goals have been relatively clear – although not necessarily always rational. The only new development is the generalization of international violence by stateless entities, and the scale of the violence.

The countries that have endured extended periods of terrorism have usually been the victims of semi-organized resistance movements within the country. These attacks, such as the Irish Republican Army (IRA) in Britain or the Euzkadi ta Azkatasuna (ETA) in Spain, have often focused on clear regional issues, often with at least some international sympathy for the cause. Seldom did the terror group focus on loss of life; rather, the aim was maximum press exposure with minimum deaths, which were usually seen as counterproductive.

The impact of these attacks on economic growth seems to have been small. British growth in the early 1980s, when I was living in London, seemed unaffected by the IRA bombings. Although there may have been some reduction in visits to the likeliest targets, most tourists were undeterred. Personally, although I was actually close enough to one bomb to hear it explode, I did not change my behavior.

Spain provides a better example, since the terrorism was regional and thus there is a clear control region with which to compare performance. Studies suggest that after 15 years of ETA attacks, the Basque region lost an average of about 10 percent on the level of regional production. The impact was significant, but not overwhelming. Some of that growth was probably redirected toward the rest of Spain.

LESSONS FOR THE FUTURE

Individuals and economies recover quickly from terror attacks. I was back at work in Lower Manhattan within two weeks of running out of the WTC after the first plane hit. (Given what is now known about toxins in the air, that was probably too soon for my own good.) The city never shut down, although the stock exchange was out of action for about ten days. Spending patterns were altered – I stopped flying for a few months – but any money I saved on travel went into other purchases (such as a new car so I could get out of town more quickly). The impact of terror attacks on the overall economy is limited, and appears to diminish with multiple attacks.

CONCLUSION

What is clear is that the individual firm cannot rely on the government to prevent terrorism, but must develop plans for dealing with the aftermath. Adequate security helps, but could any of the firms in the WTC have done anything to prevent 9/11? What they could have done is to provide adequate recovery plans for disaster – whether natural or man-made. Those firms that survived, did.

BIBLIOGRAPHY

Abadie, Alberto and Javier Gardeazabal. 'The Economic Costs of Conflict: A Case Control Study for the Basque Country.' National Bureau of Economic Research, Working Paper No. 8478. September 2001. Pp 1 – 32.

Barros, Carlos P., Guglielmo Maria Caporale and Luis A. Gil-Alana. 'ETA Terrorism: Police Action, Political Measures and the Influence of Violence on Economic Activity in the Basque Country.' February 2006. Pp 1 – 27.

Becker, G.S. and K. Murphy 'Prosperity Will Rise Out of the Ashes.' *Wall Street Journal*, October 29 2001.

Blomberg, S. Brock, Gregory D. Hess and Athanasios Orphanides. 'The Macroeconomic Consequences of Terrorism.' CESIFO Working Paper No. 1151. March 2004. Pp 1 – 38.

Bram, Jason, Andrew Haughwout and James Orr. 'Has September 11 Affected New York City's Growth Potential?' *FRBNY Economic Policy Review*. November 2002. Pp 81 – 96.

Brown, Jeffrey R., J. David Cummins, Christopher M. Lewis and Ran Wei. 'An Empirical Analysis of the Economic Impact of Federal Terrorism Reinsurance.' November 2003. Pp 1 – 57.

Chen, Andrew H. and Thomas F. Siems. 'The Effects of Terrorism on Global Capital Markets.' *European Journal of Political Economy*. 2004. Vol. 20. Pp 349 – 366.

Drakos, Konstantinos and Ali M. Kutan. 'Regional Effects of Terrorism on Tourism: Evidence From Three Mediterranean Countries.' Center for European Integration Studies. 2001. Pp 1 – 43.

Enders, Walter and Todd Sandler. 'What do we Know About the Substitution Effect in Transnational Terrorism?' April 2002. Pp 1 – 25.

Fielding, David. 'Counting the Costs of Intifada: Consumption, Saving and Political Instability in Israel.' *Public Choice*. September 2003. Vol. 116, No. 3 – 4. Pp 297 – 314.

Fleischer, Aliza and Steven Buccola. 'War, Terror, and the Tourism Market in Israel.' *Applied Economics*. 2002. Pp 1335 – 1343.

Foresman, George, Department of Homeland Security press conference, May 31 2006, http://www.dhs.gov/xnews/releases/press_release_0922.shtm.

Frey, Bruno, Simon Luechinger and Alois Stutzer. 'Calculating Tragedy: Assessing the Costs of Terrorism.' CESIFO Working Paper No. 1341. November 2004. Pp 1 – 31.

Gupta, Sanjeev, Benedict Clemens, Rina Bhattacharya and Shamit Chakravarti. 'Fiscal Consequences of Armed Conflict and Terrorism in Low- and Middle-Income Countries.' International Monetary Fund, WP/02/142. August 2002. Pp 1 – 28.

Ito, Harumi and Darin Lee. 'Assessing the Impact of the September 11 Terrorist Attacks on U.S. Airline Demand.' February 2004. Pp 1 – 24.

Lakdawala, Darius and George Zanjani. 'Insurance Self-Protection, and the Economics of Terrorism.' National Bureau of Economic Research, Working Paper No. 9215. September 2002. Pp 1 – 26.

McKibbin, Warwick J. and Alexandra A. Sidorenko. 'Global Macroeconomic Consequences of Pandemic Influenza.' Lowy Institute for International Policy. February 2006. Pp 1 – 70.

Nitsch, Volker and Dieter Schumacher. 'Terrorism and Trade.' DIW Berlin: German Institute for Economic Research. June 2002. Pp 1 – 20.

Raby, Geoff. 'The Costs of Terrorism and the Benefits of Cooperating to Combat Terrorism.' Australian Government Department of Foreign Affairs and Trade. February 2003. Pp 1 – 11.

Sandler, Todd and Walter Enders. 'An Economic Perspective on Transnational Terrorism.' February 2002. Pp 1 – 37.

2 Terrorism: a short-term phenomenon?
Michael Minor

Fear not for the future, weep not for the past. (Percy Bysshe Shelley)

INTRODUCTION

In the heat of the moment, events can assume a larger-than-life quality and seem destined to change our lives, our country, perhaps even the world order, permanently. Arguably, when it comes to terrorism, we are still in the heat of the moment. Will terrorism permanently and fundamentally alter our political and economic landscape, and the way we do business? In this chapter I argue that two similar phenomena have occurred in the post-World War II period. Both of these phenomena turned out to be important but not breathtaking. I argue that, ultimately, we will find that terrorism's impact is similar – important but not profound.

When I was studying risk assessment some years ago, I learned that we can divide risks into two major categories (there is even a Society for Risk Analysis, believe it or not). First, there are huge or cataclysmic events that change many lives on a permanent basis. Luckily, these events, like the tsunami that hit Asia, do not happen very often. Then there are other negative events which occur frequently, but their effect is temporary or mild. There are many earthquakes, but thankfully only a few do more than jeopardize the family china.

I was asked to speak about the effect of terror on business to a conference at Texas A&M University. This was the Business, Terrorism and Homeland Security Workshop on 7 June 2005, and the Bush School of Government put it on. As I was thinking about what to say, I was drawn to doing two things. The first was to put the question of terror's impact in a historical or comparative context, and the second was to give my thoughts on whether terrorism belonged to the 'seldom happens, big impact' or the 'often happens, little impact' type of event.

We will take these questions separately. First, is there anything we can compare terrorism to – at least when we are discussing the effect of terrorism on business continuity? In fact, I think there are useful comparisons to be made. I am comparing terrorism to two earlier near-global phenomena – expropriations and privatizations – and if we use these phenomena for comparative purposes, we do not have to go too far back into history.

Each of these three phenomena (expropriation, privatization and terrorism) belongs mostly to the post-World War II period, although there are earlier examples. I will go through the reasons why we may be able to draw parallels.

THE WAVES OF BUSINESS UPHEAVAL

Here is a little background. Expropriation, formally the taking of a private holding by a government, has been a shattering experience for many people and businesses, for example during the founding of the Soviet Union in 1917, Mexico in 1936–38, China in the late 1940s and Cuba in 1959. Some 1705 multinational firms experienced forced divestiture in developing countries from 1960 to 1979 (Kobrin, 1982). Peru nationalized Belco Petroleum in 1985, and we shall see that there are continuing acts even today. For example, in 2006 Bolivia nationalized its natural energy resources. President Hugo Chavez in Venezuela has expropriated an abandoned valve factory as well as a paper mill. There may be a push in Brazil for the same thing to happen.

In the 1960s and 1970s, these expropriations frightened both businesses and home country governments. Although it is beyond our interests to examine the phenomenon exhaustively, basically this was a reaction by host country governments (often of smaller, poorer states) to the seeming ability of multinational corporations to invest as and where they wanted, send the profits home, and do relatively little in the way of improving the local economy in the process. Coupled with this, there was often a popular movement of protest which, though directed against the government, usually included the foreign multinationals, so the local government could hope to deflect criticism against itself toward the foreign companies.

In the 1960 and 1970s, expropriations spread through a substantial chunk of the developing world. In the early 1970s, perhaps as many as 30 countries were expropriating some foreign investment every year (see Figure 2.1). Every large business had to do some measure of contingency planning. What if they were taken over? What would happen? Were there any actions that businesses could take to help keep this from happening to them?

We will not concern ourselves with the specific actions businesses took, because after this very substantial wave of activity during these two decades the number of countries participating in expropriation fell off dramatically. In the 1980s there was very little

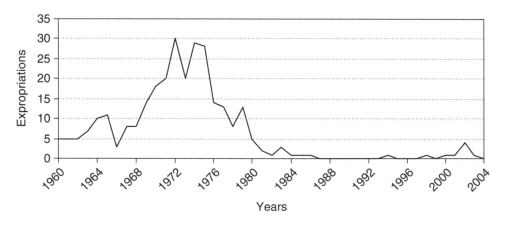

Source: Compiled from data supplied by Kobrin (1984), Minor (1994), and Coyle et al. (2005).

Figure 2.1   The number of countries expropriating 1960–2004

activity – a trend which has continued, more or less, to this day. Figure 2.1 shows the rise and then the decline in expropriation quite clearly.

PRIVATIZATION

Privatization (which peaked in the 1990s) excited businesses and governments. In many ways, privatization is the opposite of expropriation. In this case, governments – many in developing countries but also in the richer states – saw private business as the solution rather than the problem. In a nutshell, the idea was that businesses were likely to be better at generating jobs and profits than governments. Therefore, many businesses run by states at the time were turned over to private businesses, either via sale or, in some cases, virtual giveaways. (A German friend tells of being lobbied to take over an inefficient business in East Germany for virtually nothing except for the obligation to keep all those poorly trained employees at work, using out-of-date machinery.)

In both cases some businesses and industries (those that were expropriated or privatized) were deeply affected. Even businesses and governments which were not direct actors could analyze both phenomena and what their response should be. For example, Chile was an early privatizer and other Latin American governments could use the Chilean experience as a guide to what might happen if they took the privatization road. Recently I and my co-authors argued (Ramachandran et al., 2003) that there is a 'demonstration effect' operating and the privatization idea diffused across countries – much like a new product or fashion trend diffuses across a market. Stephen Kobrin (1985) made much the same argument about expropriation 20 years ago.

In this paper on privatization, we found that at least over the first decade or so of privatization activity, the number of countries expropriating continued to build although the rate of increase began to level off. By now, we would argue, many of the privatizations that could happen have already happened (Ramachandran et al., 2003).

EFFECTS OF EXPROPRIATION AND PRIVATIZATION

That is a skimpy background, I admit. What were the effects of these phenomena on the world in general? Did these phenomena profoundly change the world? In the case of expropriation, I think there was a somewhat negative effect on the world economy, as businesses, for fear of being expropriated, shifted their potential foreign investments to relatively 'expropriation-proof' markets or delayed investment opportunities and just stayed home. The effect was stronger, of course, in industries where there was significant expropriation. There is nothing like seeing a competitor booted out of a market to make a business weigh its options carefully.

In the case of privatizations, some countries got more than their 'usual share' of foreign investment as foreign businesses found good opportunities to make foreign acquisitions. Some investments that would have otherwise gone to country X went to country Y instead. However, it is also likely that somewhat more money from the rich countries was 'drawn out' to make these investments than would otherwise have been the case. Other foreign investments might have been made earlier than they would otherwise happened. So privatization has probably had a stimulating economic effect overall. Again, this effect was not spread evenly across either countries or industries.

To sum up, expropriation probably had a chilling effect on the world economy for a decade or two. Privatization has probably had a stimulating effect, and we are about halfway through the second decade of 'the privatization era'. We should expect that there will be additional privatization and a corresponding salutary – but generally not too critical – effect. Giving both of these phenomena their due, they probably changed investment strategies somewhat for a fairly large number of companies. There is some controversy about whether either phenomenon changed the lives of citizens for the better or not, but I suppose that means there is some consensus that there was an effect.

In retrospect, though, the amount of fundamental and permanent change in the world economy was not breathtaking. This is not to say that certain countries, industries or businesses were not profoundly affected – they were – but we are discussing a global impact (or lack thereof).

COMPARING TERRORISM

What about terrorism viewed from the perspective of having analyzed expropriation and privatization? My interpretation is that 20 years from now, terrorism will look very much like expropriation and privatization. What I mean is this. Terrorism will profoundly affect certain countries and certain businesses. It has already affected certain industries in a major way (the airlines come to mind). Major incidents such as 9/11 will have a depressing effect on the global economy and – I want to be very sensitive here – friends and relatives of victims will grieve for decades, even generations. This applies to Chechnya, India and the US – everywhere terrorism has left victims.

On an economic level, though, the global economy will generally continue to grow. This growth is not likely to be stopped – although it may be slowed – by terrorism, any more than expropriation stopped it (nor did privatization kick it into the stratosphere).

Some preliminary, admittedly scattered, but tantalizing studies show that this is the case. For example, one of my students (Dania, 2005) demonstrated that there was relatively little effect on portfolio investment in India as a result of the number of terrorist attacks there.

Similarly – and on a much larger and more general scale – another student (Coyle, 2006) showed that there did not seem to be any substantial effect on the US economy or, for that matter, on several economies in Asia as a result of terrorist incidents.

Neither of these studies is conclusive and both leave something to be desired from a methodological standpoint. Nonetheless, both point in the same direction and they are supported by the anecdotal information.

CONCLUSION

It should be noted that, despite my argument, it is always possible that there simply have not been enough incidents of terror for a cumulative effect to build that results in a crushing, permanent blow to an economy. Gladwell (2000) makes a persuasive argument that in fashion, ideas, even diseases, there is a 'tipping point' at which a phenomenon 'takes over'. Below that point, there is hardly a ripple. Above that point, a phenomenon takes off. He gives the example of the declining popularity of classic brushed-suede shoes called Hush Puppies, which suddenly became in vogue again. When a few people began wearing them, the shoes suddenly became hip in the clubs of downtown Manhattan and thereafter sales quadrupled. He also cites the declining crime rate in New York City, in which murders and total crimes plummeted during a five-year period. Like the few who started the shoe trend, it took a small number of people to change and influence behavior with dramatic results. Gladwell calls these 'epidemics in action'. My favorite example is the rise in suicides in Micronesia, which apparently grew from extremely rare to the highest per capita in the world, following the example of one boy who influenced an extremely popular gruesome activity.

Others have suggested that diseases are taken seriously only when the number of deaths reaches 30 000, or perhaps an analogy that makes more sense is that the US government defines a 'rare' disease as one that affects fewer than 200 000 people (Marcus, 2006). From this perspective, I may be correct, but only to a point: if and when terrorist incidents reach a tipping point, from that point forward businesses (and perhaps the economies in which they exist) will not exhibit the resilience shown thus far. Therefore, we ask if there is a tipping point. Unfortunately, the 'tipping point' argument is not really a good explanation, neither is it a useful predictor. We can only use it as an explanation after the fact.

In the meantime, we have to deal with the facts as they have thus far revealed themselves. So we have periods of anomalies where it seems that 'things have changed fundamentally' but, it turns out, the general upward economic trend remains more or less the same, and there are often signs that aggressive actions can have unforeseen consequences that call for caution. For example, two of the countries most affected by Bolivia's recent nationalization and its energy resources are not oil multinationals – but Brazil and Argentina. In fact, Brazil imports about 40 percent of its natural gas from Bolivia and is concerned about both security of supply and price. Bolivia's move has in fact caused a rift between Brazil, Argentina, Bolivia and Venezuela – the South American nations most opposed to the United States – and there are other signs as well. The costs of radicalization to moderate and somewhat secular Muslim countries like Indonesia, Bahrain or Egypt are becoming apparent in their economies. For instance, terrorism is discouraging the once flourishing tourism industries in Turkey, Egypt and Bali.[1] I think the experiences of expropriation and privatization can give us hope that the global economy is robust and will survive these more-chaotic periods. The forces of moderation will prevail in the end.

NOTE

1. I am grateful to Bill Hancock for this suggestion.

REFERENCES

Coyle, E. Thomas Jr. (2006), 'The impact of terrorism on East Asian business', working paper.
Coyle, E. Thomas Jr., Michael S. Minor and Laura Serviere (2005), 'Expropriation re-re-visited', working paper.

Dania, Akash (2005), 'Country risk and ADR volatility – diversification in the Indian Sub-Continent', working paper.
Gladwell, Malcolm (2000), 'The tipping point: how little things can make a big difference', Boston, MA: Little Brown.
Kobrin, Stephen (1982), 'Trends in forced divestment of foreign affiliates, 1960–1979', The United Nations Centre on Transnational Corporations Reporter, **13,** 13–38.
Kobrin, Stephen (1984), 'Expropriation as an attempt to control foreign firms in LDCs: trends from 1960–1979', *International Studies Quarterly*, **3** (September), 329–48.
Kobrin, Stephen (1985), 'Diffusion as an explanation of oil nationalization', *Journal of Conflict Resolution*, **29,** 3–32.
Marcus, Amy Dockser (2006), 'Common cause: a woman fights to unravel mystery of her rare disease', *Wall Street Journal*, (29 June), A1–A13.
Minor, Michael S. (1994), 'The demise of expropriation as an instrument of LDC policy, 1980–1992', *Journal of International Business Studies*, **25,** 1, 177–88.
Ramachandran, Mohan K., Michael S. Minor and Angela Hausman (2003), 'Globalization and the diffusion of policy ideas: or the domino effect rides yet again', working paper.

3 Business continuity and enterprise value

Peter Leitner

Chance favors the prepared mind. (Louis Pasteur, 1854)

INTRODUCTION

Most discussions on enterprise value focus on how to create it, while questions of business continuity usually pertain to bankruptcy and business failure. These discussions usually involve normal business conditions driven by competition, product innovation and management quality, which are heavily influenced by macroeconomic factors like growth, inflation and credit availability. They are, therefore, a normal part of a market economy and are generally well understood.

In this chapter, however, I focus on preserving enterprise value during abnormal conditions following an extreme event. An extreme event may be improbable in the short run, but more likely in the long run, and its effects are potentially catastrophic to the firm. By potentially catastrophic, I mean the firm might not continue as a going concern, and its surviving assets – if any – may be worthless. Examples of such extreme events include a global influenza pandemic, a Category 5 hurricane in an important commercial area and a major terrorist incident.

It is important to emphasize the double-barreled effects of an extreme event. Damage to personnel ranks, factories and office buildings, as well as communication and transportation infrastructure, can hamper a firm's ability to supply the market. But impaired business and consumer confidence can wreak havoc with demand from the market. In the extreme, panic can cause shortages of some products and services, while fears of inflation or deflation can be self-fulfilling prophesies that distort the economy far beyond the loss of production, distribution and communication capacity.[1] Most business leaders are unprepared for such an environment and its deep and lasting effects on their firms' enterprise value.

So, what is enterprise value and why is it important in the face of disaster? Simply stated, it is the perceived worth of a firm's assets, tangible and intangible. It is important because it is the glue that binds employees, vendors, customers and financiers together so that the firm can operate. If one or more of these essential players think the firm has lost value, they will distance themselves – perhaps completely – which can trigger a cascade of abandonment by the others, causing the firm's value to sink even faster. It is the commercial and industrial equivalent of a bank run. Preserving enterprise value is thus a matter of enterprise survival. Indeed, it is managing the ultimate corporate risk.

In this chapter, I shall examine the concept of enterprise value and its preservation, and consider how the modern firm is particularly vulnerable in the twenty-first century. But I shall begin with the role philosophy plays and its critical importance in preserving enterprise value before, during and after an extreme event.

19

PHILOSOPHY MATTERS: THE BOARD AND MANAGEMENT

Preserving enterprise value begins with the philosophy of its board of directors and its management team. By this I mean how seriously they take the risk and how deeply they understand the ramifications. However, despite directors' and officers' fiduciary duty to their shareholders, they all too often focus on the short run – with its pressing need to generate earnings – and too little on the long run.

This failure to take the long view, and to focus instead on the short run (when extreme events are less likely to occur) results from the relatively tranquil period of 1950–2000, which were the formative years of directors, officers and managers of most firms today. In other words, most current business leaders have lived charmed lives, spared from the searing experiences of war or plague, and the economic collapse that so often follows. Knowing only relatively good times, they lack the survival instincts – perhaps even the paranoia – about which former Intel chairman and chief executive officer (CEO) Andy Grove wrote and was widely quoted more than a decade ago.[2] This is in stark contrast to the previous generation of leaders, so let us consider what it was like 50 years ago through the lens of one firm.

Price Waterhouse & Co. (now PricewaterhouseCoopers), the public accounting firm, was a partnership led by veterans of World War I and staffed by veterans of World War II. Most had faced the horrors of war first hand and all lived through the privation of the Great Depression, which ruined the world economy between the two wars, and which most believed would resume when hostilities ceased in 1945. These considerable experiences expressed themselves in subtle but important ways in which the partners led the firm.

Consider the annual partner meeting, when they all met to discuss and make important decisions like expanding into new markets, distributing capital and electing new partners (this of course pre-dated conference calls, videoconferencing, webcams and Skype). Today such a meeting would be considered an opportunity to network and perhaps play a little golf, and at worst an inconvenience. But to the partners of Price Waterhouse it was a white-knuckled and serious affair: the entire leadership, the brain trust of the firm, would be together in one room. If anything were to happen to the building – explosion, fire, collapse – or to the city where they gathered – nuclear bomb, hurricane – the firm would be wiped out. Such risks did not stop them from meeting, but they prompted the partners to anticipate problems, plan around them and otherwise hedge as best they could.

This often meant meeting in second-tier cities less prone to catastrophic events like a nuclear attack, which was at the front of people's minds in the mid-1950s. Furthermore, it meant meeting only long enough to conduct their business before quickly dispersing. And no more than two partners were allowed to fly on the same aircraft to or from the meeting (or any other time, for that matter), to minimize the impact of their loss if their plane crashed.

Whether this describes accountants' paranoia or leadership wisdom is a matter of context. Like most people of that era, the partners and staff of Price Waterhouse were prudent and conservative realists (philosophically, not necessarily politically) who knew first hand that bad things happen, sometimes worse than imaginable, and that survival comes only from preparation, improvization and a dollop of good luck. They did not lose sleep over these risks, but they did not blithely ignore them, either. Today there is little of this philosophy in our boardrooms and executive suites, as few who lived through the two world wars and the global depression presently lead companies.

Many firms instead operate as if 9/11 was a one-time event; as if pandemic influenza will be felled by modern medicine; and Hurricane Katrina was more of a partisan brawl than a reminder that nature can overwhelm our ability to forecast storms, evacuate cities, rescue survivors and rebuild quickly. And despite these fresh memories, and expert warnings to expect more of the same, there is a profound lack of prudent and conservative realism. Yet this is essential to preserve enterprise value and ensure business continuity.

ENTERPRISE VALUE: CREATING AND DESTROYING IT UNDER NORMAL CONDITIONS

I previously defined enterprise value as the perceived worth of a firm's assets, both tangible and intangible. This is true, though oversimplified. A more formal definition is:

Enterprise Value = Debt + Shareholder Value

This formula expresses enterprise value from the liability and ownership side of the balance sheet, instead of the asset side, and is preferred because it reveals not only the assets' market value but also how they are financed. As such, it reminds us that debts must be repaid before shareholders receive their capital, and that there is a cost for the capital used to buy assets.

The cost of capital is the interest rate lenders require on borrowed funds, plus the rate of return shareholders require for risking their funds while investing in the firm's stock. Therefore, enterprise value is the total value of the firm, regardless of who provided the firm's capital and thus has a claim on the firm's assets.

In understanding enterprise value, however, it is important to realize that it bears little relation to the amount of funds stockholders and lenders provide to the firm. Indeed, enterprise value may be more or less than the total funds provided, reflecting instead the expectation of free cash flows generated by the assets in the future.

For example, a new firm raises $100 million from investors and lenders and uses $80 million of it to build a factory, buy raw material and acquire another small company, leaving $20 million in cash. The book value of its assets, therefore, is $100 million dollars. But if the company's prospects are considered very high, its enterprise value may be more – perhaps considerably more – than $100 million. This is because the firm's assets are expected to generate a perpetually growing stream of net cash flows that equate to a value greater than $100 million. Indeed, that is what every entrepreneur and investor hopes for, otherwise there would be no incentive to start the business and invest funds in the first place. However, sometimes a firm's prospects dim or its future cash flows are very uncertain; this means the firm may be worth less than what it invested in its assets, even though it paid $80 million for them and the rest is in cash.

We therefore estimate the enterprise value of a firm by summing its expected future cash flows, which are discounted by the firm's cost of capital, and then adding to this sum a final estimate of the firm's terminal value. In other words, the firm's value equals all of its risk-adjusted future cash flows. Let us now briefly examine how enterprise value is created or impaired under normal conditions.

To create enterprise value, the firm must generate more cash than it needs to pay for all of its costs to operate the business, as well as invest in and finance it. This is known as free cash flow, that is, the cash available to shareholders after all other cash requirements are satisfied. If a firm generates free cash flow consistently over time, its enterprise value will rise along a similar trajectory. This is why so many publicly traded firms are focused (some might say obsessed) with quarterly net income. If earnings per share increase at or above the market expectations, the share price will rise; if they do not, it will fall. Yet generating free cash flow consistently over time is very difficult to do because competition and innovation, as well as macroeconomic factors like inflation, require the firm to reinvent itself on a continuous basis.

Most firms struggle with this from time to time, almost surely generating negative cash flow and thus destroying enterprise value. This cannot continue indefinitely, though some firms operate like this for years with their enterprise value eroding like soil under steady rainfall, until bankruptcy is their only option. But this is the extreme. Most firms either fix their problems or merge with a stronger company.

In summary, and under normal business conditions, enterprise value is created when a firm uses its assets to generate more cash than it needs to pay for operating, investing in and financing the business; enterprise value is destroyed when it does not generate enough cash, usually due to the forces of competition, innovation and macroeconomics.

ENTERPRISE VALUE: DESTRUCTION IN ABNORMAL CONDITIONS

In the previous section, I examined how enterprise value is created or destroyed in normal business conditions, showing that it depends on how much free cash flow the firm is expected to generate in the future, both near-term and long-term, and that even though periods of value destruction are common, failure of the firm is unusual. Yet these are normal conditions, when business problems usually require years to develop and even more years to remedy. So let us consider how things differ in abnormal conditions following an extreme event.

EXTREME EVENTS AND GENERAL EFFECTS ON THE FIRM

1. Speed: the loss of enterprise value is nearly instantaneous, causing a chain reaction among and between employees, customers, vendors and financiers that will manifest itself as an unraveling of the social and financial bonds that normally tie them together. Many will lose confidence in the firm's survival and will cut their losses by abandoning it.
2. All alone: the damage from an extreme event will most likely affect other firms as well, in addition to communications and transportation infrastructure, so rescue and recovery resources – both private and public sector – will be in high demand, thinly spread, and thus of little help. Indeed, the armies of consultants, lawyers,

lenders and investors who normally work to save troubled firms, to say nothing of the bankruptcy court system, which provides an orderly legal process to sort out the problems of troubled firms, will be overwhelmed.

3. Beyond hope: the damage to the firm's operating assets, such as production capacity, infrastructure and workers, may be so great that recovery is simply impossible. For example, a firm that relies on one factory or concentrates its brain trust in one vulnerable location, if they are lost, will most likely be unable to continue as a going concern in the aftermath of an extreme event.

In sum, the damage will occur quickly, leaders should expect little help from the government or others, and the situation may be terminal. Leaders should also anticipate that extreme events will:

● cause large numbers of employees to abandon their jobs to remain with their families;
● render vendors unable to supply essential inventory and services on which firms depend on to operate; and
● force lenders, who will undoubtedly face financial catastrophe themselves, to demand immediate repayment of corporate debts and, if necessary, to exercise their rights to seize and liquidate assets.

In such an environment, whatever enterprise value that remains will be tenuous at best.

PRESERVATION THROUGH PREPARATION

Enterprise value can be preserved and business continuity assured only through preparation. This requires a commitment to a philosophy of prudent and conservative realism, followed by strong corporate governance and management, appropriate business planning, and realistic measurement of enterprise value and value-at-risk.

Strong Governance and Management

Preparation must be a cooperative effort between the board of directors, which represents the shareholders' interests, and the management team, whose fiduciary duty is to preserve and enhance value. Indeed, both leadership tiers share this duty to investors and other stakeholders, but it begins with a balanced, independent and seasoned board of directors. Yet at these levels of the organization, the risk to enterprise value is rarely well managed, or even known, especially in private firms.

A survey of senior financial officers (chief financial officers – CFOs, treasurers, controllers) in private middle-market firms, which represent the vast majority of companies in the US, revealed that most did not know their firm's enterprise value. Of those who said they did, the study showed that most relied on dubious sources of valuation information.[3] Therefore, the vast majority of our economy's top financial leaders neither know their firm's value nor how much of it is at risk.

Appropriate Business Planning

Strategic business planning for preserving enterprise value and ensuring business continuity – which must occur at the board and senior management level, not delegated downward – goes far beyond redundant information technology (IT) systems and insurance. Key areas for examination include the firm's business model, its capitalization and its supply chain. For example, with the board's assent management can:

- Transform the firm into a network model, with operations and personnel (including the management team) distributed across wide geographic areas to lessen the impact of an extreme event. This could also include favoring vendors and targeting markets that are similarly distributed so that concentration risk is mitigated.
- Capitalize the business so that it can withstand an instantaneous and sustained loss of enterprise value, which means using less debt and more equity than would be advisable under normal economic conditions.
- Accumulate inventory and essential conversion supplies so that the firm can continue to operate if its supply chain is temporarily interrupted. Indeed, firms' efficiency achievements in the past 30 years – such as reducing raw material and finished goods inventories from months- to hours-worth of supply on hand – may normally be a source of pride, but are counterproductive in survival conditions.
- Assume that traditional hedges like property and casualty insurance contracts and tradable derivatives may fail, along with insurers and trading counterparties themselves. Even under ideal conditions, such hedges require time for adjudication or clearing, and thus may provide too little liquidity, too late to save the firm.

By ensuring the firm has a more resilient business model – capitalization, supply chain and hedging strategy – its prospects for preserving enterprise value and ensuring business continuity are greatly enhanced. Yet there is also a new and very powerful tool that firms can use in addition to the steps suggested above and traditional strategic planning methods.

Prediction markets, known also as decision markets and information markets, can greatly enhance the ability of firms to anticipate, mitigate and recover from extreme events that have potentially catastrophic consequences. Generally speaking, they function like futures markets – not unlike markets for commodity futures – drawing their predictive power from a pool of many market participants, each of whom has some capital at risk. While still in their infancy, prediction markets can provide the board of directors, senior management and corporate risk-management personnel with a highly effective means of anticipating an extreme event and thus minimizing its effect on the firm. Depending on their specific design, these markets can:

- predict the likelihood that a specific event will occur;
- forecast the likely effects on the firm; and
- assess the likely success of the options available to the firm and from which management must choose.

Unlike insurance and related traditional risk management tools, which are usually static analyses based on estimates of probability and costs of such an event, prediction markets – like other free markets – dynamically consume and produce valuable information. The information these markets consume is the aggregate of all available information about a given subject (be it the future price of pork bellies or the likelihood of an avian flu pandemic). The information these markets produce is price changes that reflect new information about the given subject. Therefore, by pooling the knowledge of many people and providing a market mechanism they can use to act on individually, a highly accurate prediction emerges.

Realistic Measurement of Enterprise Value and Value-at-Risk

Once a firm makes enterprise value analysis a regular part of its planning and operating decisions, it should measure value-at-risk, or VaR. Traders of securities and commodities use VaR to forecast portfolio losses in specific circumstances, such as an interest rate hike or geopolitical event, and then hedge their positions accordingly. Securities analysts perform similar tests on publicly traded stocks, in essence measuring how much value an investor will lose if a firm encounters trouble.

The principle of VaR applies to commercial and industrial firms, too. One first measures the company's enterprise value and then uses probabilistic-driven scenarios to estimate how much value would be lost due to reductions in net cash flow and the cost and time needed to rebuild. Hedges are then identified, priced and acquired.

The role of VaR in preserving enterprise value during an extreme event is like a system stress test. How much of a shock to revenue, costs and cash flow can be withstood in scenarios that are perhaps unlikely in the short run but highly likely in the long run? Consider, for example, a company that manufactures industrial components and whose customers are other firms that are also based on Long Island, 50 miles east of New York City. The firm's enterprise value is $100 million, of which $60 million is debt borrowed from a local bank.

If a Category 5 hurricane hits the firm's headquarters and its nearby manufacturing plant, management estimates that at least $50 million of enterprise value will be destroyed (that is, its value-at-risk is $50 million). This is because its free cash flow will be deeply negative (not only from its inability to supply customers, but from their reduced demand, too) and it will take two years and $15 million to rebuild the lost plant.

Yet management's VaR analysis reveals a more troubling problem: this storm would shave off so much enterprise value that its lender would have the right to recall its loan, which would then be worth more than the entire firm. Management would effectively lose the firm, as the bank would control its assets and would move to sell them quickly to the highest bidder. What can management do to hedge its $50 million VaR due to a Category 5 hurricane? Here are four possible ways that mitigate risk and thus preserve enterprise value and ensure business continuity:

1. Use less debt. Since the damaged firm would be worth less than the debt it owes the bank and a Category 5 hurricane striking Long Island is considered highly probable, then the firm should replace some or all of its debt with equity capital. This removes the possibility that the bank will call its loan and force the liquidation of the firm.
2. Refinance the loan. Since the loan recall will be influenced by the bank's exposure to other businesses damaged by the storm, a firm that cannot replace debt with equity

should refinance its debt with a lender that has less exposure to Long Island businesses. They may be more patient if a Category 5 hurricane strikes the region, and less apt to call in the loan.

3. Move the operation. Since Long Island lies directly in the path of a likely hurricane and has little land mass to dissipate a storm's energy, the firm could move 50 miles north or west of Manhattan, to parts of Connecticut, New York State or New Jersey, where hurricanes are less devastating – yet the firm would easily reach its Long Island customer base.

4. Develop new markets. Using their existing product line, the firm could seek new customers well outside of Long Island to mitigate the damage to demand if a major storm strikes.

As this example shows, VaR reveals not only just how much value is at risk, but also secondary risks that may otherwise go unrecognized. It is therefore essential that possible primary risks are identified – severe weather, terrorist attack, pandemic – and secondary risks are understood and hedged as well.

IT'S DIFFERENT THIS TIME: ENTERPRISE VALUE IN THE TWENTY-FIRST CENTURY

The importance of managing enterprise value, as well as the risk to enterprise value, is rising. This is not only because experts forecast an increase in catastrophic events, but also because modern firms are more vulnerable if an extreme event occurs.

The rise in vulnerability stems from their nature: most new companies are knowledge-based – often comprised largely of brands, patents, alliances, contracts and other intellectual property, all of which are intangible assets. Even manufacturing companies – both old and new alike – rely on research and development, marketing alliances and outsourcing agreements, instead of being fully-integrated firms that comprise plant, property and equipment.

The significance of this evolution to a service and information economy is that firms whose assets are largely intangible will see their enterprise value evaporate almost instantly in a crisis. This is because the entire premise of a knowledge-based firm is the unique combination of employees, vendors, customers and financiers that magically yield cash flow from a proprietary pool of brands, patents and other intellectual property. The only tangible asset the firm may own is an office building or corporate campus, which is hardly enough to prop up impaired market value.

This is very different from the nineteenth and twentieth centuries, when corporate assets were nearly all tangible – inventory, plant, property and equipment. If a steel maker, for example, failed for economic reasons, such as inferior product quality, labor unrest or weak pricing, the business could completely stop operating and lie idle, but a fully-functioning steel mill would remain. This asset could then be sold to entrepreneurs who thought they could succeed in the steel business, but only because the core assets of the failed company were tangible, still functional and easily transferable.

Today, a knowledge-based firm may fail – for any reason – and one can buy its collection of brands and patents and other intellectual property, but it is nearly impossible to recreate the unique combination of relationships between employees, vendors, customers and financiers that once made those assets worth more than their book value. Those relationships evaporated either slowly, as the firm failed for economic reasons, or instantly, when it was affected by an extreme event. In either case, when trouble occurs knowledge-based firms often unravel before reorganization is possible, as the collapse of Arthur Anderson from the Enron scandal's collateral damage exemplifies.

We also recently witnessed the mass extinction of knowledge-based firms at the end of the 'dot-com' and telecom boom in 2000 and 2001, before 9/11, when legions of firms of all sizes quickly perished, leaving little behind even of liquidation value. We should thus expect a similar loss of enterprise value, including entire firms and perhaps an entire industry or two, in the wake of an extreme event.

CONCLUSION

In this chapter, I have examined the concept of enterprise value and its creation and destruction, under normal business conditions and following an extreme event. I have emphasized the importance of a board and management philosophy that is prudent, conservative and realist, and stressed the role of preparation – through strong governance and management, business planning and value-at-risk measurement – in preserving enterprise value and ensuring business continuity. Finally, I have emphasized the new-found vulnerability that knowledge-based firms face in the twenty-first century, given that they largely comprise intangible assets.

As the invisible glue which holds a company together, enterprise value has long been recognized by financiers as the best measure of its success. But a firm now bears risks that eclipse even the greatest competitive or macroeconomic threats: extreme events that can damage its enterprise value so quickly and irreversibly that the firm will fail. Managing enterprise value for business continuity is therefore managing the ultimate corporate risk.

NOTES

1. We may chuckle today about the shortage of duct tape in New York City following the anthrax attacks in 2001, or fume about gasoline priced at $3 per gallon, but most American business people are unaware of the economic effects that can follow an extreme event. For example, in Germany inflation was so high after World War I that some businesses paid their employees twice a day – at noon and again at day's end – because goods were scarce and their prices often rose several times each day.
2. Grove, Andrew (1996), *Only the Paranoid Survive,* Currency Books, New York, NY.
3. Waterford Advisors LLC (2006), 'Value and valuation: are private firms prepared for mission-critical decisions?', Princeton, NJ, January.

4 The legal impact of homeland security on business
Greg McNeal

Ignorance of the law excuses no man. (John Selden, English Statesman, 1584–1654)

INTRODUCTION

Homeland security means managing and preparing for emergencies. Similarly, businesses either prepare for the worst disasters or attacks, or suffer the consequences. This chapter seeks to evaluate the legal issues related to planning for, responding to and recovering from homeland security incidents.[1] The chapter provides this information in a manner which business leaders can act from and apply. Because each business circumstance is different, this chapter will not provide a comprehensive review of each possible incident. A comprehensive review can only come from a business engaging in the planning process. Instead, this chapter highlights and explains common issues so businesses can identify and further explore those issues with legal counsel.

OBLIGATIONS TO PREPARE FOR INCIDENTS

In preparing for homeland security incidents, business leaders owe a duty to their organizations to assess current levels of vulnerability, plan for emergencies and periodically review those plans. In the preparation phase business leaders are also responsible for ensuring that their organizations have in place the capacity to comply with legal and regulatory obligations related to their sectors. Following an incident, business leaders must focus on preventing loss, mitigating losses, and reducing legal liability if a loss occurs. Comprehensive incident-related planning that integrates legal counsel is the key to navigating potential liability flowing from a homeland security incident.

Potential Routes of Liability

It is nearly certain that businesses addressing or involved in homeland security incidents will face the potential of legal liability. Following the 1993 World Trade Center (WTC) bombing more than 175 civil lawsuits were filed.[2] These lawsuits sought damages from the attack totaling over $1.9 billion.[3] After the Centennial Park bombing lawsuits were filed against park operators for failure to provide adequate security. Most recently, following the attacks of 11 September 2001 (and despite a comprehensive victim compensation scheme), over 70 plaintiffs sued for injuries and property damage.[4]

Business liability resulting from homeland security incidents may arise under principles similar to some theories of landowner liability. These theories include a duty to maintain a safe workplace, voluntary assumption of duty, contract and negligence.[5]

Furthermore, businesses may be held liable to shareholders, vendors and others under an evolving theory of negligent failure to plan, which is an expanded theory of simple negligence.

The duty to maintain a safe workplace and to comply with regulations requiring preparation for terrorist attacks presents a series of questions. For example, in the industrial field most plants or refineries have considered the potential of an attack, and have written plans and implemented safeguards against terrorist attacks.[6] These response plans, while necessary to prepare, may constitute an admission of foreseeability.[7] To further illustrate, consider facilities that handle toxic chemicals and have a duty of assuring environmental safety 'akin to their "general duty" of maintaining a safe workplace for their workers'.[8] These facilities are specifically required to take measures to prevent releases.[9] In the event of a terrorist attack, the question arises whether courts 'will infer . . . a duty to plan for terrorist attacks as well?'[10]

Employers may also be held liable for failing to maintain a safe work place under the 'general duty clause' of the federal Occupational Safety and Health Act. 'The general duty clause requires employers to provide workers with a place of employment free from recognized hazards that cause or are likely to cause death or serious physical harm to employees. Over the past two decades, the Occupational Safety and Health Administration (OSHA) increasingly has relied on the general duty clause to impose potentially significant penalties and fines on employers [including a record fine of $20 million].'[11]

In other contexts plaintiffs have attempted to hold owners and operators of buildings responsible for the design, construction and maintenance of structures to 'withstand the spread of fire and to avoid collapses caused by fire'.[12] Building owners have been subjected to suits asserting that owners and operators 'should have designed and effectuated fire safety and evacuation procedures to provide for the safe escape of more people'.[13] These instances and differing methods of recovery highlight the requirement for a business to engage in thorough assessment, planning and review of its facilities and emergency action plans.

The tort concept of 'negligent failure to plan' is a new theory that expands the legal concept of simple negligence. While much has been written on the concept by risk planning consultants and lawyers, no scholarly attention has been dedicated to the concept by legal journals. There is no specific case law as of yet to support the doctrine in a homeland security incident context. Nonetheless, it is worthy of attention since many experts see another terrorist attack as a foreseeable occurrence for which businesses must prepare. Key to this legal concept is the fact that the assertion of negligence is not premised upon an allegation that the business failed to stop an attack or prevent an incident and its associated damage. The concept is instead negligence premised upon a failure to prepare the business to handle the incident with a minimal loss of life or property. Of course, if the method of attack was foreseeable, such a suit might prevail on the basis of a failure by the business to put in reasonable measures to prevent the attack. Depending upon the nature of the foreseeable threat, such reasonable measures could include barricades to prevent vehicle-based explosives, or metal detectors to prevent weapons from being brought into a facility.

The legal basis for lawsuits claiming a failure to plan for an incident includes common-law negligence, corporate negligence liability, and in some circumstances personal liability for corporate officers. Under common-law negligence there must be a duty owed, a breach of that duty, and the breach must be the proximate cause of the loss. These are settled concepts which can be discussed at length with legal counsel.[14] Courts have not yet discussed the question of required planning for homeland security incidents. Nonetheless, broad rules of duty and liability for preparing for specific disasters do exist.[15] These standards should also be reviewed with legal counsel throughout the planning process.

Corporations may be held liable for negligent acts in a fashion similar to liability for individuals.[16] Moreover, when a corporation's agents act within the scope of their corporate duties or responsibilities and commit a negligent act, the corporation may also be held liable for those actions.[17] Where the corporation owes a third party a duty, such as under a fiduciary relationship, and 'the corporate agent fails to perform that duty, the injured third party may recover for that failure'.[18]

In general anything related to its corporate duties is a basis for a suit against a corporation.[19] For example, 'failure to provide adequate safeguards for a corporate asset . . . may be considered a breach of a corporate duty, for which recovery would be granted to an injured third party'.[20] A business may also be liable for a failure to provide security or for providing security which was inadequate to protect against catastrophic incidents. For example, in a facility with a parking garage, a plaintiff may bring a suit against a business for failure to provide security where a bomb or similar terrorist attack was foreseeable, or for failure to provide adequate mail screening when mail bombs or similar attacks are foreseeable. In an information security context, a business may find itself in court if its computer systems are used in a terrorist attack or terrorist activity, and it failed to provide reasonable safeguards to protect against such a foreseeable attack or activity.

Importantly, foreseeability does not hinge upon the fact of a prior occurrence of the action giving rise to a suit, although that fact may prove important to a court. For example, a gas station customer in California who was 'robbed, beaten and stabbed by a gang member filed a lawsuit alleging that the station lacked adequate safety measures for its customers'.[21] The station argued it had no duty to protect him from criminal acts. 'The California Court of Appeals in 2003 held that the case should proceed to a jury because there was evidence of prior violent crimes at the store and in an adjacent park that could have created a duty . . . to take steps to protect its customers'.[22] On the other hand, in an Idaho court, evidence of prior acts was of no consequence to the court. There a defendant landlord argued that a lawsuit against him should be denied because 'the plaintiff failed to come forward with any evidence that prior similar incidents of criminal activity had occurred in the building or in its vicinity'.[23] The court then elaborated upon a string of cases from across the country rejecting what it termed as the notion that 'every dog gets one free bite before its owner can be held to be negligent for failing to control the dog'.[24] The trend, when it comes to security and business planning is that the courts are indicating there are no free passes.

It may seem unreasonable to hold businesses accountable for the criminal acts of third parties, or 'acts of God'. However, such incidents do not break the chain of responsibility and the duty of care for corporations unless the intervening acts were unforeseeable.[25] 'Today it is foreseeable that another terrorist attack could occur, so corporations will be liable for negligence if they do not exercise due care to protect employees, vendors, shareholders, customers and other potential plaintiffs against this risk of harm. The fact that an act of terrorism is criminal in and of itself will not insulate corporations from liability.'[26]

These potential routes of liability highlight the need for business leaders to conduct thorough planning. The business judgment rule operates in most jurisdictions to protect corporate officers who plan responsibly. The business judgment rule 'is a presumption that in making a business decision the directors of a corporation acted on an informed basis, in good faith and in the honest belief that the action taken was in the best interests of the company. Absent an abuse of discretion, that judgment will be respected by the courts. The burden is on the party challenging the decision to establish facts rebutting the presumption.'[27] The rule only applies where there was an actual decision made, it does not protect for omissions. Thus to prevail in court, a plaintiff must show that: '(1) the directors did not in fact make a decision; (2) the directors' decision was uninformed; (3) the directors were not disinterested or independent; or (4) the directors were grossly negligent.'[28] In a homeland security incident context, this means that courts will focus their inquiry on management's efforts in arriving at their preparation decisions rather than on the wisdom of the decisions. Courts will not protect decisions where directors did not take seriously their obligations in reaching decisions or did not exercise due care. Thus, the substance of a business decision will be immune from challenge if, and only if, the directors were diligent in making their decision. Diligence requires thorough planning and preparation in accordance with industry standards.

Assessment of Capacity and Vulnerabilities

Given the potential legal liability business leaders can face, appropriate planning for homeland security incidents is a requirement. The first step business leaders must take in planning for a potential homeland security incident is to assess their current ability to handle such an emergency. Legal advice and input is critical to developing a confidential plan which will protect the business from future liability. The Federal Emergency Management Agency (FEMA) has produced a guide for business and industry. This FEMA guide[29] and its recommendations may constitute the minimum requirements to meet industry standards for planning. Another possible industry standard is the National Fire Protection Association Standard 1600 (NFPA 1600). This voluntary code was recommended to the Department of Homeland Security by the American National Standards Institute (ANSI), as the national standard for private sector preparedness. Importantly, 'even if Congress does not enact NFPA 1600 as the statutory duty of care for private employers, employers still should be mindful that courts ultimately may adopt that standard in negligence suits as the measure of what can be expected of the reasonable employer'.[30] Business leaders should be mindful of both of these standards and at a minimum should ensure compliance with their guidance.

In planning, the FEMA guide states that '[a]t the very least, you should obtain input from all functional areas'. Specifically listed in the guide is the 'legal' functional area. In the abstract it may seem like common sense to include legal counsel throughout each phase of homeland security incident preparation; however all too often what occurs in practice is a 'legal review' added to the end of a process rather than incorporated throughout. While following this practice may save money and time, it is a sure-fire way to ensure that critical legal and regulatory issues will be missed. When planning for homeland security incidents, the legal advice of counsel is critical throughout the process.

The FEMA guide recommends analyzing capabilities and hazards, and using such data to determine the business's capability for handling an incident. Included in this phase are:

- A review of internal plans and policies such as evacuation plans, security procedures, insurance programs, hazardous materials plans, and so on.[31]
- Meetings with outside groups to inform the business about potential incidents and resources.[32]
- Identification of applicable federal, state and local regulations.[33]
- Identification of critical products, services and operations.[34]
- Identification of internal and external resources and capabilities.[35]
- A review of insurance polices with carriers.[36]

These steps likely constitute the minimum due diligence which business leaders are expected to undergo in the assessment phase. A failure to assess each of the items detailed in this list may expose the business to liability for not meeting the standard of care required of business leaders. However, a comprehensive assessment does not stop with the review and identification detailed above. Business leaders must also conduct a vulnerability analysis to assess potential incidents, their likelihood and their impact on the business. Again, the FEMA guide provides straightforward steps:

- List potential emergencies, taking into account history, technology, geography, human error and regulations.[37]
- Estimate the probability of an incident occurring.
- Assess the potential human, property and business impact.[38]
- Assess internal and external resources.[39]

Together, the identification and assessment phase will form the basis for the development of a plan for preparing for, preventing and responding to homeland security incidents. Business leaders, however, should not rely only upon their internal expertise, they should also seek the advice of outside experts. Key among these outside experts is legal counsel, who should be integrated throughout the process to identify potential legal and regulatory hurdles. It may even be advantageous to have legal counsel lead the assessment to protect the information developed from potential disclosure.[40] To protect against potential lawsuits, 'all efforts should be documented so the business has a record of the expense, effort, time and expertise invested in developing and implementing policies and practices'.[41]

The experience of the 1993 WTC bombing litigants provides an example of the importance of integrating legal counsel and demonstrates how assessment documents may find their way into court. Following the bombing, plaintiffs alleging various injuries and damages sought WTC building security plans and documents from the Port Authority (PA).[42] Specifically, the plaintiffs sought a PA[43] review designed to 'address exposure to terrorist acts in all PA-owned facilities . . . address vulnerabilities, identify alternatives and solutions, present recommendations to each facility's management, and obtain a response from each facility'.[44] This review listed a series of possible methods of attacking the WTC which were almost identical to how the actual attack occurred. The review also revealed that government security agencies concurred with the report's findings, and that the PA had ordered a review by private consulting firms, and these firms issued summary reports that also concurred.[45]

The court held that the PA, unlike most private landlords and businesses, performed essential government functions, meaning that some information related to its activities could be kept from the public under the doctrine of 'public interest privilege'.[46] However, despite its quasi-governmental status, the court did not grant a full privilege. It instead determined that the privilege only applied where the PA could demonstrate the specific public interest which would be jeopardized by disclosure of the information. Unfortunately for business leaders, no such public interest privilege exists, meaning that many if not all planning documents may find their way into court. However, the attorney–client privilege remains and its protections are nearly inviolable.[47] Therefore, because so much of the activity involved in conducting an assessment involves legal and regulatory issues, and in consideration of the potential for litigation following a homeland security incident, it is advisable to work closely with legal counsel in developing the assessment. This will not only ensure adequate attention to legal issues but also will protect the assessment's confidentiality.

Planning for Incidents

Planning for homeland security incidents is a comprehensive process integrating the elements of the assessment phase into a concrete actionable plan. The planning phase includes development of a written plan, communicating incident response procedures to personnel, developing incident response documents and conducting training. The goals of the plan are to prevent losses, mitigate the impact of losses when unavoidable and limit legal liability in the event of a loss.

In developing a plan businesses should consider procedures and activities that will prevent losses or will mitigate unavoidable losses. Examples of such procedures include:

- security systems and personnel;
- alarms and other means of notifying emergency personnel that an incident has occurred;
- protection systems such as fire suppression;
- emergency power generations; and
- hazardous material response training, equipment and procedures.

Other procedures may include retrofitting measures such as upgrading structures and relocating key equipment, materials and records off-site or in protected storage.[48] To mitigate losses businesses should ensure they have adequate insurance, a continuity of management plan, and a recovery of operations plan. Such plans will assure the chain of command, maintain lines of succession for key personnel, and include procedures for moving to alternate work sites.[49]

Businesses may be liable to vendors, customers, shareholder, employees and other potential plaintiffs for failure to prevent losses.[50] Liability arises when the risk of loss was foreseeable to management. The scope of such loss may include lost revenues due to an inability to continue operations and provide products or services to customers.[51] Businesses should consider making contractual arrangements with vendors for post-emergency services, and have 'backup' vendors located in different geographic regions from regular vendors.

A key part of the process also includes periodically reviewing the plan developed by the business. Threats and potential vulnerabilities are in a state of constant flux and what was not foreseeable one day may become foreseeable the next. Business leaders when implementing a loss prevention or mitigation plan must ensure that they have also put in place a schedule for periodic review. Such action not only ensures that the plan is responsive to changes in the incident context, but also ensures that leaders are meeting their legal obligations to prepare the business.

OTHER INCIDENT-RELATED OBLIGATIONS

Business leaders owe a responsibility to their organizations in response and recovery efforts. This duty extends to the company in the form of post-disaster actions to reduce liability, speed recovery efforts, cooperate with government officials, reduce the impact of the disaster, and look-out for the interests of employees. Business leaders have an equal responsibility following an emergency to ensure they comply with their regulatory obligations. These include reporting requirements, providing material in accordance with pre-determined agreements and plans, a fiduciary responsibility for disaster recovery which may have been undertaken by the government, and criminal liability for certain actions.

As discussed above, there are a variety of legal issues and potential areas for liability for those businesses which negligently fail to prepare for incidents. Moreover, questions arise in non-tort-related instances, such as whether parties should be excused from their contract obligations in the face of a terrorist attack, or whether they can be held liable for delays in the performance of those contracts. Businesses should review their agreements with commercial partners to determine what provisions exist for homeland security incidents and who will bear responsibility in the event that such an incident occurs. Similarly, leases should be reviewed to determine what obligations businesses will incur if they are no longer able to access their facilities because they have become crime scenes or environmental disaster areas.

Businesses providing critical services to municipalities, such as fire, Emergency Medical Services (EMS), or other traditionally public functions should review their 'public–private partnerships'. In some instances, the existence of such a partnership may make the community ineligible for federal assistance. Businesses should work with local government officials to structure their arrangements as contract costs to ensure that eligible entities can be reimbursed under federal disaster programs.

Homeland security regulations impact nearly every type of business, whether that business works directly with the government or not. In the area of employment law, the businesses obligation to ensure workplace safety requires business leaders to ensure they are investigating their employees. In particular, businesses operating chemical facilities, mass transit or other critical infrastructure are particularly affected by the obligation to ensure their employees are who they say they are, and are not a threat.

Questions regarding employees also arise in the context of homeland security incident-related shutdowns and labor. First, business leaders must ensure that legal counsel reviews their agreements with unionized employees to ensure provisions are in place for homeland security incident-related shutdowns. Also, the business should be aware of regulatory obligations. For example, the Worker Adjustment and Retraining Notification (WARN) Act requires employers to give its employees 60 days advance notice of a plant closing.[52] The purpose of the statute is to give workers transition time to seek alternative jobs and, if necessary, seek retraining to allow them to compete successfully in the job market. Under the WARN Act, the required 60-day notice period may be reduced or eliminated if the closure was caused by 'business circumstances that were not reasonably foreseeable as of the time that notice would have been required'.[53] The unforeseen business circumstances must be 'caused by some sudden, dramatic, and unexpected action or condition outside the employer's control'.[54] Again, the foreseeability of the event or incident comes to the fore. In providing guidance, the Department of Labor has been hesitant to create pre-set rules as to what constitutes unforeseen business circumstances, and instead encourages a case-by-case examination of the facts.[55]

In the context of environmental and hazardous materials obligations new regulations affecting use and storage of chemicals, transportation of hazardous materials, and compliance with current regulations all present issues which must be addressed by business leaders in consultation with legal counsel. If an incident involves hazardous materials the actions of public and private entities are governed by extensive regulations. Included amongst these are the regulations of the OSHA and the Environmental Protection Agency (EPA). 'Both public and private entities may be charged with first response to a HAZMAT occurrence.'[56] Moreover, interesting questions arise regarding corporate procedures for dealing with local, state and federal officials in the event of an environmental or 'hazmat' incident. For example, what if a state official orders a business to commit an act which violates federal environmental laws? This state official may justify their order by informing the business that 'the laws' have been suspended for the emergency. Can businesses rely on the orders of the local official who does not have the authority to suspend federal regulations? What if those orders result in a loss of life or property? If the laws have citizen suit provisions, will the reliance upon orders of a local official constitute a valid defense? These questions raise serious issues of liability and financial impact and are worth exploring with counsel so as to develop clear policies and guidance for employees.

Business leaders should also prepare to use the law as a sword. If emergency responders act improperly and harm a business, attorneys for that business should be cognizant of the standards which emergency responders must follow and be prepared to recover if the responders were grossly negligent. 'Potential claims in the aftermath of disasters include wrongful death, negligent planning or actions during the disaster, civil rights violations resulting from improper use of authority, exceeding the scope of proper practice for emergency management, failure to properly distribute aid, monetary damages resulting from loss of business during an evacuation, and many more.'[57] Business leaders and their attorneys should be prepared to raise these claims in the event of injury, damage or loss.

CONCLUSION

Homeland security incidents present legal and regulatory challenges that must be addressed prior to an incident occurring. Planning for homeland security incidents is a comprehensive process that should incorporate or be directed by legal counsel. New homeland security regulations, coupled with evolving theories of negligence and foreseeability, have changed the obligations and responsibilities of business leaders. Accordingly, there is a need to consider and evaluate nearly every business decision and critical activity through the lens of homeland security incident preparedness. A business that waits until after a disaster to address the legal issues which may arise during an incident may find it is incapable of sustaining operations and, worse, may be liable to negligence suits. In this context, an ounce of prevention truly is worth a pound of cure.

NOTES

1. This chapter uses the term 'homeland security incident' to describe any emergency or incident which impacts upon a business and may, but does not necessarily, fall under the purview of the Department of Homeland Security. These include terrorist attacks, major disasters such as hurricanes, tornadoes, earthquakes and other storms, and accidents for which it may not be initially clear whether the incident was an accident or an act of terrorism, including hazardous material incidents, radiological accidents and explosions. This list is not exhaustive, and business leaders should strive to plan using an 'all-hazards' approach to prepare appropriately for the full spectrum of potential liability from emergencies and homeland security incidents.
2. *In Re World Trade Center Bombing Litigation*, 709 N.E. 2d 452 (2d Circuit) (1999) (consolidated by judicial order).
3. See, Pacelle Mitchell (2004), 'Onslaught of civil suits begins in World Trade Center Bombing', *Wall Street Journal*, 28 June, B1, B10.
4. *In Re September 11th Litigation*, 280 F.Supp. 2d 279 (S.D.N.Y.) (2003).
5. Melinda L. Reynolds, 'Landowner liability for terrorist acts', 47 Case Western Reserve University Law Review 155 (providing an expansive discussion of landlord liability for terrorist attacks and associated policy issues).
6. Oreilly, James T. (2006), 'Allocating the private-sector costs of a future 9/11', 20 Natural Resources and Environment 43, 45.
7. Ibid.
8. Ibid.
9. Schierow, Linda-Jo (2006), *Chemical Facility Security*, CRS Report for Congress, 12 January, p. 15. This explains that The Clean Air Act §112(r) imposes a general duty on chemical facilities producing, processing, handling, or storing any 'extremely hazardous substance' to detect and prevent or minimize accidental releases and to provide prompt emergency response to a chemical release in order to protect human health and the environment. The Clean Air Act (CAA) requires owners and operators of chemical facilities to prepare Risk Management Plans (RMPs) that summarize the potential threat of sudden large releases of certain chemicals. The CAA also requires chemical facilities to have plans in place to prevent chemical damage caused by a chemical release.
10. Ibid.
11. Lindsey, Kevin, *'Legal trends: crisis alert'*, SHRM Online, http://www.shrm.org/hrmagazine/articles/0806/0806legaltrends.asp#ek#ek, accessed 3 August 2006.
12. McGraw Hill §5.03[1] citing 280 f. Supp. 2d at 299; and Pristin, Terry (2004), Commercial real estate; US landlords face post-9/11 standards', *New York Times,* 11 February.
13. Ibid.
14. Prosser & Keeton on the Law of Torts § 53.
15. See, Burk, Dan L. and Laurence H. Winer (1989), 'Failure to prepare: who's liable in a data processing disaster? 5 *Computer and High Technology Law Journal* 19; FEMA (1993), 'Emergency management guide for business and industry: a step-by-step approach to emergency planning, response and recovery for companies of all sizes', FEMA 141/October (hereinafter FEMA Guide).

16. *Grow Farms Corp. v. National State Bank* (1979) 167 NJ Super 102, 400 A2d 535.
17. *O'Shea v Pacific Gas & Electric Co.* (1936) 18 Cal App 2d 32, 62 P2d 1066.
18. Leahy Monique C.M, *Tort Liability for Failure to Provide Computer Disaster Recovery Measures*, 29 AM. JUR. PROOF OF FACTS 3d 53.
19. Ibid.
20. Ibid.
21. Lindsey, *supra*, citing *Claxton v. Atlantic Richfield Co.*, 108 Cal. App. 4th 327 (2003).
22. Ibid.
23. *Sharp v. W.H. Moore*, Inc.118 Idaho 297, 301 (Idaho, 1990).
24. Ibid.
25. McGraw Hill §5.03 (citing *Klages v. Gen. Ordnance Equip. Corp.* 367 A.2d 304 (Pa. Super. Ct. 1976).
26. Ibid.
27. *Aronson v. Lewis*, 473 A2d 805, 812 (Del 1984).
28. Fletcher Cyclopedia of the Law of Private Corporations, §1036.
29. FEMA Guide, *supra*.
30. Lindsey, *supra*.
31. See ibid., p. 11 for the complete list.
32. Ibid., p. 11.
33. Ibid., p. 12.
34. Ibid.
35. Ibid., pp. 12–13
36. Ibid.
37. Ibid., pp. 14–15.
38. Ibid., pp. 15–16.
39. Ibid.
40. See, McGraw Hill Homeland Security Deskbook §5.05[1] Note 2 (stating companies should 'obtain outside counsel to oversee the audit process so they can claim attorney–client privilege for the information developed').
41. Ibid.
42. In re World Trade Center Bombing Litigation, 93 N.Y.2d 1, 4 (N.Y. 1999).
43. The landlord for the World Trade Center.
44. Ibid., p. 5.
45. Ibid.
46. Ibid., p. 8. (This explains that: 'a public interest privilege inheres in certain official confidential information in the care and custody of governmental entities. This privilege permits appropriate parties to protect information from ordinary disclosure, as an exception to liberal discovery rubrics . . . The justification for the privilege is that the public interest might otherwise be harmed if extremely sensitive material were to lose this special shield of confidentiality').
47. However, very specific circumstances exist where waiver of the privilege can occur. It is therefore critical that attorneys and business leaders closely monitor distribution and disclosure of information which they intend to keep confidential.
48. FEMA Guide, p. 43.
49. Ibid.
50. McGraw Hill, §5.03[3].
51. Ibid.
52. 29 U.S.C. § 2102(a).
53. Ibid.
54. Ibid.
55. *Hotel Employees and Rest. Employees Int'l Union Local 54 v. Elsinore Shore Assocs.*, 173 F.3d 175, 180 (3d Cir.)(1999).
56. 29 C.F.R. § 1910.119 and 29 C.F.R. §1910.120. Also, for an extensive discussion of hazardous materials operations see, Nicholson, William C. 'legal issues in response to terrorism incidents involving hazardous materials: The Hazardous Waste Operations and Emergency Response ("HAZWOPER") Standard, Standard Operating Procedures, Mutual Aid and The Incident Management System'.
57. William C. Nicholson, 'Emergency management and law', http://training.fema.gov/EMIWeb/edu/docs/EM%20and%20Law.doc, accessed 14 July 2006.

5 Legal liability when businesses are unprepared for disasters*

Kevin Lindsey

It is easy to dodge our responsibilities, but we cannot dodge the consequences of dodging our responsibilities. (Sir Josiah Stamp, British Businessman, 1880–1914)

INTRODUCTION

Organizations that still think an emergency management plan is a 'nice-to-have' rather than a 'must-have' could be in for a rude awakening if victims of workplace crises haul them into court for negligence. Catastrophic terrorist attacks. Violent crime. Ravaging hurricanes and floods. A global influenza pandemic. Remember the good old days, when business-continuation planning focused primarily on figuring out what to do if key executives were incapacitated? Today, companies need to broaden their emergency planning to encompass a wide range of potential catastrophes, first and foremost to protect their people but also to preserve their property and profits. Moreover, failure to plan may expose organizations to legal liability.

Unfortunately, many organizations are not prepared. In August 2005, AT&T reported in its fourth annual survey – 'Disaster planning in the private sector: a look at the state of business continuity in the US' – that on average a third of companies in the country do not have a disaster recovery plan. Among the companies surveyed that do have plans, approximately 25 percent of them had neither updated their plans nor tested them within the previous year, while 17 percent said they had never tested their plans. Only 11 percent said they change their operational methods when the federal government raises its terrorist alert level. Companies need to overcome their reluctance to think ahead and plan. With terrorist attacks and reports of avian flu cases capturing headlines, now is the time to prepare for the unimaginable.

TODAY: LIABILITY FOR OUTSIDERS' CRIMINAL ACTS

Many business leaders erroneously believe that they do not risk legal liability for criminal activity committed by individuals they do not manage. In reality, employers may be held liable for criminal acts committed by third parties under the 'general duty clause' of the federal Occupational Safety and Health Act and on theories of negligence under state law. The general duty clause requires employers to provide workers with a place of employment free from recognized hazards that cause or are likely to cause death

---

* Reprinted with the permission of *HR Magazine*, published by the Society for Human Resource Management, Alexandria, VA.

or serious physical harm to employees. For more than two decades, the Occupational Safety and Health Administration (OSHA) has increasingly relied on the general duty clause to impose potentially significant penalties and fines on employers. For example, OSHA levied a record fine of $20 million on a company for an explosion at a petroleum refinery based in part on a violation of the Health and Safety Act's general duty clause. As for state law negligence claims, several states have expanded the scope of employers' legal duty to protect customers and their employees from criminal activity in the aftermath of known criminal activity at or near their places of business. In *Claxton* v. *Atlantic Richfield Co.*, 108 Cal. App. 4th 327 (2003), for example, a gas station customer who was robbed, beaten and stabbed by a gang member filed a lawsuit alleging that the station lacked adequate safety measures for its customers. Atlantic Richfield argued that it owed no duty to Claxton to protect him from criminal acts. A California Court of Appeals (108 Cal. App. 4th 327) in 2003 held that the case should proceed to a jury because there was evidence of prior violent crimes at the store and in an adjacent park that could have created a duty for Atlantic Richfield to take steps to protect its customers. The case was subsequently settled.

Workers' compensation laws limit the remedies available to employees for injuries sustained at work, but most such statutes have an intentional tort exception. Over the past decade, courts have been more open to finding that an employer's violation of safety rules is an intentional tort. For example, the New Jersey Supreme Court in *Mull* v. *Zeta Consumer Products*, 823 A.2d 782 (2003), upheld a lower court's decision allowing an employee to bring a negligence claim directly against her employer for OSHA violations. Also, in *Ursua* v. *Alameda County Medical Center*, 2004 U.S. Dist. LEXIS 22925 (N.D. Cal. 2004), a physician was fatally injured while examining a disorientated woman with known violent propensities. The State of California's Division of Occupational Safety and Health had previously directed the medical center to install surveillance cameras and to increase the number of security personnel because violent patients had inflicted injuries on employees. The court first denied the hospital's motion to dismiss, relying on the hospital's failure to increase the number of guards as directed. Although, after discovery, the court ultimately granted the hospital's motion for summary judgment, the legal proposition from the first decision still stands; the court did not overrule itself on that point. These cases highlight three emerging trends. First, in certain instances employers arguably have a legal duty to protect people (both employees and customers) from criminal acts by outsiders. Second, the defense that workers' compensation is the exclusive remedy for workplace injuries will not always prevail. Third, there is a growing, if tempered, willingness among courts to expand employers' liability for criminal acts committed against their employees.

TOMORROW: LIABILITY FOR TERRORIST ACTS?

More recently and significantly, there is increasing public interest in imposing an even broader duty of care on employers – a standard that would not only cover companies operating in high-danger areas or in light of known risks, but would also apply to anyone running a business in today's disaster-prone world. The days of private businesses operating with complete immunity from liability for injuries resulting from acts of terrorism or natural disasters seem to be numbered. Noting that the private sector owns approximately 85 percent of the nation's critical infrastructure, the National Commission on Terrorist Attacks upon the United States, also known as the 9/11 Commission, in 2004 issued a report titled 'National Planning Scenarios'. The report urges both the private and the public sectors to develop plans for catastrophic events such as hurricanes, terrorist acts and the plague. The commission later retained the American National Standards Institute (ANSI) to develop a national standard for preparedness for the private sector to be regulated by the Department of Homeland Security.

ANSI recommended that homeland security recognize the National Fire Protection Association Standard 1600 (NFPA 1600). This is a voluntary code that sets forth a comprehensive process for devising and implementing a crisis-management plan. Although, historically, compliance with NFPA 1600 has been voluntary, there are three reasons to believe it will become mandatory and lead to greater legal exposure for employers.

First, in the Intelligence Reform and Terrorism Prevention Act of 2004, Congress urged homeland security to promote adoption of voluntary national preparedness standards for the private sector. Second, the 9/11 Commission report urged insurance and credit-rating industries to rate companies based on NFPA 1600 compliance. Third, the 9/11 Commission report clearly and strongly suggested that companies failing to comply with NFPA 1600 are operating their businesses in a negligent manner. 'We believe that compliance with [NFPA 1600] should define the standard of care owed by a company to its employees and the public for legal purposes', the report said. 'Private-sector preparedness is not a luxury; it is a cost of doing business in the post-9/11 world.' Even if Congress does not enact NFPA 1600 as the statutory duty of care for private employers, employers still should be mindful that courts may ultimately adopt that standard in negligence suits as the measure of what can be expected of the reasonable employer.

NOT QUITE AN EMERGENCY

If your organization is behind the curve with respect to implementing NFPA 1600, do not be too alarmed. You are by no means alone. Most likely you have at least a rudimentary plan for dealing with workplace emergencies. You may be able simply to modify your program, incorporating NFPA 1600 into current business practices with the help of guidance available on the Internet or through training. NFPA 1600 requires steps that are common to any broad-based organizational initiative:

- Develop an executive policy.
- Appoint a program coordinator.
- Create an advisory committee.
- Conduct a risk assessment.
- Develop a plan.
- Continually evaluate and modify the plan in response to emerging risk factors.

The NFPA 1600 framework is adaptable to developing policies and protocols for responding to a pandemic influenza outbreak or to currently unforeseen types of emergencies. If your existing program for business continuity and disaster management does not contain any of these elements, seriously consider including them. The Department of Homeland Security Website (www.dhs.gov) provides employers with a very straightforward, NFPA-compliant sample emergency plan. It outlines practical steps and common-sense measures for businesses, and it includes easy-to-use templates to help companies plan for emergency situations. The Website provides links to additional resources offering detailed information on business continuity and disaster preparedness. Information about NFPA 1600 and NFPA workshops can be found on the organization's Website, at www.nfpa.org. NFPA also offers workshops on NFPA 1600 on a regular basis. Specific information on how businesses can respond to pandemic influenza can be found at www. pandemicflu.gov and www.cdc.gov/business.

HR FRONT AND CENTER

Human Resources (HR) leaders play a vital role in the successful planning and implementation of NFPA 1600-style emergency management planning. HR professionals will be called on to understand and strike the proper balance among myriad federal and state laws regulating employee leave, wages and hours, privacy and benefits. Application of the Worker Adjustment Retraining and Notification Act may become an issue, in addition to policies and practices governing quarantine, absenteeism and termination. What is more, HR staff will have to anticipate and deal with the emotional toll that crises can take on a workforce. Emotional issues arising from a crisis can emerge days, weeks or even months after the event. Apropos of the latter, consider the recent experience of a large national retailer. A store employee's disgruntled spouse, in a drug-induced rage, drove his vehicle through the front door of the store shortly after midnight, narrowly missing an employee. He exited the vehicle with his hand in his pocket in a way that suggested that he was carrying a weapon. Adhering to protocols and prior evacuation drills, the store manager led an evacuation to the designated safe location and contacted the police. The police arrived promptly and arrested the spouse before anyone was injured or more damage was done. Surveillance video of the damage caused by the individual was forwarded to the police within 24 hours of the incident. Management immediately dispatched additional resources to make repairs and open up the store. By the following afternoon, there were no visible signs of the substantial damage.

Problem solved, right? Not quite. Some of the store's employees were having difficulty coping with the stress and anxiety caused by the event. Some said they felt powerless, others said they experienced a sense of impending danger and constant anxiety. No two employees responded to the situation in exactly the same way. Fortunately, HR staff members had engaged in crisis management role playing before the event occurred. As a result, they had taken several proactive steps and were able to respond promptly with counseling services and had a plan for managing leave and privacy issues. The store's sales volume and profitability were unaffected. Clearly, HR's role in the crisis management team served the company well.

LIVING WITH THE PLAN

We cannot live our lives in a constant state of fear. We all know that. Succumbing to fear and attempting to anticipate every imaginable danger should not be the goal of the emergency management planning process. On the contrary, emergency management planning seeks to strike a proper balance between our going about our normal business and appropriately managing potential risk. Remember when we were children? Most of us thought nothing of participating in fire drills, tornado drills or earthquake drills during school hours. How many of us, however, have participated in such drills at our place of employment? As natural disasters and the attacks on the World Trade Center and the Pentagon attest, emergencies can occur while we are at work, yet as discussed above a significant proportion of employers fail to conduct such exercises. Emergency management planning did not interfere with our ability to function at school when we were kids. With just a little more responsibility and preparation, emergency management planning need not interfere with our ability to conduct and enjoy business either.

6 The impact of threats and catastrophes on corporate governance: how to minimize disruption, mitigate the risks and manage business recovery and continuity proactively
Gad Selig

I do not believe you can do today's job with yesterday's methods and be in business tomorrow. (Nelson Jackson)

INTRODUCTION

Over the past few years, there has been a lot of talk and discussions about business threats based on man-made and natural disasters and security breaches such as 9/11, tsunamis, Internet identity and information theft and increasingly violent hurricanes such as Katrina.

The Department of Homeland Security was established by President George W. Bush in 2002 to improve inter-agency coordination in case of threats and disasters as well as a funding mechanism to help state and local governments start or improve their own emergency preparedness and response programs. As a result of the federal government actions and the increased awareness of the potential negative impacts of terrorist attacks, natural disasters, industrial accidents (such as Bhopal, India and Chernobyl, Russia), industrial espionage and other causes of threats, business organizations must be prepared to do their part to protect their assets, minimize business disruption and institute business continuity and protection programs as an integral component of corporate governance.

The issues, opportunities and challenges of effectively governing an organization's operations and functions, customer demands, investments, regulatory compliance, resources and business continuity has become a major concern of the board and executive management in enterprises on a global basis.

According to the International Association of Accountants: 'Corporate governance is the set of responsibilities and practices exercised by the Board and Executive Management with the goal of providing strategic direction, ensuring that plans and objectives are achieved, assessing that risks are proactively managed and mitigated and assuring that the enterprise's resources are used responsibly and that they are safe' (IT Governance Institute, 2003).

Corporate governance represents a journey (not an end state in itself), which focuses on sustaining value and confidence across the business. There are not always 'right' or 'wrong' answers in dealing with threats and catastrophes and their impact or potential impact on corporate governance. However, in the review of the literature, there is general

43

consensus that there are a number of corporate governance principles and practices which, if followed, can better prepare organizations to detect, analyze and proactively mitigate and manage threats and the associated risks of the impact of either natural or man-made catastrophes and disasters. These principles and practices can speed up the recovery process and minimize potential disruptions and losses. They include, but are not limited to, the following:

●   Identify and classify potential threats and their risks using intelligence systems, processes (for example data collection and analysis; threat and/or impact assessment and evaluation; information dissemination to the right individuals; identifying triggering events for potential action: and using enabling technologies to facilitate decisions and corrective responses.
●   Institute a risk management and mitigation policy and process to assess the impact (for example high, medium or low) probability of occurrence (for example high, medium or low) of potential catastrophes and disasters on the organization, and develop a mitigation and contingency plan. At a minimum, a contingency action plan should be developed for the high-impact and high-probability situations. It is almost impossible to cover all threats with contingency plans.
●   Develop a business-continuity plan and a disaster-recovery plan.
●   Develop a corporate and information security plan and policy.
●   Identify individual roles and responsibilities (by name and title) for each component of the plan and test it periodically.

These principles and practices can serve as a guideline for organizations to select and tailor the appropriate approach applicable to their environment, prioritize actions and ensure that the right resources are available at the appropriate time and place. With some astute planning and a deep understanding of business vulnerabilities and risk tolerance, it is possible to develop a pragmatic and effective business protection plan that will minimize disruptions, financial and human losses.

CORPORATE GOVERNANCE – DEFINITION, PURPOSE AND BENEFITS

Corporate governance formalizes and clarifies oversight, accountability and decision rights. Governance is a collection of management, planning and performance reporting, measurement and review processes with associated decision rights, which establish policies, processes, procedures and controls and performance metrics over key investments, business operations, business continuity and compliance with regulations and laws.

The purpose of corporate governance is to do the following:

●   Separate ownership and control of an organization and assure checks and balances between them.
●   Assure responsible utilization, protection and security of resources, assets and owners' equity.
●   Ensure that executive management delivers on its plans, budgets and commitments.

- Establish and clarify accountability and decision rights (clearly define roles and authority for the board, executive management and others involved).
- Manage risks proactively and be better prepared to mitigate threats and/or recover from disasters.
- Improve organizational performance, compliance, maturity and staff development.
- Improve customer service, overall customer responsiveness and satisfaction.
- Assure that performance measurements are established, monitored and acted upon.

Effective governance is critical for business success and provides the following benefits (IT Governance Institute, 2003; Pultorak and Kerrigan, 2005):

- Formalizes and clarifies oversight and accountability to ensure more effective, efficient and ethical management.
- Improves planning, synergy, coordination, communications and performance across the organization.
- Improves overall effectiveness and productivity.
- Optimizes assets and human capital resources.
- Advances organizational effectiveness and maturity.
- Facilitates compliance and audits (for example SOX, FDA, HIPPA).
- Contains threats and improves the readiness and responsiveness of the organization to threats, catastrophes and disasters.

The role of the CEO and the executive management team is complex and requires a balance between achieving sustainable growth, optimizing organizational effectiveness and assuring business continuity. Some of the critical success enablers include strong leadership and motivational skills, scalable business processes, pragmatic and realistic balanced scorecard metrics and controls, and the use of enabling technologies (IT Governance Institute, 2005).

As Michael Cinema, president and CEO of Etienne Aigner Group stated:

> The Board of Directors is well aware of its role to oversee the company's organizational strategies, structures, systems, staff, performance and standards. As president, it is my responsibility to ensure that they extend that oversight to the company's information technology as well, and with our growing reliance on IT for competitive advantage, we simply cannot afford to apply to our IT anything less than the level of commitment we apply to overall governance (Weill and Ross, 2004).

It is difficult to quantify accurately the cost of security breaches, disasters and catastrophes, but events such as 9/11, Katrina, tsunamis and industrial thefts cause millions of dollars of losses including the following:

- Business losses and disruptions, damaged reputations and weakened competitive positions.
- Schedules not met, higher costs, poorer quality, unsatisfied customers.
- Business continuity may be disrupted.
- Loss of assets and lives.

- Disruption in supply lines, operations and information technology systems and services.

THE CRITICAL PILLARS OF EFFECTIVE CORPORATE GOVERNANCE

Effective corporate governance is built on three critical pillars. These pillars include leadership, organization and decision rights; flexible and scalable processes; and the use of enabling technologies (Selig, 2006).

- Leadership, organization and decision rights – defines the organization's structure, roles and responsibilities, decision rights (decision influencers and makers), a shared vision and interface and integration touch points:
    - Roles and responsibilities are well defined with respect to each of the governance components and processes, including emergency steering groups, command and control, response teams, single point for communications, and so on.
    - Clear hands-off and interface agreements exist for internal and external work and deliverables.
    - Motivated leaders and change agents with the right skills and competencies.
    - Audit and sanity checks.
- Flexible and scalable processes – the corporate governance model places heavy emphasis on the importance of process implementation and improvement:
    - Processes are well defined, documented and measured (for example business continuity planning; security detection and analysis of threats, catastrophes and disasters; risk management and mitigation; contingency plans, and so on).
    - Processes define interfaces between organizations and ensure that workflow effectively spans boundaries or silos (organization, vendors, geography and technology).
    - Processes should be flexible, scalable and consistently applied with common sense.
- Enabling technology – leverage leading tools and technologies that support the major governance components:
    - Processes are supported by information requirements.
    - Tools provide governance, communications and effectiveness metrics to facilitate decision support.

RISK ASSESSMENT, MANAGEMENT AND MITIGATION

Risk analysis is the systematic identification of potential areas of threat or concern. There are three primary aspects of risk management to be considered:

- Risk identification and analysis.
- Risk quantification.
- Risk response, mitigation and contingency plan development.

In order to address threats and their risk impact, each of potential threats should be identified in terms of the following items:

1. Causes and classification of threats:
    - man-made (for example terrorism, espionage);
    - natural or 'acts of God';
    - industrial accidents.
2. Business continuity:
    - disruption of business processes;
    - loss of physical locations;
    - lack of or inadequate disaster prevention/recovery plans;
    - discontinuity of business;
    - discontinuity of IT services;
    - loss of vital assets – physical, human, intellectual property, other.
3. Security breaches:
    - physical;
    - logical;
    - information technology.
4. Theft:
    - physical property;
    - intellectual property;
    - assets.

For each potential threat or risk, ask these questions, and then assign a value of high, medium or low:

- What are the possible triggers for these risks?
- What is the probability (time or money) that this risk will occur?
- What would be the impact on the organization if this risk should occur?
- What can be done to mitigate the risk (for example avoid, mitigate, share with a partner or vendor, contingency)?

For risks with high probability and high impact, develop contingency and continuity plans (see Appendix 6.1 for details).

Responses to threats generally fit into one of the following categories:

- Avoidance: eliminate the risk by eliminating the cause.
- Mitigation: reduce the monetary value of the risk by reducing the probability, impact or both.
- Acceptance: simply accept the consequences.

There are several responses to potential risks:

- Outsourcing: get additional products or services from outside.
- Create multiple centers of excellence on a global basis in multiple locations (avoid putting all of your eggs in one basket).

- Contingency planning: define action steps that will be taken in the event the risk event occurs, and estimate the costs associated with that action.
- Alternative strategies: consider changing the approach.
- Insurance: may protect against financial losses associated with certain types of risk.

BUSINESS CONTINUITY AND PROTECTION PLANNING

A business continuity and protection policy, plan, process and related templates should be developed, disseminated (to select constituents in the organizations) and updated periodically for all critical business units and functions. A business continuity and protection plan must contain a number of components: business impact analysis, risk assessment, mitigation and management, preparing for emergencies and business recovery processes. (See Appendix 6.1 for details.)

STEPS IN MAKING GOVERNANCE AND BUSINESS CONTINUITY REAL AND SUSTAINABLE

The following prerequisites will help to make business governance and continuity more real and help transition enterprises to a higher level of business continuity readiness and effectiveness (Board Effectiveness Partners, 2004; Wearing, 2005; Oltsik, 2006).

- The board and the executive leadership team must be committed to implementing and sustaining a robust governance and business continuity environment.
- Do your homework: educate yourself on past, current and emerging governance and business continuity best practices.
- Complete an assessment of the 'current state' of the level of business continuity and protection maturity, and identify any gaps. The Capability Maturity Model Integration (CMMI) developed at the Software Engineering Institute (SEI) at Carnegie Mellon University represents a five-level maturity assessment and evaluation model to help organizations assist their level of effectiveness based on leading companies' best practice. They range from Level 1 (ad hoc with virtually no process discipline in the threat and risk management area) to Level 5 (Optimized Maturity where an organization has developed and implemented a formal policy and process for threat and risk management and mitigation) (Software Engineering Institute, 2002 and 2005).
- Develop a 'future state' business continuity, protection and related governance blueprint (where you want to be) and always keep it in focus.
- Develop, adopt, integrate, leverage and tailor current and emerging best-practice models, frameworks and standards to make them work for the enterprise.
- Decompose the business continuity plan and guideline components into well-defined phases and work packages, assign an owner and champion to each component, and develop a prioritized roadmap and action plan that concentrates on delivering a series of short-term incremental deliverables to facilitate deployment, create visibility and demonstrate progress.

- Assign roles and responsibilities for the various components to key personnel.
- Test the business recovery plan.
- Communicate the plan to the organization.

CONCLUSION

Business continuity and protection should be a critical component of corporate governance. There are not always 'right' or 'wrong' answers in dealing with threats, catastrophes and corporate governance. There is general consensus that there are a number of corporate governance and risk management principles and practices which, if followed, can better prepare organizations to detect, analyze and proactively mitigate and manage the impact of threats, natural or man-made catastrophes and disasters.

The material in this chapter can serve as a guideline for organizations to select and customize the appropriate approach applicable to their environment. The business continuity and governance area requires continuous improvement and updating as new threats evolve. It truly represents a journey that never ends.

APPENDIX 6.1   BUSINESS CONTINUITY AND PROTECTION PLANNING (BCPP) GUIDELINE

(Modified and consolidated from FFIEC, 2003; Marcus and Kaiser, 2006)

1.0   Preparing the Plan.
2.0   Initiating the BCPP Project.
    2.1   Project Initiation Tasks.
        2.1.1   Review of Existing BCPP.
        2.1.2   Benefits of Developing a BCPP (Value Proposition and Marketing).
        2.1.3   BCPP Policy Statement.
        2.1.4   Decision Authority and Approvals.
        2.1.5   Communications Plan.
    2.2   Project Organization.
        2.2.1   Charter – Objectives, Timetable, Budget, Deliverables, Scope, Authorization.
        2.2.2   Appoint Project Manager and Team.
        2.2.3   Reporting Requirements and Metrics.
3.0   Assessing Business Risk and Impact of Potential Threats and Emergencies.
    3.1   Threat Assessment.
        3.1.1   Environmental Disasters.
        3.1.2   Terrorist or Other Deliberate Disruptions.
        3.1.3   Loss of External Services – Supplies, Utilities, Raw Material.
        3.1.4   Equipment or System or Information Technology Failures.
        3.1.5   Serious Security Breaches.
        3.1.6   Other Emergencies.

5.2.3   Prepare Specific Recovery Plans – Detailed Resumption, Recovery and Restoration.
5.2.4   Communicate Status of Recovery.
5.2.5   Business Recovery Tasks.
   5.2.5.1   Power and Other Utilities.
   5.2.5.2   Premises, Fixtures, Furniture (Facilities Recovery Management).
   5.2.5.3   IT and Communications Systems and Facilities.
   5.2.5.4   Production Facilities and Equipment.
   5.2.5.5   Operations.
   5.2.5.6   Distribution, Warehousing, Logistics and Supply Chain Management.
   5.2.5.7   Sales, Marketing and Customer Service.
   5.2.5.8   Engineering and Research and Development.
   5.2.5.9   Finance, Administration and Security.
   5.2.5.10 Other +++.
6.0   Testing the Business Recovery Plan and Process.
   6.1   Planning the Tests.
      6.1.1   Test Multiple Scenarios Based on Different Threats.
      6.1.2   Evaluate Results, Identify Gaps and Improve.
7.0   Education, Training and Plan Updating.
   7.1   Develop Organizational Awareness and Training Programs.
   7.2   Develop Vehicles for Dissemination Information.
   7.3   Develop Budget and Schedule for Plan Updates.
   7.4   Plan Distribution, Audits and Security.

REFERENCES

Board Effectiveness Partners (2004), *A Roadmap: Strengthening Corporate Governance,* Insights, Chapter 1, Version 2.0, January.
'The business continuity plan template and guide', http://www.bcpgenerator.com/.
'Business continuity planning model', http://www.drj.com/new2dr/model/bcmodel.htm.
'Business continuity planning guidelines', http://www.yourwindow.to/business-continuity/contents.htm.
Federal Financial Institutions Examination Council (FFIEC) (2003), 'Business continuity planning', March http://72.14.207.104/search?q=cache:J2O1ENzyQ4QJ:www.occ.treas.gov/efiles/disk2/book.
IT Governance Institute (2003), *Board Briefing on IT Governance Report,* 2nd edn, Rolling Meadows, IL: ITGI.
IT Governance Institute (2005), *Governance of the Extended Enterprise: Bridging Business and IT Strategies,* New York: J. Wiley & Sons.
Marcus, Alfred and Sheryl Kaiser (2006), *Managing Beyond Compliance,* Garfield Heights, OH: North Coast Publishers.
Oltsik, Jon (2006), 'Enterprise rights management: a superior approach to confidential data security', white paper published by the Enterprise Strategy Group, May.
Pultorak, David and Jim Kerrigan (2005), 'Conformance performance and rapport: a framework for corporate and IT governance', NACD – *Directors Monthly,* February.
Selig, Gad J. (2006), *Information Technology Strategy and Governance,* Courseware Workbook, Fairfield, CT: GPS Group.
Software Engineering Institute (2002), *Capabilities Maturity Model Integrated – Staged and Continuous Model – Version 1.1, Documet Numbers CMU/SEI-2005-TR-011, CMU?SEI-2002-TR-028, CMU/SEI 2002-TR-029*SEI, Carnegie Mellon University, 2002 and 2005.

Wearing, Robert (2005), *Cases in Corporate Governance*, Thousand Oaks, CA: Sage Publishing.
Weill, Peter and Jeanne Ross (2004), *IT Governance: How Top Performers Manage IT Decision Rights Results*, Cambridge, MA: Harvard Business Press.

PART II

REAL DANGERS DEMAND REAL ANSWERS

CHAPTER 7   THE THREAT OF TERRORISM

Fred Burton sets the scene for this section of our book by outlining the terrorist threats that confront our country and especially American businesses. He focuses his analysis on al Qaeda and the Islamic jihadist conflict with the West. He explains the rationale for the radical Islamists' strategy and specifically the origins of the 9/11 attacks. As homeland security is improved and hard targets become more difficult to harm, the jihadists have shifted their priority to easier quarry. This increases the vulnerability of businesses and the public in general. Fred Burton traces the rapid evolution of Islamist terrorism, beginning in the 1990s, into a centrally planned and coordinated movement. Today the threat is even more dangerous than before, in part due to the war on terror's success in turning al Qaeda into a decentralized network of anti-Western sympathizers and copycats. Homegrown and self-directed terrorists in Europe and the secular Muslim countries have increased the danger of global business operations. Fred draws from his deep experience in intelligence work to define, quantify and prioritize the danger of terrorist attacks on businesses, their customers, and government facilities and services that make doing business possible.

CHAPTER 8   TRANSCENDING THE CONSEQUENCES OF TERROR ON BUSINESS

Dean Alexander looks to the future and helps us put the real dangers of terrorism into a larger perspective. He shows us the path that business leaders can follow to assure their organizations' continuity of operations, even in the event of a devastating attack like 9/11. Improved physical security, better communications with customers, pre-emptive legal remedies, and protection of company supply chains are the basic requirements for business survival.

CHAPTER 9   THE IMPACT OF DISEASE AND PANDEMICS ON BUSINESS CONTINUITY

Elin Gursky at Anser Analytic Services in Washington, DC is one of the country's leading experts in biodefense. She provides us with historical background and perspective about disease management, public health and the threat of pandemics and biological attacks. She writes about the threat to public health posed by pandemics such as H5N1 influenza and what such a nightmare might do to business continuity throughout the United States and other nations. Her assessment of the medical community's lack of ability to cope with such severe emergencies is sobering. People in the United States have access to the best medical care in the world, but this excellent system will prove to be totally inadequate in the face of a major outbreak of infectious disease. Such a situation will create a tremendous dilemma for businesses. Should employees come to work or stay home in isolation to avoid becoming ill? How can medical care professionals render services while minimizing the risk to their lives and to those of their co-workers and families? Elin Gursky explores these issues and leaves us with a sense of impending crisis.

CHAPTER 10   TELEWORK IN THE FACE OF A PANDEMIC

Paul B. Kurtz, former White House expert on information protection, heads the Cyber Security Industry Alliance based in Washington, DC. He is a veteran authority in his field. This chapter explains how the threats posed by pandemics and other national disasters also represent opportunities for both business and government to dramatically improve the productivity of workers and managers. The United States may face an impending labor shortage with the expected mass retirement of the baby-boom generation. Many of these individuals will elect 'semi-retirement' and become teleworkers. This gap will also be partially filled by those currently unemployable due to family demands, physical handicaps and personal preferences. Like the semi-retired, these people are also potential teleworkers. Temporary measures in response to a pandemic will expedite this process and make telework a permanent feature of the electronic virtual workplace.

CHAPTER 11   IMMEDIATE EFFECTS OF TERRORISM ON BUSINESS

Dean Alexander summarizes the major impacts of catastrophic terrorism, especially the 9/11 attacks on businesses in New York and nationwide. He points out that some industry sectors have actually benefited from the onset of terrorism. Professor Alexander quantifies these effects in real terms, outlining the financial losses and gains on market segments, industries, individual companies, and even some specific merger and acquisition deals.

CHAPTER 12   PROSPERING IN THE SECURE ECONOMY

Greg Pellegrino and Bill Eggers show business and government leaders how terrorism and homeland security creates opportunities for smart organizations to look at potential catastrophes in a new and constructive way. Indeed the glass is half full as well as being half empty. More than just 'spin doctoring', our two brilliant consultants from Deloitte challenge management to embrace the new realities and turn these negatives into competitive advantages in the global marketplace.

7 The threat of terrorism
Fred Burton

Courage in danger is half the battle. (Titus Maccius Plautus, Roman Playwright, 254–184 BC)

Mankind today is on the brink of a precipice, because humanity is devoid of those vital values for its healthy development and real progress. (Sayyid Qutb)

INTRODUCTION

In an ideal world, one could set out to write a chapter on 'the threat of terrorism' by defining, first, exactly what that threat consists of: the actors, the targets, the goals and the recommended countermeasures. But as we all know, the world we are living in is far from ideal. There is no single, monolithic 'terrorist threat', but rather a universe of actors – ranging from al Qaeda to regional insurgencies, separatist movements, grass-roots criminals and 'lone wolves' – who may or may not represent a terrorist threat to a particular government, business or traveler of a certain nationality at any given point in time. Terrorist threats are not static; they are fluid and prone to evolutionary cycles. Grasping this principle is the first step toward effective security.

However, this chapter is being written in the midst of – and in the context of – the US–jihadist war. While there is no universal terrorist threat, there is a universally recognized terrorist threat, stemming at this moment from al Qaeda. But for the psychological blow that was struck in the United States on 11 September 2001, it is highly unlikely that the book you hold in your hands would have come into being – or indeed, that the need for such a manual even would have been recognized. The threat posed by al Qaeda is not always clearly understood in the United States or much of the West. However, one of the enduring consequences of 9/11 was that it stripped from Americans the illusion (carried by many) that they would always be safe, under any circumstances. The attacks forced an intense and ongoing discussion about the nature – and reality – of terrorism and more clear-eyed methods for ensuring safety and business continuity.

In my view, al Qaeda no longer qualifies as a strategic force in its own right – meaning that it is no longer capable of reshaping global patterns and relationships, as it did on 9/11. As an organization, it has been too severely disrupted and degraded for that. But that is not the same thing as saying that al Qaeda is a spent force. Abu Musab al-Zarqawi – who for some time was al Qaeda's most effective commander in the field in Iraq – is dead, as are many others who at various times were said to be the organization's 'number three', leader. But Osama bin Laden and Ayman al-Zawahiri remain at large and, at the time of this writing in November 2006, are fairly vocal. They are not entirely irrelevant to the global scene. It is not clear how important or effective their periodic broadcasts are in shaping the behavior of sympathizers or 'grass-roots jihadists' around the world at this time, but it is significant that terrorist cells and apparent plots, relating to al Qaeda in various ways, continue to be disrupted. Thus, in at least one of its goals – establishing itself as 'the base' for future terrorist groups and actions – al Qaeda indeed may have succeeded.

AL QAEDA: THE FACE OF TERRORISM

The story of al Qaeda's evolution – or more properly stated, devolution – offers valuable insights into the nature of terrorist threats in the West and other parts of the world today.

It is difficult to say that al Qaeda, before 9/11, was a strictly unified organization: it had a pattern of co-opting and cooperating with existing regional groups and insurgencies, such as Jemaah Islamiyah, that remained distinctive in their own right. But it is fair to say that al Qaeda was a cohesive organization: The core groups were well-known to each other, many having served together as mujahideen in the Afghan–Soviet War. Prior to 9/11, this group engaged in centrally planned operations and, in their travels abroad, frequently connected with other veterans of the Afghan jihad or alumni of bin Laden's training camps, forming the glue that pulled various cells together. At other times, 'The Base' provided support to semi-autonomous local or regional groups and approval for locally planned operations – in effect, outsourcing certain operations as needed.

This was quite important, considering the grandiose nature of the plan being hatched. In order for the core group to be operationally secure and effective, they had to remain few in number – and to be extremely risk-averse. After all, one does not build a successful organization by liberally sharing trade secrets, recruiting employees without a direct operational need or mindlessly ignoring risks – self-destruction would result. And al Qaeda did not self-destruct.

Rather, it set for itself a lofty goal: to be the vanguard of radical Islamism, seeking to re-establish the Caliphate of old. To do this, al Qaeda needed to force the United States – the strongest military power in the world – to withdraw from Muslim lands, thus weakening the secular regimes (which bin Laden and his allies viewed as 'apostates') the United States was supporting. Having accomplished that, the stage would be set for the 'apostates' to be overthrown in risings by the Muslim masses and supplanted.

It is crucial to recognize that al Qaeda's most devastating blow was struck not against the regimes in Riyadh, Cairo or other key Muslim countries, but against a country that might be described as a peripheral – or enabling – player, by bin Laden's calculus. Hatred of the West was not the primary motivating factor, any more than striking the World Trade Center or the Pentagon and killing 3000 people was the end goal in itself. Rather, this was a means to an end in a much bigger plan. Without understanding the ultimate goal or those to whom al Qaeda wished to send a message, it would be difficult or impossible to make sense of the group's actions or to take any meaningful countermeasures.

The targets al Qaeda chose during the course of this unrecognized war fit perfectly into the strategy. Prior to 9/11, there appears to have been a marked preference for 'hard' targets – such as US military facilities in Saudi Arabia, US embassies in Kenya and Tanzania, and the USS *Cole*, anchored off the coast of Yemen. These types of targets work well, when they can be hit, because they send an immediate, clear political message. The pool of possible perpetrators is usually much smaller – and the actual culprit more quickly identified – than when softer targets like schools or nightclubs are targeted.

'HARD' TARGETS	'SOFT' TARGETS
• Government Institutions • Military Assets	• Places of worship • Entertainment • Schools • Public transport • Hospitality industry
VALUE	VALUE
• Highly symbolic • Well-recognized • Clear message to enemy	• Numerous • Poorly defended • Attract crowds
DRAWBACKS	DRAWBACKS
• Usually well-defended (increasingly so after 9/11)	• Symbolic value questionable

Source: Strategic Forecasting, Inc.

Figure   7.1

For al Qaeda, hard targets represented the most direct means toward its desired end – assuming, of course, that the United States was listening.

As it eventually became apparent, the United States was not listening as well as al Qaeda had hoped. Something more drastic – a spectacular strike – was needed in order to draw the desired response from Washington and strike a note of empowerment that would resonate with the Muslim masses.

With 9/11, both hard (the Pentagon) and soft targets (the World Trade Center towers) were struck, and as before there was a clear political message – and with the soft targets, an immense death toll. (The strikes were likely more successful than al Qaeda had anticipated – but even had those targets not been on US soil, destruction of such a degree would have been impossible to ignore.) There was a heavy degree of symbolism here as well: the World Trade Center was a symbol of economic wealth – a key element in the United States' global strength – that was recognized around the world. As a target, it was a choice that still carries meaning for businesses that seek to protect their supply chains in the globalized market.

Bin Laden himself has indicated on several occasions that al Qaeda views its war against the United States as a long-term war of economic attrition – referring specifically, in an October 2004 videotape, to 'our plan to bleed America to the point of bankruptcy, with God's will'.

POST-9/11 DEVOLUTION

There were two crucial responses to the 9/11 attacks. One was immediate: a confused (though understandable) reaction by both the public and private sectors in the United

States, which were gripped by the fear that everyone and everything was under threat. Without differentiating between strategic targets and how they tied into al Qaeda's goals, there was concern that schools, shopping malls and other such targets – none of them recognizable within the Muslim world or serving a strategic purpose beyond the sheer 'terror' aspect – would be struck. As a result, no one felt safe – and as is often the case with knee-jerk reactions, money (in both the public and private sectors) was thrown at the problem.

The second response evolved over time, as a result of the US-declared 'global war on terrorism': al Qaeda, disrupted and hunted, did indeed make a pronounced shift toward soft targets, though not in the haphazard way that Americans seemed to fear. Rather, there appeared to remain a certain cohesion in the way that many targets were chosen.

One explanation for this is that al Qaeda – stripped of its physical training camps and gathering places in Afghanistan, went virtual, using the Internet and online publications such as *Maaskar al-Bataar* as a means of continuing to nurture and guide aspiring jihadists.

Some of the articles in *Maaskar al-Bataar* are particularly pertinent. For instance, an article in Issue 7 (March 2004) on targeting humans stated: 'The primary targets should be Jews and Christians who have important status in the Islamic countries . . . Our advice is to start with unprotected soft targets and the individuals from countries that support the local renegades.' Later editions of the magazine provided quite detailed tactical recommendations for carrying out assassinations and kidnappings. In other literature, targeting guidance placed increased emphasis on symbolic individuals – including Western business executives – and bin Laden has personally advised that jihadist 'youth should strive to find the weak points of the American economy and strike the enemy there'.

The shift to soft targets also can be explained as the natural outflow of the decline in al Qaeda's capabilities. No longer able to handpick and personally oversee the details of key operations (as bin Laden claimed to have done with the 9/11 attacks), the organization was left more reliant on grass-roots-level operatives who would respond to its ideological exhortations and strike out at targets within their reach.

When we speak of 'grass-roots jihadists', we are referring to cells with a local leadership that carry out attacks in a country with which they have a long association. This is quite different from the 9/11 model, in which al Qaeda's central command deployed a team to the United States expressly for purposes of conducting an attack – nor can grass-roots actors properly be referred to as 'sleeper cells'. That would mean they had been placed in a country long ago and were expected to take no operational acts whatsoever until 'activated' by their chain of command. Examples of the grass-roots model can be found in the 7 July 2005 attacks in London or the April 2006 series of attacks in the Sinai Peninsula. In some cases, it appears that members or leaders of the cells in question have been trained at terrorist camps or fought in a jihad somewhere, but they are, for the most part, citizens of the targeted country who have been inspired by al Qaeda, and the cells have done their recruiting locally. Moreover, they choose targets and conduct operations only in the countries where they live.

Tactically speaking, this is a perfectly logical evolution. Grass-roots jihadists can take moral guidance and targeting tips from afar, but some of the more sophisticated tricks of the trade can be mastered only with practice. Bin Laden ran training camps in Sudan and Afghanistan where students learned to build explosives and handle rocket-propelled

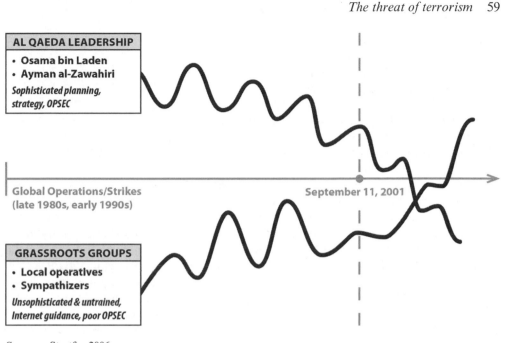

AL QAEDA LEADERSHIP
- **Osama bin Laden**
- **Ayman al-Zawahiri**

Sophisticated planning, strategy, OPSEC

Global Operations/Strikes
(late 1980s, early 1990s)

September 11, 2001

GRASSROOTS GROUPS
- **Local operatives**
- **Sympathizers**

Unsophisticated & untrained, Internet guidance, poor OPSEC

Source: Stratfor 2006.

Figure   7.2

grenade launchers; the skills practiced by covert operatives and which are needed to take out well-defended targets require similar practice. The ability of today's grass-roots jihadists to learn and practice such hands-on skills is severely limited – at least, if they want to remain below the radar of local law enforcement. Therefore, we have seen local groups and grass-roots actors plotting against predictable 'soft targets', such as hotels and transportation systems, where the odds favor successful strikes. Judging from arrests in several Western countries, it appears that several plots involving economic targets also have continued to be formed.

Though a precise depiction of this process is impossible, a notional representation of al Qaeda's evolution could look something like this:

Obviously, the successful strikes following 9/11 have all occurred outside the United States, and there has been a marked preference for 'soft targets' in places beyond the Iraq theater:

- Synagogue (Djerba, Tunisia, 2002).
- Nightclubs (Bali, Indonesia, 2002).
- Hotel (Nairobi, Kenya, 2002).
- Housing complexes (Riyadh, Saudi Arabia, 2003).
- Jewish community center, Spanish restaurant, hotel (Casablanca, Morocco, 2003).
- Hotel (Jakarta, Indonesia, 2003).
- Synagogues (Istanbul, Turkey, 2003).
- Rail system (Madrid, Spain, 2004).
- Corporate offices and housing (Yanbu and al-Khobar, Saudi Arabia, 2004).

- Hotel (Taba, Egypt, 2004).
- Rail system (London, UK, 2005).
- Restaurants (Bali, Indonesia, 2005).
- Hotels (Amman, Jordan, 2005).

Interestingly, al Qaeda has claimed responsibility for a great many of these post-9/11 attacks – even though the core leadership was, by definition, far less involved in the planning and execution of these operations than it was in others, prior to and including 9/11, for which it initially denied responsibility.

There is, within this shift, another trend worth noting: the immediate costs of the US–jihadist war have been slowly but steadily pushed into the private sector. In many cases, soft targets are, by their very definition, difficult to protect. Imagine the costs and inefficiencies of screening every handbag and backpack being carried onto a busy metro subway system, for example. Moreover, what owner of a four-star hotel chain could easily contemplate doing away with door-to-door limousine services in the interest of increasing stand-off perimeters? In some instances, the methods required by effective security exist in tension with, or even at odds with, what has traditionally been considered good business practice or a competitive advantage within industries. Yet, as more attention was given to 'hardening' government installations and key infrastructure, the costs of effective security became ever more necessary – and routine – for business.

THE REALITY OF TERRORISM

The reality of terrorism today is, naturally, much more complex and nuanced than a study of al Qaeda alone would suggest. In every part of the world, there are groups and individuals – for example, Jemaah Islamiyah in Southeast Asia; the Liberation Tigers of Tamil Eelam in Sri Lanka; the Maoist Naxalites and Kashmiri separatists in India; Chechen insurgents in Russia; narco-terrorists in Colombia and other parts of Latin America – who use violence and terrorist tactics for certain ends. Some of these groups have specific political goals; others are primarily criminal organizations that act with financial motivations. From a distance, however, these can appear much the same. Add in the existence of 'lone wolves' – violent individuals who plan or carry out attacks on their own, sometimes acting out of psychosis – and it becomes clear that we are living in a very unsafe world.

Nevertheless, the lessons learned immediately following 9/11 still apply. It obviously is impossible for government or business to defend against every permutation of possible threat, yet it is necessary for both to take all prudent security steps in a given operating environment. For multinational corporations, the concerns can be particularly acute. A failure to evaluate and take steps to mitigate potential threats is a liability that they cannot sustain in the post-9/11 world: the costs to the company and the brand – in terms of insurance premiums, loss of personnel, facilities or inventory – is simply too great.

The logical solution to this problem is a 'threat matrix'. This is an intelligence-based tool that assesses threats by aligning actors with both motivations and potential targets in a given operating sphere. As we have seen in the study of al Qaeda, having a grasp of the audience to whom a terrorist wishes to speak when he carries out an attack – and differentiating true terrorists from criminals who seek mainly to line their own pockets, or from local groups who exploit corporations for their own political ends – is essential in recognizing the assets that may indeed be under threat, and for planning appropriate strategies.

The concept of a threat matrix is quite simple. In application, however, it can be devastatingly complex, particularly for entities with global operations or extended supply chains to protect. The underlying prerequisites are solid situational awareness in the regions where one operates or is considering doing business, as well as a grasp of local perceptions – of your company, industry, nation or government – in a given environment. Moreover, one should recognize that these perceptions can shift over time as a result of exogenous factors, and that terrorists and criminals can learn from and copy each other's effective techniques.

To illustrate the point, one could argue that a series of hostage-takings in post-Hussein Iraq were in some respects quite similar to others that have been carried out in the Niger Delta and in Colombia in recent years. In all three examples, foreign workers have been kidnapped and held hostage for a time. But the proper response and countermeasures for a company in Nigeria would have been quite different from those in Iraq or Colombia. In the Delta, hostage-takings have frequently been carried out by local tribes seeking to force concessions from the foreign oil companies operating in the region or the national government in Abuja – and sometimes both. In Latin America, foreigners have occasionally been taken hostage – along with hundreds of native Colombians – by the Revolutionary Armed Forces of Colombia and held for ransom. This tactic has long been used to fund the guerrillas' side of the civil war. And in Iraq, it was – at least for a time – rather difficult to distinguish readily between actions by local criminals (who exploited the chaos following Saddam Hussein's fall and the ensuing insurgency to turn kidnaps-for-ransom into a cottage industry) and al Qaeda-linked jihadists (who brutally beheaded their victims in front of video cameras). With one set of actors, negotiations for the release of foreign contractors and aid workers could be quietly (if reluctantly) pursued and their safe release secured; with the other, negotiations would not only be unthinkable but likely would not have worked under any circumstances. Where one group was motivated by financial gain, the other was motivated by ideology and power for its own sake.

Moreover, the pre-emptive security measures undertaken by a company sending workers into a dangerous zone could vary significantly, according to the nature of the threat. In Colombia, where well-connected locals are more apt than foreigners to be targeted, one might advise steering clear of certain types of social gatherings; in Saudi Arabia, where Islamist militants specifically hunted and targeted Western expatriates in 2004, one might have advised seeking safety in numbers.

This discussion does not even begin to take into account the global threats posed by organized crime syndicates, pirates and other types of criminals, who are usually more prone to hijacking a company's shipping containers or inventory than targeting its employees – at costs mounting into the billions per year. Of course, terrorists also can be adept in these techniques: consider the attention paid to cargo threats following the bombing of Pan American Flight 103, which was brought down by a bomb hidden in a piece of luggage. Similarly, in the post-9/11 era, preventing a dirty bomb from being smuggled into the United States in a commercial shipping container became a top priority for US Immigration and Customs Enforcement.

For businesses with complex, global operations, assessing terrorist and criminal threats is work best conducted with an outside partner, for a variety of reasons. For one thing, a professional audit of one's security practices by an outsourced provider makes sense from a liability perspective; this is merely due diligence. For another, experienced corporate regional security officers realize that they face at least two professional hazards: at one extreme, they might 'go native', becoming unable to see the significance of events that have become commonplace in their sphere of operations; at the other, they can overreact to perceived threats that are not significant, and thus sacrifice their own effectiveness. An outside perspective – from a source capable of providing situational awareness in unfamiliar areas and perspective on larger trends and patterns that might be difficult to detect at close range – can help to maintain the balance toward the middle of the spectrum.

CONCLUSION

Dealing with terrorism is an inescapable part of doing business in the post-9/11 world. Obviously, al Qaeda did not invent terrorism nor pioneer its most effective tactics; in most respects, it has merely been an apt student of pre-existing groups and methodologies. Nevertheless, the 9/11 attacks ushered in a new era of awareness on both sides of the divide: terrorism has been made both more visible and more virtual in the years since those strikes. Stated differently, Americans will never again be quite so confident of their own safety, particularly when traveling abroad, after having suffered the psychological blow of being attacked on their own soil. And not only al Qaeda sympathizers, but radicals of other brands, have been educated by the public discourse, the 'virtual training' manuals, jihadist websites and other materials that have appeared on the Internet. The education and training that were once reserved for the committed few have been made much more widely – even if not as effectively – available for the many. The genie will not be returned to its bottle.

Even more important, the United States' 'global war on terrorism' has meant that government defenses (of both the homeland and government assets and personnel abroad) have been strengthened – not necessarily perfectly, but to a significant degree. The natural result of this process has been that the terrorist threat has been deflected to other parts of the world and toward other, 'softer' targets. A perfect example of this is the triple bombings that were carried out at hotels in Amman, Jordan, in November 2005: Western businesses were struck both directly and indirectly, because they were symbolic targets within the reach of a jihadist group, and the attacks sent specific messages to multiple audiences. In this example, the jihadist group did have links to al Qaeda, but that need not always be the case: smart terrorists, like businesses, have limited resources and always will seek the greatest 'bang for their buck'.

The view held by Stratfor, a global intelligence firm where I serve as a vice president, is that al Qaeda, as a strategic force, has been drastically weakened since the onset of the US–jihadist war. But in many ways, that has driven al Qaeda's remnants and follow-on groups underground. They are simultaneously less cohesive and less effective, but potentially more widespread and harder to detect and disrupt. In many respects, their behavior can closely resemble that of more common criminal groups, and vice versa.

As a result of this, the lessons of 9/11 will continue to be important for years to come, for businesses that seek to protect their profits and their people. Terrorism has become a fact of our existence: the face may change and the degree of risk may rise or fall with variations in time and place, but we should not expect it to dissipate completely.

POSTSCRIPT

Since the chapter was originally written, in 2006 'the threat of terrorism' has changed drastically in the minds of many Americans and those fighting jihadist and insurgent forces around the world. The names of Osama bin Laden and Ayman al-Zawahiri still carry some currency, but that of Abu Musab al-Zarqawi – for several years the scourge of coalition forces in Iraq – has become a faint memory for most, if it is remembered at all. Iraq itself, from which the last deployments of American forces are now anticipating their departure, has been replaced in the headlines by the war in Afghanistan. And even there, in the drive toward an exit for military forces, foreign powers now publicly discuss what once would have seemed an unthinkable option: political accommodation with the Taliban. The Taliban itself remains potent, making frequent use of terrorist tactics, but it is – notably – a relatively decentralized and fragmented force rather than a strictly hierarchical organization.

Organized groups named as prominent and well-known examples in this chapter have fared poorly in recent years. The al Qaeda node in Saudi Arabia was decapitated, so to speak, several times over; and while the militant Wahhabi strain undoubtedly survives to some extent within the kingdom, its more notable activities of late have occurred south of the border, in Yemen. In southeast Asia, Jemaah Islamiyah, which splintered in 2003, suffered the losses of high-profile operatives like Noordin Mohammed Top and Dulmatin in 2009 and 2010. Sri Lanka's 25-year civil war has ended, as has the strategic threat posed by the Liberation Tigers of Tamil Eelam. The Revolutionary Armed Forces of Colombia (FARC), though still active, was weakened by a series of setbacks in 2008 – including the capture of sensitive computer files and the losses of some of its best-known hostages, freed by a Special Forces raid – and has never fully regained its strength. The list goes on.

But terrorist threats remain very much a part of the global landscape, and have devolved to new forms, much as we outlined in 2006. Al Qaeda has not mustered another multipronged airplane attack against the United States, but a young Nigerian named Umar Farouk Abdulmutallab very nearly succeeded in his attempt to bring down a Detroit-bound plane on 25 December 2009. Only a few weeks before that incident, a US Army major, Nidal Malik Hassan, killed 13 people and wounded many others in a shooting rampage at Fort Hood, Texas. Both men had been in contact with a radical-ized Islamist in Yemen, Anwar al-Awlaki – a thought influencer perhaps comparable to bin Laden.

The notion of training camps has not been entirely supplanted by the Internet, and some appear to have produced graduates whose names are well known to the US counterterrorism community. For example, Najibullah Zazi and Faisal Shahzad, both naturalized US citizens, were accused in separate plots of planning to blow up New York City subway trains and landmarks in 2009 and 2010. But US-born citizens – among them Randall Todd Royer (convicted on federal charges in 2004) of the so-called 'Virginia jihad network' and Daniel Patrick Boyd, alleged ringleader of the North Carolina 'Triangle Terror' cell, arrested in 2009 – equally have been accused of attending training camps abroad as well as attempting to start camps of their own on US soil.

The terrorism case files in FBI offices have by no means grown slimmer over the years. If anything, they are increasingly filled with unmemorable names of both foreign- and American-born suspects, accused in plots that when carried to fruition have been deadly but (in comparison to 9/11) quite small; efficient but not terribly symbolic. The shift toward grass-roots jihadists and 'lone wolf' actors can be clearly seen – at least, at this stage of the cycle.

For I remain as convinced today as ever of the principle stated in the introduction to this chapter: 'Terrorist threats are not static; they are fluid and prone to evolutionary cycles. Grasping this principle is the first step toward effective security.'

8 Transcending the consequences of terror on business
Dean Alexander

A danger foreseen is half avoided. (Thomas Fuller, British Clergy and Historian, 1608–1661)

INTRODUCTION

The broad ramifications of terror on business will be discussed accordingly in this chapter: terror costs in terms of outlays and rising transaction costs; security at a business location; interactions with customers; ramifications on sourcing, inventory and logistics; and legal issues.

COSTS

Terrorism is relatively easy and inexpensive to activate yet very difficult and extremely costly to counter. These costs are ongoing and likely will rise in the future.

The costs arising from 9/11 have run into the hundreds of billions of dollars if one includes direct and indirect effects. Some of the costs, such as security and military expenditures fueled by those incidents, are foreseen to increase annually. Private sector security costs alone are estimated at $100 billion yearly. *Fortune* magazine estimated that economic 'friction' due to terrorism, as exemplified in higher expenditure by business – logistics, insurance, workplace security, information technology, travel and transportation, and workforce – will cost companies about $150 billion annually.

Other terror-related costs attach even though they are outside the security rubric. In fact, some expenditure is entirely defensive though not security related. At the time of this writing, the American Hospital Association projected that US hospital systems will require nearly $10 billion to react adequately to a massive biological, chemical or nuclear terror attack.

Terror attacks against economic targets have resulted in significant financial costs worldwide. The Provisional Irish Republican Army (IRA) exploded a large bomb outside the Baltic Exchange in London in April 1992, killing three and injuring about 90. The incident caused damage and disruption estimated to amount to at least several hundred million dollars. A Provisional IRA bomb blast at a large shopping center in Manchester, England, injured 200, damaged hundreds of businesses, and caused some $300 million in damage.

Terrorist incidents against the Jakarta and Bombay Stock Exchanges in recent years have also caused shattering financial costs. Multiple terrorist attacks against Israeli targets – transportation, entertainment, and restaurants – during the Second Intifada caused a decline in tourism of some 50 percent.

Business, too, is cognizant that it has limited financial resources with which to reduce terrorist threats. In turn, the tension between providing sufficient security without expending excessive resources has gained greater resonance. This balancing act will continue to plague government and business.

Businesses have made cutbacks in other departments due to greater security demands at corporate facilities, points-of-sale and elsewhere. When possible, companies pass on disparate security costs to customers. Such fees are forwarded either directly (through a security fee) or indirectly (prices are raised but with no disclosure as to the reason).

As there is now a security surcharge on airline tickets, so too other businesses deemed soft targets of terrorism (for example restaurants and movie theaters) may impose security fees. Security charges have been instituted at some restaurants in Israel, where numerous suicide bombers wreak heavy human and financial tolls.

Businesses face higher costs when government raises terror warnings. For instance, increased threats result in increasing security forces within airports with requisite added costs.

The costs of compensating terrorist victims' families are matters that will be increasingly relevant should terrorist attacks proliferate, particularly in the United States. Unlike the persons killed and injured during the 1993 World Trade Center (WTC) attacks and the 1995 Oklahoma City bombing, the 9/11 victims (or their families) received compensation.

While some compensation was provided for some of the victims of the 1998 bombings of the US embassies in Kenya and Tanzania, the projected $5 billion allocated to the 9/11 victims is unprecedented. As such, it is likely that some level of compensation will attach to a future, large-scale terror attack occurring on US soil or overseas.

Because terrorists and their sympathizers use the economic system, businesses closely investigate their employees, customers, suppliers and partners. These investigative activities have resulted in greater costs to companies (for example paying outside firms to investigate employee backgrounds or having internal staff to monitor employee e-mail and Internet use). Furthermore, these measures have led to friction between employees and employers.

SECURITY AT BUSINESS LOCATIONS

After 9/11, a business site – be it a store, office, or factory – can be characterized differently. There is now greater cognizance that the battlefront of terrorism has entered into business environs: restaurants, theaters and malls have been bombed; office buildings have been attacked by car bombs and planes; factories and facilities have been sabotaged; and personnel have been kidnapped and assassinated.

These facts have led businesses to spend more resources – manpower, money and time – to counter and assuage the terrorist challenge. Additional security measures external to the site (for example concrete barriers and fences) and within a business location (for example metal detectors and closed-circuit television – CCTV cameras) have introduced a better awareness that terrorist threats affect the ways in which businesses protect themselves.

It is difficult, though, to protect the business site against perpetrators. This is particularly so with those masquerading as legitimate suppliers, customers and employees. Moreover, defending against suicide bombers and those without concern for their fate post-operation is highly complex.

Increased security in transportation systems, particularly in shipping and trucking, resulted in: higher transaction costs; interference with tight production schedules as supplies are not delivered as expected; closing or decreasing production routes; and accelerating delays. Since 9/11, trucks are subject to closer scrutiny by law enforcement officials than before the attacks. Truckers' licenses and transportation manifests are examined more carefully. Bridges, tunnels and highway toll facilities are under expanded surveillance. Public–private developments in improving logistics within a security framework have helped the situation.

Business tends to focus substantial attention on the most recent threat at a business site, while often ignoring future challenges. Following the 9/11 attacks, the commercial aviation sector implemented wide-reaching changes in its security framework. Unfortunately, security at other transportation modes (for example passenger trains, buses and subways) has not yet received adequate attention. Sadly, only major attacks on disparate settings will initiate greater focus on less protected targets. An example of this was the increase in security at trains and subways in Europe and the United States after 9/11.

Terror's spurring of broader security and national security concerns has other implications as well. A country may claim that accelerated security measures and requirements imposed on foreign companies are non-tariff barriers and inviolate of trade law. For example, in January 2004, the US government pronounced that foreign carriers might be required to attach armed air marshals on specific US-bound flights.

While trade law allows for governments safely to implement measures to protect domestic consumers, extensive use of 'terror safety', arguments may lead to future challenges. The existing trade agreements between the United States, Mexico and Canada are affected by increased border security. Such security measures, while important – and even necessary – may indeed give rise to international challenges.

Companies that do not undertake security measures and adopt emergency preparedness procedures may lose customers. Clients may avoid doing business with companies that have sub-par or, worse, non-existent, security measures. Firms that invest in security products and services – such as shopping mall operators that place security officers at all entrances – may tout these measures to current and prospective clients. Some corporate jet service providers have cited their security features in their advertising as a way to attract customers.

The introduction (or escalation in the use) of security measures at a business site also affects the receptivity of the business to customers. A fortress-like setting could be a turn-off because it might be viewed as unattractive and difficult to maneuver within (for example barriers at the entrance). Some consumers may view additional security as a sign that a particular location, such as a shopping mall, is a potential terrorist target.

There is some evidence to suggest that customers who may venture to eat at a restaurant or shop at a department store may do without these services temporarily following terror attacks. Declining attendance at Israeli cafes and restaurants subsequent to suicide bombings at such establishments supports this assertion.

Such a business shift was also witnessed during the 2002 sniper attacks in the Washington, DC area. Although carried out by two individuals without apparent ties to terrorism, the attacks effectively 'terrorized' the region and affected commerce. More specifically, the sniper attacks led to more home deliveries of groceries and meals. A similar change in business is conceivable should terrorists conduct sniper-like rampages in the US and elsewhere.

Another element worth considering is whether a terrorist attack against a global retailer or restaurant chain justifies closure of all outlets within the same country, continent, or worldwide. Companies must weigh up whether similar security measures should exist worldwide. Another calculation is whether political risk disparities warrant different security responses provided that security thresholds exist.

Given the specter of terrorism, it seems reasonable that businesses address the issue of how they will respond in the event of a terrorist attack. This is particularly important for customers (and employees) who may be present at a business during an incident.

INTERACTIONS WITH CUSTOMERS

Informing Customers of Threats

Since 9/11, employers have given more attention to informing employees on how to react in case of a terrorist attack. The natural progression of such education is for employees to instruct customers on how to respond in the event of a terrorist incident. By making customers aware of how to behave in such trying circumstances, a company demonstrates several things. First, the firm acknowledges that it is aware of terror risks facing the community. Second, the company shows it is undertaking some security measures. Third, and most importantly, the firm is concerned about the safety of its customers.

The prospect of a restaurant's customer reading a notice at the end of a menu – 'In case of a terrorist attack, hit the floor and crawl to the nearest exit' – is rather far fetched. However, during the autumn of 2002, hundreds of Moscow theater goers were taken hostage by Chechen terrorists, who stormed the House of Culture Theater. The incident demonstrated that a business – a theater in that instance – must be aware that it may become a target of terrorism. As such, firms should consider various approaches including security and public affairs components. Perhaps the term 'emergency', rather than 'terrorist attack', suffices in a warning instruction.

Therein lies the tension of a firm's duty to inform and aid its customers, while not scaring them away unnecessarily or creating unreasonable tension. Even before 9/11, the Washington, DC subway had public service notices requesting customers to be vigilant about suspicious objects and terrorist suspects.

By acknowledging that a customer might be at risk, the business potentially takes upon itself the obligation to provide a minimum level of security. Should a company fail to undertake security measures while a direct competitor does, and injury occurs, the plaintiff may have a stronger case. At the same time, a customer who has knowledge of the risks, and proceeds nonetheless, might not win a lawsuit.

Customers as Threats

At first glance, a business owner does not know whether a customer is a terrorist. The product or service the customer is purchasing will warrant whether the business owner should undertake special care in investigating the customer – or at least find out how the customer intends to use the product or service. There are also issues of what legal and moral obligations businesses have to 'uncover' prospective terrorists.

A company can rarely determine whether a customer has opened a bank account to obtain wire transfer of money from terrorist funders. Also, it is difficult to adduce whether a client is buying sophisticated technology or an unusual product (for example a short-wave radio that can hear planes) for terrorist purposes. Among issues that might be considered are whether the products and services have dual uses.

Given fears of another 9/11-like aviation attack against Washington, DC, particular security measures are imposed on customers who fly into (or from) Reagan/National Airport. For example, the '30-Minute Seat Rule' mandates that all passengers must stay in their seats for 30 minutes before arriving at that airport, and for the initial 30 minutes following departure from that airport. During these periods, passengers are not permitted to use the lavatories nor roam around the plane. Non-compliant passengers face potential arrest and pilots are required to modify their flight plans.

In the autumn of 2002, the FBI requested colleges and universities to provide extensive information about foreign students, including their names, citizenship, places and dates of birth, addresses, and overseas contact information. While the US Department of Education allows higher education institutions to provide some student information (for example name, address, telephone number and place of birth) to law enforcement officials, other information (for example social security numbers, citizenship and ethnicity) generally requires a subpoena or court order.

Educational service providers feel the tension between cooperating with their government's attempt to protect the nation and the rights of some customers: foreign students. Expanded US government investigation of foreign student applications and registration requirements has resulted in a decline in the number of overseas students on US campuses. Failure by universities to comply with laws mandating cooperation with government investigations may result in the imposition of sanctions.

Other Customer Issues

A customer can become a terrorist victim (for example a passenger on a plane or a customer on a train that is targeted by a terrorist). Given this possibility, customers place more demands on businesses to provide adequate security than they did prior to 9/11. As noted earlier, customers may reduce patronage at a victimized firm following a dramatic terror attack. Customers will find alternate products or services that reduce the possibility of subsequent threats or attacks (for example use of e-mail, phone, videoconferencing instead of flying). For a period, demand for more expensive (for example corporate jets) or even less convenient services (for example buses) will take hold as customers may seek to avoid the victimized provider or its sub-sector.

Customers do not expect that a store where they shop will employ a terrorist sleeper cell member. Also, consumers do not imagine that a company is a front for terrorist groups. It is also relevant to consider whether companies view protecting customers as more important than safeguarding workers.

Customers are part of the solution in that they can alert business owners of possible threats. Customers can also contact law enforcement authorities if they are concerned about a company's activities.

SOURCING, INVENTORY AND LOGISTICS

Interruptions to distribution systems immediately following the 9/11 incidents caused companies to re-examine just-in-time inventory techniques (which involves delivery of parts to the assembly line only when they are needed). Still, the use of international and multiple domestic sources for manufacturing and the prevalence of just-in-time practices makes it arduous to modify these currently ingrained elements of production.

Yet, a number of corporations are increasing inventories and building additional storage facilities in light of terror threats. While raising the levels of inventories may force increased costs in such outlays, they may buffer firms by allowing for ample supplies of key components, even in the event of a major terrorist attack.

According to Joseph Martha and Sunil Subbakrisha of Mercer Management Consultants, manufacturers, retailers and suppliers will be well advised to take into consideration a few strategies regarding sourcing, inventory and logistics issues, such as:

- Inventory management: manufacturers will need to carry more buffer inventory in order to hedge against supply and production-line disruptions.
- Sourcing: manufacturers should be more selective about where their critical parts are coming from. A sourcing strategy will have to vary by location.
- Transportation: manufacturers and retailers should consider broadening their shipping arrangements.

As broad security initiatives have been launched, manufacturers, shippers and freight forwarders increased responsibility for container contents and security. Companies are called upon to conduct better investigation of customers, suppliers and vendors. Secure transport containers with tamper-proof seals are increasingly used. Such measures may cause delays in shipping; they may affect inventories, arrival of component parts and assembly of final products.

Government–industry partnerships, such as the Customs–Trade Partnership Against Terrorism (C-TPAT), allows for securing and facilitating trade. Such steps also aid in instilling resilience in the supply chain process.

Impact on Revenues

Another related aspect is the decline in revenue that may occur as potentially suspicious transactions are eschewed – be they deposits from potentially unsavory customers or imports from emerging markets. The fear of doing business with individuals in high-risk countries may result in companies concentrating greater sales efforts in industrialized and newly industrialized nations or utilizing foreign subsidiaries and third parties to undertake riskier deals.

American foreign policy will always impact, to some extent, upon the capacity of US firms to conduct business abroad. Expanded US government scrutiny of foreigners as possible terrorists post-9/11 has engendered some negative feelings towards the United States and US products. Also, what appears to some countries (for example France and Germany) as American expansionism or interventionist actions globally (for example Iraq and Afghanistan) could make foreign consumers less receptive to US products and services.

Already, some non-US enterprises have seized pent-up demand for non-US products and services by developing their own brands. This was witnessed with the introduction of several alternatives to Coca-Cola. Also, products with a pan-Arab or Islamic positioning have expanded in the post-9/11 environment. Unfortunately, some anti-Americanism has been ingrained in selected overseas markets since well before the post-9/11 era.

LEGAL IMPLICATIONS

There are many legal implications that relate to the impact of terror on business. Among some of these legal issues are: government procurement procedures and protests following awards of homeland security contracts; privacy concerns relating to customer information, industry's acquisition thereof and government's interest in such data; businesses' treatment of employees, customers and partners as inquiry into potential terrorists or their supporters widens; compliance with vast post-9/11 legislation affecting how business is carried out (for example doing business with the Department of Homeland Security – DHS, importation procedures, food safety issues and money laundering rules); adequate disclosures on the counterterror capabilities of homeland security products and services; and potential liability firms may face due to having inadequate security, crisis management and emergency training procedures in place.

Also, it is difficult to ascribe liability and project potential recovery in the aftermath of a terror attack. A particularly interesting case involves potential recovery by the leaseholder of the WTC, who contends that the two planes that crashed into the buildings constituted two separate attacks. Under such reasoning, the leaseholder would be entitled to a maximum recovery of some $7 billion from insurers, about $3.5 billion for each plane. In contrast, the insurers argue that the attacks comprised one attack, and thereby, only $3.5 billion – at the high end – could potentially be recovered. At the time of this writing, this dispute has been brought before a court but has yet to be resolved.

Potential lawsuits by 9/11 victims and their families against selected entities were partially stymied or pre-empted by autumn 2001 legislation. Legislation insulated some companies and organizations that otherwise might have been subject to various levels of financial liability. The Air Transportation Safety and System Stabilization Act of 2001 (ATSSA), included language that limited the damages American Airlines and United Airlines – hosts of the four hijacked planes – could suffer due to suits arising under the 9/11 incidents.

Under the ATSSA, victims' families were permitted to make claims under the Victim

Compensation Fund. As of January 2004, the 11 September Victims Compensation Fund was expected to provide some $5 billion in compensation, with awards ranging from $250 000 to nearly $7 million for victims who perished. Awards for those injured during the 11 September incidents ranged from $500 to $7.8 million. Those who opted out of the ATSSA could pursue claims, but as cited above, limits on possible awards – such as the insurance levels that airlines had on 9/11 – would attach.

Other post-9/11 legislation and proposed laws contain language that restricts lawsuits and prevents punitive damages in suits arising from terrorist events. Other rules potentially absolve or reduce liability to providers of homeland security products and services from liability should the Department of Homeland Security give its imprimatur on the firm's offerings.

With reference to lawsuits connected to the anthrax attacks, the families of postal workers affected may be prevented from suing the US Postal Service as the law already provides for some measures to compensate victims in such circumstances. Nevertheless, plaintiffs may pursue other suits, as in the case of the son of a Washington, DC postal worker who died following exposure to inhalation anthrax. More specifically, in November 2001, Thomas L. Morris III filed a $37 million wrongful-death action against Kaiser Permanente in Maryland, claiming that a Kaiser physician did not recognize and treat the anthrax symptoms of his father, Thomas L. Morris Jr., but rather directed him to take Tylenol for his symptoms. Tylenol is a brand name for an over-the-counter pain reliever. Acetaminophen, which is marketed worldwide under a variety of brand names.

It is also worth highlighting that there is precedent for families of victims killed during a terrorist attack to file a civil action in US courts against the perpetrators, the terrorist groups and their state sponsors. In addition, victims' families have been successful in suing US-based hate groups for crimes carried out by their members. American plaintiffs sometimes have difficulty recovering on successful claims due to sovereign immunity defenses. Nevertheless, some of these obstacles have been resolved by US legislation freeing some monies for such awards.

In 2003, a US court ruled that Iran must pay $313 million to the survivors of an elderly American woman killed during a suicide bombing in Jerusalem in 1997. The court found that Iran had supported the perpetrators of the attacks – the Islamic Resistance Movement (Hamas) – with funding and training. Other Americans who have won judgments in US courts relating to terror acts abroad include another victim of a suicide bombing, killed in Israel in 1995, and an American journalist kidnapped in Lebanon in 1985.

A nearly decade-long United Nations embargo was lifted on Libya in 2002, following its agreement to pay $2.7 billion in compensation to the relatives of those killed during the explosion of Pan Am Flight 103 over Scotland and its aftermath. In January 2004, the Libyan government formally agreed to provide $170 million to the families of those killed during the 1989 downing of Union des Transport Aériens (UTA) Flight 772 in Africa.

In August 2002, some 600 families of those killed during the 9/11 attacks filed suit against various Saudi Arabian interests, including banks, charities and royal family members for their alleged support of al Qaeda. The suit sought hundreds of billions of dollars in damages. In another suit arising from the 9/11 incidents, plaintiffs sought over $1 trillion in damages in claims against bin Laden, al Qaeda and Iraq.

CONCLUSION

The analysis of the consequences of terrorism on business described here complements an analysis of how terrorism changes business. In this chapter, we have explored some influences on business following a major terror attack such as 9/11. Volatility in currencies and stocks, delays and cancellations of transactions, disparate effects on labor, shaken consumer behavior and industry hesitation are among the initial ramifications of catastrophic terror.

Industry responses to terror ranged from declines in demand for particular products and services to accelerated interest in certain sectors, such as homeland security companies. Consolidation among such terror-fighting firms was contrasted with weaknesses – including bankruptcies – among industries negatively affected by terrorism. Additional effects of terrorism on business – higher transaction and security costs; new security dynamics at a business location; evolving customer–industry dynamics; effects on sourcing, inventory and logistics; and multiple legal issues – were highlighted.

In the future, terrorism will inflict additional human casualties, financial costs and manifold consequences on industry. Businesses, however, can contribute to lessening such dangers if serious attention and sufficient resources are deployed.

9   The impact of disease and pandemics on business continuity

*Elin Gursky**

Medicine is the only profession that labors incessantly to destroy the reason for its existence. (James Bryce, British Politician, 1838–1922)

There are no such things as incurables; there are only things for which man has not found a cure. (Bernard M. Baruch, American Economist, 1870–1965)

INTRODUCTION

The possibility now exists of a pandemic, acts of deliberate terrorism with biological, chemical or radiological agents, or some other type of catastrophic event that can cause mass illness and fatality. The potential for such a scenario to trigger a serious and sustained negative impact to the global economy is irrefutable. Although seasonal spikes in disease and absenteeism are a routine concern, the business community should now vigorously reassess its personnel health policies and institute plans that protect both its workforce and its continuity of operations in the face of an atypical and large-scale event.

THE INTERSECTION OF DISEASE AND SECURITY

The history of mankind mirrors the receding and surging of major disease outbreaks. Influenza pandemics, plagues, smallpox, polio and tuberculosis are but a few examples of communicable diseases that have decimated populations, inflicted a host of debilitating symptoms such as blindness and paralysis, caused high premature death rates and contributed to unstable economies and governments.[1] Plague entered Europe via the trade routes from Asia during the late Middle Ages. Its annihilation of over one-quarter of the population caused labor shortages and economic decline and depressed progress and social reform for much of the fourteenth century.[2] The pre-Columbian civilizations of Central and South America were devastated by European colonization and the African slave trade, which introduced new diseases from the Old World, such as smallpox.[3] The relationship between disease and governance is bidirectional. In periods of good health, societies have prospered, elevated their educational levels and improved their standards of living. Globally, regions with the lowest political, social and economic stability have been distinguished by their inability to establish an infrastructure that promotes health and prevents disease.[4] A sick workforce is not a productive workforce.

Despite profound achievements in medical science, pharmacology and public health in the middle and late twentieth century, threats from disease remain, more than ever, key political and economic concerns. Globalization and the rapid movement of people, goods and agricultural products provide a fertile venue for the transmission of diseases. Bird flu in Asia and Ebola in Africa are geographically pervasive health concerns because few corners of the planet remain isolated from trade and travelers. As such, outbreaks of contagious disease – wherever they occur – become an immediate worry to America's health, security and economy.

MORBIDITY, MORTALITY AND MONEY

Events in the first years of the twenty-first century depict a new threat environment. Deliberate acts of terrorism, including the 9/11 attacks on the Pentagon and World Trade Center, along with the Madrid and London bombings, resulted in 3000 deaths.[5] The 2001 anthrax attacks, for which attribution has never been determined, resulted in 22 individuals infected and five deaths. Although considered a disease incident of relatively small scale, its health consequence impact was large. Over 40000 individuals potentially exposed to anthrax spores required a course of preventive antibiotics of prophylaxis.[6] Normal climatic cycles, and possibly global warming, may account for the recent (and forecasted) pattern of unusually horrific natural disasters:[7] The 2004 tsunami in Indonesia, the 2005 earthquake in Pakistan and Hurricanes Katrina and Rita on the US Gulf Coast in 2005 left over 330000 dead and millions more displaced.[8]

Irrespective of the breadth of the human toll, these and other tragedies have exacted a large economic burden. As a result of the 2001 anthrax attacks, of 282 US mail distribution centers,[9] two – Hamilton, NJ and Brentwood in Washington, DC – were closed for nearly three years until proven to be 100 percent free of anthrax contamination.[10] The cost of this clean-up is estimated to be in excess of $100 million for the US Postal Service. Decontaminating the Hart Senate Office Building and other Capitol Hill offices cost the Environmental Protection Agency and its contractors nearly $42 million.[11] Additionally, public health departments across the United States – not just in the five anthrax epicenters – were deluged with anthrax-related medical questions, media expectations and demands from the 'worried well' that redirected their focus away from routine, day-to-day responsibilities such as preventing local disease outbreaks.[12]

The 2003 outbreaks of severe acute respiratory syndrome (SARS) caused global economic shocks estimated at $54 billion in lost trade, travel, tourism and related healthcare costs.[13] SARS led to a 19 percent drop in international visitors in Singapore and a 10 percent drop in China, according to the World Tourism Organization.[14] The discovery of bovine spongiform encephalopathy (mad cow disease) in a cow in Washington state in December 2003 caused a 9 percent decline in US retail beef prices[15] in the following months as Japan, South Korea, Taiwan, Malaysia and Singapore prohibited the importation of American beef.[16] Hurricane Katrina (August 2005) decimated the New Orleans hospital system. Almost one year later, 80 percent of the hospitals' pre-Katrina bed capacity remained lost. At the six-month point, only three of nine acute-care hospitals had reopened, yielding a capacity of 456 staffed beds to serve the post-hurricane population of 158000.[17] Additionally, more than three-quarters of the safety-net clinics in the New Orleans area were closed, and many of those that have reopened have limited capacity.[18]

The convergence of disease and economy resurfaces with the emergence of the H5N1 avian influenza virus. First observed in a limited outbreak in 1997, this novel virus – for which there is no human immunity – was laboratory confirmed in 203 individuals across nine countries between 1 December 2003 and 30 April 2006. The tendency to dismiss the severity of this disease can be immediately countered by grasping the magnitude of the 56 percent case fatality rate this illness carries.[19] Except for one cluster, all cases have occurred as a result of bird-to-human transmission.[20] Nevertheless, efficient human-to-human transmission remains an ominous threat. Typically fatal in poultry,[21] H5N1 in Asia and Europe has resulted in the culling of 200 million birds with an estimated $20 billion worth of consequences for the countries affected[22] and portends staggering ramifications for poor farmers who rely on this industry for income and subsistence.[23] Fear of bird flu has resulted in a drop in tourism to some destinations in Asia and Turkey.[24]

Seasonal flu kills 36000 to 40000 Americans and hospitalizes more than 200000 at a cost to the US economy of over $10 billion in lost productivity and direct medical expenses.[25] The possibility of an avian influenza pandemic on the scale of the 1918 Spanish flu has led experts to hypothesize that as many as 90 million Americans would contract the disease, resulting in 1.9 million deaths.[26] There is no vaccine, and there are enough antivirals such as Tamiflu and Relenza – the efficacy of which is questionable – to cover only 2.3 million Americans.[27] America's already overburdened hospitals and public health departments will be hard pressed to administer these medications rapidly and effectively on a large scale (to a mass population).[28] Moreover, there is but nascent policy regarding who should receive these limited medical countermeasures, historically a decision biased in favor of the elderly and infirm. The H5N1 virus, reminiscent of the 1918 Spanish flu, changes this paradigm. Dubbed highly pathogenic avian influenza, this new virus is particularly virulent in those under 40 years of age, whose healthy immune systems inadvertently kill its host in the battle to kill the invading pathogen. This scenario confounds the usual debate supporting the distribution of scarce medical resources: should they be allocated to society's most vulnerable (historically the elderly and young children), or to its most valuable (the physicians who will treat the sick, the truckers who will haul the food, and the utility workers who will supply the power and water)?

INFLUENZA PANDEMIC: WHY THE BUSINESS COMMUNITY MUST BE CONCERNED

There are three influenza types: A, B and C. A has been responsible for the greatest rates of mortality. Influenza A originates in wild aquatic birds, from which it derives the moniker 'bird flu'. The influenza virus is a remarkable example of nature's ability to evolve.

Influenza A consists of two surface coverings or glycoproteins termed neuraminidase (NA) and hemaglutinin (HA). Through a process of 'shift' and 'drift', they 'reassort' (swap genetic material) and rearrange into novel viruses. Pandemics occur when new or novel viruses erupt in a population that has no immunity to that strain. Antigenic drifts are frequent, minor antigenic changes that are responsible for the annual or seasonal outbreaks of influenza. Antigenic shifts account for major changes in HA and NA. These shifts led to three major influenza outbreaks or pandemics in the twentieth century: the

1918 Spanish flu (H1N1), the 1957–58 Asian flu (H2N2) and the 1968–69 Hong Kong flu (H3N2), the last of which caused approximately 34 000 deaths in the United States.[29]

The Spanish flu stands out as one of history's greatest tragedies. It claimed the lives of 50 million to 100 million people globally (these figures may be an underestimate, due to under-reporting from some countries). In two waves lasting almost two years, a fifth of the world's population was infected.[30] The influenza pandemic was responsible for more deaths than World War I. Of the US soldiers who died in Europe, half fell to the influenza virus and not to the enemy. An estimated 43 000 servicemen mobilized for World War I died of influenza.[31]

Most of us living today have little remembrance of widespread disease and illness. Iron lungs, polio and scarlet fever appear only in textbooks or period novels. The 1918 flu was a killer of unprecedented proportions. People unknowingly infected with the virus would leave for work in the morning and never return home, their precipitous death due to overwhelming viral replications over the course of mere hours. On a single day in the city of Philadelphia, 759 people died, surpassing the combined average 485 deaths per week from all causes (illness, accidents, suicides and criminal acts). Hospitals refused patients, despite bribes – although medical care was useless against this disease. Doctors and nurses died in large numbers, and the piles of bodies exceeded the number of coffins. Eventually, corpses overflowed the hospital and city morgues. Bodies were left in people's homes on beds, in closets, on porches and in corners of rooms. Help was needed, but few could be persuaded by urgent pleas for hospital volunteers. Nuns were released from their holy obligations and were allowed to break vows of silence and spend nights away from the convent to offer their service to hospitals. Disease and fear gripped everyone, from telephone workers to gravediggers to shipworkers.[32] America was in the grips of fighting two wars – the battle abroad and invading disease at home. The war on the home front involved an enemy that American science and medicine was not prepared to defeat.

Influenza is spread through respiratory secretions. Inhaled virus attaches to the inner lining (epithelial cells) of the upper respiratory tract. Once an individual is infected, the virus begins to replicate in the body. Over one to four days, an individual begins developing clinical symptoms, which can include an abrupt onset of fever, cough, sore throat, nasal discharge, myalgia (muscle ache), headache and general malaise. The time between becoming infected and first presenting symptoms is called an incubation period. It is important to understand that a person who is incubating disease but not demonstrating clinical symptoms may still be infectious – able to transmit disease to others.

Those most vulnerable to seasonal influenza – including young children, the elderly and individuals with chronic illnesses – may suffer complications such as pneumonia and ear infection. Persons 65 and older account for 90 percent of excess deaths associated with seasonal flu outbreaks.

Although the data are inexact, the 1918 influenza provides the best framework from which we can extrapolate the potential morbidity (illness) and mortality (death) rates associated with H5N1. Unlike seasonal flu outbreaks, the highest rates of mortality during the Spanish flu were seen in younger and healthier individuals, with human infectivity (attack) rates of 20 percent to 30 percent in adults and 30 percent to 45 percent in children.[33] The influenza epidemic was so severe that the average lifespan in the United States was depressed by ten years.[34]

The death rate for 15- to 34-year-olds from influenza and pneumonia was 20 times higher in 1918 than in previous years.[35] The skewed fatality rates observed in younger populations are an unfortunate attribute of a healthy immune system. In an attack of the H1N1 (Spanish flu) virus (a similar situation is now being seen with the H5N1 virus), an inappropriate (exaggerated) immune response occurred, inciting rapidly proliferating and highly activated cells into a 'cytokine storm'.[36] The result is acute respiratory distress syndrome, leading to lung failure and then multisystem organ failure and death. Thus far, more than 75 percent of confirmed deaths from H5N1 were in people aged 30 years or younger,[37] and specifically highest in the age groups 5 to 9 and 15 to 19.[38]

There are a number of reasons to approach this impending pandemic with heightened concern. The first, as indicated above, is the high fatality rate in humans. Second, the N5N1 virus, first seen in the Hong Kong Special Administration Region outbreak in 1997, demonstrated this strain's ability to pass efficiently and directly from birds to humans; an intermediate 'mixing bowl' (such as a pig) was not required for successful genetic reassortment. Third, after a quiescent post-Hong Kong Special Administration Region period, an 'historically unprecedented' number of outbreaks among poultry and wide geographic spread (presenting expanding opportunities for human exposure) emerged in early 2004. This second wave has established H5N1 as an endemic pathogen (regularly found) in parts of Asia. Fourth, the H5N1 virus is demonstrating increasing pathogenicity in poultry and is establishing itself across an expanding range of mammalian hosts, including cats, tigers, ferrets, white rabbits, leopards, rats, pigs and stone martens.[39] A 2005 World Health Organization (WHO) report notes: 'No virus of the H5 subtype has probably ever circulated among humans. Population vulnerability to an H5N1-like virus would be universal'.[40] The absence of prior immunity, the persistence of the threat posed by the H5N1 virus, the lack of preventive and curative measures and the negligible levels of surge capacity of our hospitals to accommodate a sharp and sudden demand in services will result in rapid decompensation across all aspects of American society.

All prerequisites but one – effective human-to-human transmission – indicate the grave potential for a pandemic. This last step is unpredictable, owing to the constantly changing nature of influenza viruses. Human-to-human transmission, if it does occur, may originate from one of two mechanisms: a reassortment (exchange of genetic material between human and avian viruses) or adaptive mutation (a more gradual process resulting from increased ability of viruses to bind to human cells).[41] The simplicity and adaptability of the Influenza A viruses contribute to their dangerousness and to the inevitability of a pandemic. Greater surveillance, robust research and time will yield more information about what may occur, but not necessarily the tools to prevent or halt a pandemic's destructive course. According to Dr Robert Webster, one of the world's most renowned virologists and acknowledged experts on H5N1: '[It] is just inevitable. One of these is just going to blow'.[42]

The potential impact of H5N1 on the US (and global) workforce and on business continuity becomes readily apparent. As much as 40 percent of the US workforce may remain home in attempts to reduce their exposure or to care for family members.[43] Should potentially infectious individuals be advised to report to work at the risk of infecting others? Will non-ill workers elect to remain at home to avoid their own exposure?

On a broader scale, contemplate the economic effect of large numbers of workers not reporting – or not able to report – to their jobs. How will factories be resupplied with parts and grocery store shelves restocked if goods are not moved from source to user?

In today's globalized economy, consider the potential for fear and nationalization to close international borders, making vital commodities inaccessible. How shall we keep America's businesses running during a pandemic?

PROTECTING THE PUBLIC'S HEALTH

Three levels of organization constitute the nation's public health sector. The federal level provides knowledge development, establishes nationwide health objectives and disburses funding.[44] Within the Department of Health and Human Services, a number of agencies support this effort, including the Centers for Disease Control and Prevention, the Health Resources and Services Administration and the Food and Drug Administration. Fifty state health departments provide the statutory base for achieving health objectives and do so consistent with the specific needs and population requirements designated by individual governors.

The operational backbone of the nation's public health sector is its 3000 local health departments. These agencies are charged with a wide spectrum of responsibilities to provide health promotion and health protection for acute, infectious and chronic disease. In addition to local disease outbreak control, they may offer a diverse menu of clinical activities covering mental health, maternal and child health, alcoholism and addiction, ambulance services, home healthcare, family planning, health education, indigent care and dental health as well as food inspection, animal control and housing inspections.[45]

The legacy of public health achievements – the eradication of smallpox and polio, the reduction of automobile fatalities through seat belt laws, the fluoridation of community drinking water leading to reduced dental caries – heralds its indefatigability of effort and spirit. But an unfortunate downside to reducing the incidence of leading diseases causing disability and premature death in the early part of the twentieth century was government's resultant underfunding of the public health sector in the latter part of the twentieth century. Bioterrorism, pandemics and new (emerging) infectious diseases such as West Nile virus and SARS have caught public health unprepared.

Public health departments are now severely under-resourced to meet the new threat of weapons of mass destruction, biological attacks, naturally occurring pandemics and disasters such as earthquakes and tsunamis. Unprecedented levels of federal funding following the 2001 anthrax attacks have allowed public health departments to improve some capabilities and capacities. They have begun implementing electronic information systems, increasing the size and training of their workforce and engaging in tabletop and practice exercises with other critical responder groups such as public safety and law enforcement.[46] However, many reports have indicated that rebuilding the public health sector to mitigate new threats, including biological attacks and pandemics, will require long-term strategy and process.[47]

CARING FOR THE ILL DURING A PANDEMIC

Public health agencies are not the only sector stressed by the new responsibilities and requirements inherent in today's threat environment. The US hospital system has undergone vast changes, starting with the concept of privatization and health management organizations (HMOs) in the 1970s. 'Managed care' promised to reverse continually elevating costs associated with 'illness care' by focusing on prevention and wellness. By health management, it was hypothesized, serious health problems would be discovered early and late-stage disease – often both expensive and fatal – could be forestalled or averted. Regular screenings, age-appropriate immunizations and behavioral interventions such as smoking cessation and weight control have held the promise (but perhaps not the delivery) of a healthier society and lower healthcare costs.[48]

Numerous additional forces have shaped our nation's hospitals. Cutting-edge microsurgeries and sophisticated pharmacological interventions have reduced the length of hospital stays. One-day 'surgicenters' have replaced a number of acute-care hospitals and reduced the number of hospital beds.[49] Consequently, at the time of this writing there are today only 4919 community hospitals in the country, with a total of 808 127 beds.[50] This represents a continuing decline: in 1986 the total was 1 290 000 beds, and ten years ago it was 1 062 000 beds.[51]

The demand on hospitals has burgeoned from individuals who do not have a routine source of primary care or who are either uninsured or underinsured. Data released by the Census Bureau show that the number of uninsured Americans stood at 45.8 million in 2004, an increase of 800 000 people over the number uninsured in 2003 (45 million). Six million more people lacked health insurance in 2004 than in 2000.[52] Hospital emergency rooms now provide 14 percent of healthcare to the currently uninsured population of 47 million,[53] exceeding a cost of $25 billion per year in uncompensated care borne by US hospitals.[54] Thirty percent of US hospitals are losing money; of those that are profitable, the operating margins average 1.9 percent. Forty-eight percent of emergency departments report being at or over capacity. Forty-six percent of emergency departments have spent some time on 'diversion' (needing to divert patients to other hospitals) during the calendar year, due primarily to a lack of inpatient beds.

In attempts to reduce operating costs, hospitals have adopted just-in-time inventories of consumable products and life-preserving equipment. Should a pandemic of 1918 proportions occur at a moderate level (assuming an outbreak of eight weeks' duration and a 25 percent attack rate), the following percentages of available hospital resources would be needed for influenza patients alone:

- 191 percent of non-intensive care unit beds;
- 461 percent of intensive care unit beds;
- 198 percent of ventilators.[55]

Besides lacking excess beds, money and stockpiles of medications, hospitals are severely constrained by staffing shortages: 100 000 additional registered nurses (8 percent of the workforce) are needed, and the Bureau of Labor Statistics predicts that by 2010, 5.3 million healthcare workers will be needed, over half of whom would be in positions needed to meet new demands.[56] Pandemic and epidemic response to potentially lethal diseases also will require a willing clinical workforce. During the 1994 pneumonic plague in Surat, India, as many as 76 percent of the doctors reportedly fled the city after learning of the outbreak.[57] Those who remained in the area immediately closed their dispensaries, and patients who were waiting for treatment were asked to leave. During the SARS outbreak in Canada, 25 percent of nurses stayed out of work to avoid exposure.[58] A study conducted by the Columbia University Mailman School of Public Health found that only 48 percent of healthcare workers stated that they would be willing to come to work during a SARS outbreak, 57 percent during a radiological event, and 61 percent in the event of a smallpox epidemic.[59]

Today's almost 5000 acute-care hospitals are neither staffed nor equipped to handle the surge and to provide the expandability of care required in the event of an epidemic, pandemic or other large-scale disaster.[60] If a widespread outbreak of SARS, avian influenza or another infectious disease were to occur in the United States, entire hospitals and their staffs might have to be used as isolation facilities. That scenario would lead to severe overcrowding at hospitals and the degradation of clinical services delivery.[61]

BUSINESS PLANNING FOR DISEASE OUTBREAKS

The success of most business is founded on its human capital. Sickness and health problems among working-age Americans and their families carry an estimated price tag of $260 billion in lost productivity each year, roughly 2.4 percent of gross domestic product.[62] Many American companies have extended the productivity of these assets by investing in the health of their workforce.[63] These investments have included partnering with or building onsite fitness clubs, providing free smoking cessation and weight-loss courses, holding seasonal flu vaccination clinics, and sponsoring lunch hour walking groups.[64]

Somewhat concomitantly, the country has seen a growing movement toward the implementation of paid time off. Paid time off replaces discrete vacation, sick days and other types of leave. It is credited with reducing the administrative hassle associated with overseeing multiple categories of leave time and allowing employees more flexibility in managing their time. A survey in 2005 by one human resource consulting firm of over 500 mid- and large-sized companies found that one in three now offers paid time off.[65] There is a downside to this flexibility. Anxious to preserve leave time for family and holidays, there is a propensity for ill, possibly infectious, workers to report for work.[66]

Data regarding workplace transmission of communicable diseases, especially during cold and flu season, are sobering. Forty percent of workers report having contracted flu from a colleague.[67] The *Boston Globe* reports that more people come to work sick than call in sick on certain days.[68] 'Presenteeism',[69] the practice of sick but not fully functioning workers showing up to work, may cost US companies $150 billion to $225 billion annually in lost productivity.[70]

Businesses – from small, family-owned companies to large corporations – need to develop as much independent capability and response capacity as possible to withstand the early effects of a potentially large-scale disease outbreak. There can be few promises of immediate help from any government agency. In the event of elevated disease spikes – harbingers of a potential epidemic – occurring simultaneously across the country, public health agencies at all levels of government will be severely strained in their efforts to identify, monitor and mitigate the outbreaks. Much of the initial burden for protecting employees and assuring continuity of operations will fall upon the businesses themselves.

Preparedness for pandemics and disease outbreaks will require a partnership between the public health sector and the business community. With planning, open channels of communication and acknowledgment of roles and responsibilities, each can have a realistic expectation of the other's capabilities.

Excellent references and preparedness checklists are available from the US Department of Health and Human Services, the Centers for Disease Control and Prevention and the US Chamber of Commerce.[71] Before developing a pandemic plan for business, ensure the involvement, guidance and participation of your human resources administrators and corporate counsel. Also familiarize yourself with common terms used to understand and describe communicable diseases.

Some overriding principles should guide your planning and preparedness efforts:

- Know your local and state public health officials. Meet with them regularly and determine a strategy for round-the-clock two-way information-sharing. You should be able to reach out when there are questions such as unexpected employee absences or an outbreak of illness. Conversely, your public health agency should implement methods to inform you of community-wide disease concerns so that you can share this information with your workforce and initiate important steps to maximize your operations.

- Develop a strategy to protect business operations by averting an outbreak within your office. If you become aware of epidemic rates of disease within the worksite community, a robust business decision may be to alter routine business practices to permit more telecommuting. It may be a prudent business decision to discourage workers from reporting to the worksite.

- Develop a chain of command, with appropriate senior backup, to ensure that timely decisions can be made to protect your workforce and your business. Ensure a strategy and mechanisms for communication exchange and knowledge transfer. This will include knowing – and having readily accessible – your employees' home and cell phone numbers and email addresses.

- Build leadership at all levels of your organization. Ensure that managers, supervisors and line staff have the command skills, authority, information and tools to make decisions in the event that senior executives within your business are incapacitated.

- Predetermine essential personnel who will have key responsibilities to ensure ongoing business and workforce decisions. Ensure that they are trained in their tasks and have the necessary equipment (cell phones, smart phones and so on) to function both onsite and offsite.

- Be aware that some of your employees may have special health needs. Arrange in advance with your human resources, legal and other appropriate management personnel strategies to protect all your workers' health and privacy.

- Consider events that may require your office staff to shelter in place for a time. Institute contingencies that account for personnel leadership and chains of command, sufficient supplies of food and water, basic comfort, backup power and lighting, emergency first aid and sanitation.

- Practice for catastrophe. Plans on paper and in ring binders will be useless unless tested, modified and refined. What sounded good around a conference table may fail miserably during the real event.

Note that these suggestions are scalable. Large companies may be able to institute these using their own resources. However, these capabilities can also be instituted by aggregating the resources of small companies within an office complex.

CAVEATS AND CONCLUSIONS

See appendix on page 152.

NOTES

*   The author would like to acknowledge and thank Ms Sweta Batni and Mr Phi Vu for their research assistance in preparing this chapter.
1.   For a history of infectious diseases, see Ortner, Dr Donald J., 'The history and evolution of infectious disease', Voices from The Smithsonian Associates, Washington, DC: Smithsonian Institution, http://anthropology.si.edu/staff/ortner/ortner.html.
2.   Shepherd, J. Marshall and Thomas Knutson (2006), 'The current debate on the linkage between global warming and hurricanes', *Geography Compass*, **1**, (1), 1–24.
3.   Tucker, Jonathan B. (2001), *Scourge: The Once and Future Threat of Smallpox*, New York: Grove Press.
4.   Chemical and Biological Arms Control Institute and the Center for Strategic and International Studies International Security Program (2002), 'Contagion and conflict: health as a global security challenge', Washington, DC: Center for Strategic and International Studies.
5.   Kugler, Sara (2003), 'New WTC death toll is 2752', Associated Press. Associated Press (2004), ' Madrid bomb death toll lowered to 190'. Radio Free Europe/Radio Liberty (2005),' London bombing death toll at 54'.
6.   Cole, Leonard A. (2003), *The Anthrax Letters: A Medical Detective Story*, Washington, DC: Joseph Henry Press.
7.   Shepherd, J. Marshall and Thomas Knutson (2006), 'The current debate on the linkage between global warming and hurricanes', *Geography Compass*, **1**, (1), 1–24.
8.   United Nations Office of the Special Envoy for Tsunami Recovery (2006), 'The human toll', New York: United Nations, http://www.tsunamispecialenvoy.org. Stuart, Julia (2006), 'IoS appeal: last chance to donate to quake victims', London Independent. Louisiana Department of Health and Hospitals (2006), 'Katrina missing: reports of missing and deceased', http://www.dhb.louisiana.gov/offices/page.asp?ID=192&Detail=5248.
9.   Bridges, John H., III, CHMM, CSHM, FACFE, Director of Incident Management, US Postal Service Office of Emergency Preparedness (2006), personal conversation.
10. Ungar, Bernard L., Director, Physical Infrastructure, and Keith Rhodes, Chief Technologist, Center for Technology and Engineering, Applied Research and Methods, US General Accounting Office (2003), 'US Postal Service: Clear Communication with Employees Needed Before Reopening the Brentwood Facility', testimony before the US House of Representatives Committee on Government Reform, http://www.gao.gov.
11. Shane, Scott (2002), 'Cleanup of anthrax will cost hundreds of millions of dollars', Baltimore *Sun*, http://www.baltimoresun.com/news/health/bal-te.anthrax18dec18,0,5693692.story?coll=bal-health-utility.
12. Gurksy, Elin et al. (2003), 'Anthrax 2001: observations on the medical and public health response', *Biosecurity and Bioterrorism: Biodefense Strategy, Practice, and Science*, **1**, (2), 97–110.
13. Knobler, Stacey, Adel Mahmoud, Stanley Lemon, Alison Mack, Laura Sivitz and Katherine Oberholtzer (eds) (2004), *Learning from SARS: Preparing for the Next Disease Outbreak*, Washington, DC: Institute of Medicine, National Academies Press, http://www.nap.edu/catalog/10915.html.
14. Haberkorn, Jen (2006), 'Tourism industry ponders bird flu', *Washington Times*, http://washingtontimes.com/business/20060412-091608-5731r.htm.
15. Holland, David, Leroy Stodick, Stephen Devadoss and Joydeep Ghosh (2004), 'The economic effects of mad cow disease on the Washington economy', Washington State University International Marketing Program for Agricultural Commodities and Trade Center.
16. CNN (2003), 'First apparent US case of mad cow disease discovered', http://www.cnn.com/2003/US/12/23/mad.cow/.
17. US Department of Health and Human Services, Health Resources and Services Administration (2004),

'Fiscal Year 2004 Continuation Guidance, National Bioterrorism Hospital Preparedness Program, Catalog of Federal Domestic Assistance (CFDA) No. 93.003'.

18. Bascetta, Cynthia, Director, Health Care, and Katherine Siggerud, Director, Physical Infrastructure, Government Accountability Office (2006), 'Hurricane Katrina: status of the health care system in New Orleans and difficult decisions related to efforts to rebuild it approximately 6 months after hurricane Katrina', letter to Congressional committees, http://www.gao.gov/new.items/d06576r.pdf.
19. World Health Organization (2006), *Weekly Epidemiological Record*, **81**, 249–60, http://www.who.
20. The cluster, which took place in Indonesia in spring 2006, involved one family. All eight members contracted avian influenza, resulting in seven fatalities. The disease did not spread beyond this household to any community or health care worker. US Department of Health and Human Services, PandemicFlu. gov, 'Indonesia situation update: May 31'.
21. Johanns, Mike (2006), 'Pandemic planning report', US Department of Agriculture, p. 3.
22. Lederer, Edith M. (2006), 'UN says bird flu spreading', Associated Press, ABC News, http://abcnews.
23. Ibid.
24. South Africa *Independent Online* (2006), 'UN aims to soften bird flu blow to tourism', http://www.int.iol. co.za/index.php?set_id=14&click_id=420&art_id=qw1141291441171T614.
25. US Chamber of Commerce, 'Pandemic planning', http://www.uschamber.com/issues/index/defense/pandemic_influenza.htm.
26. US Department of Health and Human Services (2005), 'HHS Pandemic Influenza Plan', http://chfs. ky.gov/NR/rdonlyres/15A4E76B-37F8-498A-9D26-3375D13BAB13/0/HHSPandemicInfluenzaPlan.pdf.
27. Schumer, US Sen. Charles E. (2006), 'As avian flu closes in on US, Schumer calls for immediate action: demands suspension of Tamiflu patent so vaccine can be mass-produced, dramatically increasing supply', press release, http://schumer.senate.gov.
28. Homeland Security Council (2006), 'National Strategy for Pandemic Influenza: Implementation Plan', Washington, DC: White House, http://www.whitehouse.gov/homeland/nspi_implementation.pdf.
29. GlobalSecurity.org, 'Homeland security: pandemic influenza', http://www.globalsecurity.org.
30. Billings, Molly (1997, 2005), 'The 1918 influenza pandemic', Stanford, CA: Stanford University, http:// virus.stanford.edu/uda/.
31. Ibid.
32. For an excellent review, see Barry, John M. (2005), *The Great Influenza: The Epic Story of the Deadliest Plague in History*, New York: Penguin.
33. Steinhoff, Mark C. (2001), 'Epidemiology: and practice of influenza', in Kenrad E. Nelson, Carolyn Masters Williams and Neil M.H. Graham (eds), *Infectious Disease Epidemiology Theory and Practice*, Gaithersburg, MD: Aspen Publishers.
34. Billings, *supra*.
35. Ibid.
36. Osterholm, Michael T., PhD, MPH (2005), 'Preparing for the next pandemic', *New England Journal of Medicine*, **352**, (18), 1839–42.
37. Phillips, Matt (2006), 'Details of flu deaths offer view into why, how the disease kills', *Wall Street Journal*, http://online.wsj.com/article/SB115080690738385086-search.html?KEYWORDS=H5N1&COLLECTION =wsjie/6month.
38. Kamps, Bernd Sebastian, Christian Hoffmann and Wolfgang Preiser (eds), 'Influenza report: age distribution of human H5N1 cases', http://influenzareport.com/ir/figures/ad060210.htm.
39. US Geological Survey (2006), 'List of species affected by H5N1 (avian influenza)', http://www.nwhc.usgs. gov/disease_information/avian_influenza/affected_species_chart.jsp.
40. World Health Organization (2005), 'Avian influenza: assessing the pandemic threat', http://www.who.int/ csr/disease/influenza/H5N1-9reduit.pdf.
41. World Health Organization (2005), 'Responding to the avian influenza pandemic threat: recommended strategic actions', http://www.who.int/csr/resources/publications/influenza/WHO_CDS_CSR_ GIP_2005_8/en/index.html.
42. Brown, David (2005), 'Scientists race to head off lethal potential of avian flu', *Washington Post*, http:// www.washingtonpost.com/wp-dyn/content/article/2005/08/22/AR2005082201365.html.
43. US Department of Health and Human Services, PandemicFlu.gov (2006), 'ABC TV movie: *Fatal Contact: Bird Flu in America*', http://www.pandemicflu.gov/news/birdfluinamerica.html.
44. Institute of Medicine (1988), *The Future of Public Health*, Washington, DC: National Academy Press.
45. Raffel, Marshall W. and Norma K. Raffel (1989), *The US Health System: Origins and Functions*, New York: Wiley.
46. Gursky, Elin (2005), 'Epidemic proportions: building national public health capabilities to meet national security threats', report to the US Senate Bioterrorism and Public Health Preparedness Subcommittee (Health, Education, Labor and Pensions Committee), http://www.homelandsecurity.org/journal/ Epidemic_Proportions_2.pdf.

47. The following reports focus on gaps in public health preparedness. Institute of Medicine (2002), 'The future of the public's health in the 21st century', Washington, DC: National Academies Press, http://www.iom.edu/?id=16741. Canada, Ben (2003), 'Homeland security: standards for state and local preparedness', Washington, DC: Congressional Research Service, http://www.law.umaryland.edu/marshall/crsreports/crsdocuments/RL31680_10082003.pdf. General Accounting Office (2003), 'Bioterrorism: preparedness varied across state and local jurisdictions', http://www.gao.gov/new.items/d03373.pdf. Gursky, Elin (2004), 'drafted to fight terror: US public health on the front lines of biological defense', Arlington, VA: ANSER, http://www.homelandsecurity.org/bulletin/drafted_gursky.pdf. Gursky, Elin (2005), 'Epidemic Proportions', *supra*. Hearne, Shelley A. et al. (2005), 'Ready or not? Protecting the public's health from diseases, disasters, and bioterrorism', Washington, DC: Trust for America's Health.
48. Amonkar, Mayur M., Suresh Madhavan, Sidney A. Rosenbluth and Kenneth J. Simon (1999), 'Barriers and facilitators to providing common preventive screening services in managed care settings', *Journal of Community Health*, **24**, (3), 229–47.
49. Toner, Eric et al. (2006), 'Meeting report: hospital preparedness for pandemic influenza', *Biosecurity and Bioterrorism: Biodefense Strategy, Practice, and Science*, **4**, (2).
50. DiCorpo, Joseph E., 'Avian flu: The "inevitable thinning of the herd?"' Assist America, http://www.assistamerica.com.
51. American Hospital Association 2006 statistics.
52. 'The number of uninsured Americans continued to rise in 2004' (2005), Washington, DC: Center on Budget and Policy Priorities.
53. Brown, David (2006), 'Crisis seen in nation's ER care', *Washington Post*, http://www.washingtonpost.com/wp-dyn/content/article/2006/06/14/AR2006061402166.html.
54. Toner, Eric et al., *supra*.
55. Ibid.
56. Health Care Leadership Council (2005), 'Health care workforce shortage: background', http://www.hlc.org/html/background6.html.
57. Shah, Ghanshyam (1996), 'Doctors and the Plague', *Indian Journal of Medical Ethics*, **4**, (4), http://www.issuesinmedicalethics.org/044ed119.html.
58. Osterholm, Michael (2006), 'Emergency and pandemic preparedness: are you ready?', American Society of Association Executives and the Center for Association Leadership, reported to Elin Gursky by Col. Randall Larsen.
59. Qurshi, K., R.R.M. Gershon, M.F. Sherman, T. Straub, E. Gebbie, M. McCollum, M.J. Erwin and S.S. Morse, 'Study finds healthcare workers in New York area may be unable or unwilling to report to work during certain types of catastrophic events', describing a paper in the *Journal of Urban Health*, **82**, (3), press release.
60. Gerencher, Kristen (2005), 'Many US hospitals called unprepared for big disasters', Fox News, http://www.foxnews.com/story/0,2933,169772,00.html.
61. California HealthCare Foundation (2003), 'US hospitals unprepared for outbreak of SARS, GAO report finds', California Healthline, http://www.californiahealthline.org/index.cfm?Action=dspItem&itemID=95183.
62. Davis, Karen, Sara R. Collins, Michelle M. Doty, Alice Ho and Alyssa L. Holmgren (2005), 'Health and productivity among US workers', Commonwealth Fund Issue Brief, http://www.cmwf.org/usr_doc/856_Davis_hlt_productivity_USworkers.pdf.
63. Anderson, Allison (2004), 'Employers make investment in workforce health', *Austin Business Journal*, http://austin.bizjournals.com/austin/stories/2004/09/20/focus3.html.
64. Ibid.
65. McCafferty, Joseph (2005), 'Banking time: paid-time-off banks make managing absences easier', *CFO Magazine*, http://www.cfo.com/article.cfm/4443603/c_4448927?f=insidecfo.
66. Lovell, Vicky (2006), 'Paid sick days improve public health by reducing the spread of disease', Institute for Women's Policy Research Fact Sheet, http://www.iwpr.org/pdf/B250.pdf.
67. Ibid.
68. Smith, Stephen (2005), 'Sick and tired at work', *Boston Globe*, http://www.boston.com/news/globe/health_science/articles/2005/12/19/sick_and_tired_at_work/.
69. Hemp, Paul (2004), 'Presenteeism: at work – but out of it', *Harvard Business Review*, **82**, (10).
70. Davis, Karen et al., *supra*.
71. PandemicFlu.gov (http://www.pandemicflu.gov/) provides comprehensive government-wide information on pandemic influenza and avian influenza for the general public, health and emergency preparedness professionals, policy makers, government and business leaders, school systems and local communities. The US Chamber of Commerce website (http://www.uschamber.com/issues/index/defense/pandemic_influenza.htm?n=ia) provides information to help guide businesses through the pandemic planning.

10 Telework in the face of a pandemic
Paul B. Kurtz

If you can keep your head when all about you are losing theirs . . . (from the poem 'If', by Rudyard Kipling)

INTRODUCTION

This chapter focuses on one of the key goals of the Implementation Plan for the National Strategy to battle and contain a pandemic influenza assembled by the White House: sustaining the infrastructure and mitigating the impact of a pandemic on the economy and functioning of society.

OVERVIEW: TECHNOLOGY AND CONTINUITY OF OPERATIONS

In the early twentieth century, more than 20 million people around the world perished in the outbreak of Spanish influenza. During this epidemic, technology played a key role in continuity of operations. An advertisement placed by Bell Canada in the autumn of 1918 urged quarantined citizens to use the phone – which was relatively new at the time for the general public – for emergencies only: 'You will thus be helping to keep the service intact to meet the urgent needs of the community in the present emergency.'[1]

In the face of a flu pandemic today, information technology (IT) should not be for emergency use only, because IT is integral to our daily lives and business operations. IT sustains and fuels the economy, and in a crisis situation it would not only help keep the public informed, but also enable us to continue working, remaining productive.

Recent years have demonstrated the wide range of bad things that can and will happen to the United States: terrorists will strike; hurricanes and earthquakes will flood and flatten cities; major accidents will happen; and health epidemics will continue to appear. Resilience in the face of these challenges – an 'all hazards' approach – encompasses protection, preparedness and recovery. In this society, information technology holds the key to all three.

This chapter covers four areas:

- First, to invest in the capability to distribute the federal workforce, which means enabling federal agency employees to function under normal and adverse conditions – not only at home, under the traditional definition of telework, but from anywhere at any time. The private sector has made great strides in this arena, for a number of reasons covered later, but the federal government is unfortunately well behind.

- Second, to use the process of planning for a possible flu pandemic as an opportunity to break down some of the institutional barriers that have prevented the federal government from keeping pace with the private sector in distributing its workforce. There is an opportunity here for a paradigm shift in the federal government, from a bricks-and-mortar mentality to a more agile, efficient workforce. The technology exists today to do so securely. Doing so would pay significant, recurring long-term dividends to the government and taxpayers well beyond just crisis management.
- Third, to address the burden that a flu pandemic would have on the overall information infrastructure, including some of the challenges of the 'last mile distribution'.
- And fourth, to offer recommendations for actions that the federal government can take, in the near and long term, to make distributed workforce capability a reality.

PANDEMIC FLU: A BIOLOGICAL WINTER

Leaving aside sensational network TV specials, emphasis is placed on the gravity of this situation by briefly describing some of the very real potential results of a flu pandemic or similar crisis.

According to the White House plan, a flu pandemic could take as long as 18 months to run its course. During this time many workers will be unable to report to their offices, either because those offices will be closed, or because they must stay at home to care for children (because schools will also be closed) or the elderly. The White House plan recommends that government and the private sector start with the assumption that up to 40 percent of staff may be absent for two weeks at the height of a pandemic wave, with lower levels for a few weeks on either side of a wave.

Travel restrictions will likely include multiple forms of mass transit, ranging from subways to air travel. The safest course for many people will be simply not to leave their homes, where eventually they may have to depend on the government to provide 'last mile' delivery of food and other supplies.

Many industries – particularly those in the service sector – will significantly reduce operations. Supply chains will be disrupted and production placed on hold. However, some industries must continue to function in order to avert social breakdown: basic utilities, of course, as well as banks, hospitals, grocery stores and so forth. Even as it comes under heavy strain at the onset of the pandemic, operation of the nation's telecommunications network will be essential for first responders to do their jobs, and for law enforcement agencies to preserve order. This is a first-order concern.

The public will need timely, reliable information about ongoing developments, because a sudden sense of both catastrophe and isolation can quickly lead to mass panic. That, in turn, would quite possibly spawn a vicious cycle of looting and destruction that increases suffering and makes ultimate recovery all the more difficult.

Most importantly, the medical community simply must have access to secure, reliable communications systems if they are to save as many lives as possible. Front-line health care providers will need to coordinate treatment services, vaccine distribution and quarantines. Academic researchers will need to exchange test results and discuss new treatment modalities. The Centers for Disease Control and Prevention (CDC) will need to be able to track virus vectors and mutating strains and coordinate with their counterparts overseas. Much of this type of communications traffic rides on today's public Internet.

THE VALUE OF A DISTRIBUTED WORKFORCE

Against this backdrop, the unforgiving reality of today's federal workforce is that most contingency plans for emergency operations are designed for a maximum downtime of two or three days. As the White House has said, pandemics play out over weeks and months. Ensuring the continuity of key government operations under that kind of an extended period is a central responsibility of the nation's leadership.

The private sector has already begun to move aggressively in this direction. In the financial community, for example, many firms moved quickly after 9/11 to disperse critical facilities outside of lower Manhattan. Now they have gone one step further, so that their workers can work any time, anywhere. For example, at the time of this writing AT&T has the following structure: 30 percent of management work outside traditional offices, another 41 percent are regular teleworkers, and 91 percent of salaried employees are teleworkers. Productivity by teleworkers increased by 12.5 percent, or one hour per day. AT&T calculated $150 million in annual benefits through higher productivity, lower overheads, enhanced retention and recruitment.[2] Note that AT&T's efforts were not limited to 'essential personnel' only.

A distributed workforce helps in all hazards – a terrorist attack, a natural disaster or an accident. As the White House implementation plan states, during a flu pandemic, 'systems that facilitate communication in the absence of person-to-person contact can be used to minimize workplace risk for essential employees and can potentially be used to minimize workplace entry of people with influenza symptoms'. During a crisis, ordinary Americans' primary and immediate concern will surely be for the safety and health of their loved ones. As the initial shock wears off, however, the ability to continue meeting their primary professional responsibilities will offer many people solace, comfort and hope.

Fortunately, the technology exists to make all this possible. Much of the private sector has already adopted collaborative, secure, mobile technologies – there are various options – that allow employees to work wherever they need to, be it at home, at an Internet cafe or on the road. There are also technologies available that do not require a wholesale change in infrastructure, for example through secure remote access. In many cases companies have had no choice; the world is an increasingly difficult and dangerous place to do business, and they have had to adopt new technologies to ensure that they can weather any storm that comes along.

However, there are also widely recognized second-order benefits to workforce distribution: increased productivity, reduced traffic congestion and fuel consumption, a cleaner environment, greater personal flexibility and a higher quality of life. These benefits are well documented by such organizations as the Telework Consortium.

A serious effort to develop a distributed workforce capability in the federal government will have a lasting impact well beyond a possible flu pandemic. In other words, implementing telework is not a one-time sunk cost. Happy employees are more efficient ones, something the Office of Personnel Management has noticed as it contemplates retention and recruitment challenges after the retirement of the baby boom generation. Workforce distribution holds the potential simply to make life better in countless ways. As frightening as a flu pandemic might be, it also provides an opportunity, and the impetus, to break down structural barriers to reform.

BARRIERS TO A DISTRIBUTED WORKFORCE

So what are those barriers? The White House plan raises the issue of telework and acknowledges its importance, and calls for updating guidance and establishing performance metrics. In fact, much of the necessary guidance exists already.

The US General Services Administration (GSA) has issued a publication entitled 'Guidelines for Alternative Workplace Arrangements' (www.gsa.gov). It covers telecommuting, hotels, virtual offices, telework centers, and so forth, and affirms that for approved teleworkers, agencies can:

- pay for broadband installation and monthly access fees;
- provide new or additional equipment, including computers; and
- provide helpdesk and technical support.

There is also the Federal Preparedness Circular (FPC) 65, from the Federal Emergency Management Agency (FEMA), which focuses on emergency scenarios and the potential value of telework in continuity-of-operations planning. However, despite this guidance, the various federal telework programs remain fragmentary and uncoordinated. According to a Government Accountability Office (GAO) analysis in July 2004, just over 100 000 employees or less than 10 percent of the civilian federal workforce teleworked; by contrast, more than 20 million people, or almost 20 percent of the adult American workforce overall, works remotely one or more days per month.[3]

The reasons for this disparity involve the budget, statutory limitations and management. The structure of the federal budget may be the biggest obstacle to the expansion of telework. There is little incentive for agency leadership to adopt telework, as any savings resulting from reduced overheads are returned to the US Department of the Treasury and cannot be applied elsewhere in an agency's operations. Enabling agencies to realize such savings appears to at least require the intervention by the Office of Management and Budget (OMB), and possibly a change in law. In addition, a recent CDW survey indicated that 55 percent of IT managers believed the Federal Information Security Management Act hampered the expansion of telework.[4] Finally, telework would require changes in the ways that managers interact and evaluate employees. Many supervisors insist on having 'eyes-on' employees, and it is known that change is hard. There are technologies available today that help with the management of telecommuters. Technologies help managers understand who signed on when and accessed what applications, and for how long. The private sector has already demonstrated that these technologies work, and work well.

That is why, as frightening as a pandemic influenza might be, it also provides a real opportunity to change fundamentally the way the federal government does business – the kind of opportunity that does not come along very often. As a kind of action-forcing event, it makes the kind of structural reforms possible that might otherwise be strangled by bureaucracy. However, only Congress, in partnership with the White House, can set this kind of process in motion, with a combination of statutory requirements, incentives, deadlines and evaluation criteria.

One thing worth reinforcing is that of all the barriers to a distributed workforce, security is not among them. Again, private industry has led the way. Two types of security are crucial for securing telework. They include network security for inter-agency communications and connections used by teleworkers, and physical security for data on mobile devices. Devices for telework that require protection include notebook personal computers, desktop personal computers used at home, handheld personal digital assistants, telephones (regular, cell, and voice over Internet Protocol – VoIP) and desktop video conferencing. Technologies to secure these devices exist at the time of this writing including encryption, virtual private networks, authentication and access control technologies.

BURDEN ON THE INFORMATION INFRASTRUCTURE

There is another factor that must be taken into consideration. Little empirical evaluation has been done of the ability of the Internet infrastructure to support the traffic created when large numbers of employees – from both public and private sector – suddenly attempt to log on. There will surely be a spike in telecommunications traffic overall at the first onset of a crisis.

The continued operation of the information infrastructure deserves critical attention as it underlies so many aspects of the White House plan. The plan states that the federal government has primary responsibility in a number of areas, including containment efforts overseas, guidance related to protective measures, and modifications to law, regulation and monetary policy in order to mitigate the impact of a pandemic. The plan pointedly does not identify the backbone of the information infrastructure as an area of primary responsibility for the federal government. This is proper, given that the private sector owns and operates the vast majority of the critical information infrastructure. However, the government must play a leading role in coordinating its continued operation during a flu pandemic, as the same pressures that would affect the nation would also affect the people who operate the Internet.

It is not known what the impact would be if, for example, even half of the 60 000-plus employees of the Department of Health and Human Services – who help coordinate the entire national health care system – were to attempt to work off-site. It is known that any limitations on their ability to do their jobs would have a cascading effect throughout the medical system, and at the worst possible time, when large numbers of Americans are in need of emergency care.

Thus, everyone must act to ensure that the basic information infrastructure itself is robust enough to handle the surge of, potentially, millions of teleworkers. If not, there is the risk of creating a virtual traffic jam for 12 hours a day.

RECOMMENDATIONS

There are a number of strategic options that could help move the federal government toward workforce distribution capability, and strengthen America's Internet infrastructure so that it is there when needed.

Given the burdens and afflictions currently facing the Department of Homeland Security, the role of other federal agencies should be closely examined, particularly by the OMB. The OMB, in coordination with the Homeland Security Council, should convene a task force to expand telework aggressively. The federal government's efforts should not be limited to enabling 'essential personnel'. They should be far more aggressive in seeking to encompass as many federal employees as possible. As was mentioned earlier, telework within the federal government is less than 10 percent, compared with more than 20 percent in the private sector. This makes no sense; in fact, it is exactly backwards considering the critical nature of many federal programs to many Americans' day-to-day lives. The federal government should at the very least seek to match the private sector's capabilities, even if it takes a crash program to do it.

The President's National Security and Telecommunications Advisory Committee and National Infrastructure Advisory Council should undertake an immediate review of the burden that a flu pandemic would have on the information infrastructure. Recommendations and plans for 'surge' capability in the opening phase of a pandemic should be assembled and ready to activate.

In preparation for the 2004 Republican and Democratic National Conventions, the Office of Personnel Management conducted emergency preparedness surveys in Boston and New York, and used them to develop program training, in partnership with other agencies, to reduce the number of employees who had to report to work in the secured arcas. The project was an unqualified success. This illustrates why the federal government should test existing distributed workforce plans now, by designating both essential and non-essential employees to work from home for a day or two. Through such exercises, managers will be able to make better-informed policy and procurement decisions. Inviting participation from the private sector would also help analyze the potential impact on contract support.

Congress should seek to remove any real or perceived barriers for federal agencies to pursue telework by pursuing a three-pronged strategy. First, it should consider legislation that enables agencies to win by participating and deploying teleworking programs. In particular, agency budgets should allow the flexibility for agencies to retain savings from teleworking and deploy them elsewhere, so that they are not punished for their success. Second, Congress should also wield a 'stick', creating the means to cut budgets for failing to take the 'carrot'. Finally, Congress should also seek to address any perceived barriers that the Federal Information Security Management Act (FISMA) has on the expansion of telework.

CONCLUSION

It is true that many agencies have made strides within their own internal operations and continuity-of-operations planning. But unfortunately they have a long way to go before they are ready to work together in a crisis like an outbreak of avian flu. Preparing for a pandemic influenza that could last up to 18 months means the federal government must ensure employees can provide essential services for an extended period of time in a distributed and resilient manner, and doing so requires an information technology infrastructure robust enough to handle the job. The workforce distribution capability that is needed today is not available, and ultimately only Congress can ask the hard questions, and use both the carrots and the sticks necessary to make telework happen.

NOTES

1. Eekhof Bill (2005), 'Lessons of 1918–19 Spanish flu epidemic guiding preparedness', http://www.myka-wartha.com/ka/news/peterborough/, 5 October.
2. Telework at AT&T, annual surveys in 2004 and 2003.
3. 2004 American Interactive Consumer Survey conducted by the Dieringer Research Group and data from the International Telework Association and Council (ITAC).
4. Thorneyer, Rob and Roseanne Gerin (2006), 'CDW survey reveals increase in telework', *Washington Technology*, 6 March.

11 Immediate effects of terrorism on business
Dean Alexander

. . . the only thing we have to fear is fear itself. (President Franklin D. Roosevelt, 1st Inaugural Address, 1933)

INTRODUCTION

In this chapter, the short-term effects of catastrophic terrorism are discussed in terms of economic and sector responses, including ramifications for financial markets and effects on business activity. Industry responses crafted thereafter include: shifts and flexibility within and among business sectors; development and expansion of homeland security companies; funding such firms; and mergers and acquisitions in that sector.

INITIAL IMPACT OF CATASTROPHIC TERRORISM: ECONOMIC AND SECTOR CONSEQUENCES

The initial economic impact of the 9/11 attacks was acute and negative, exemplified by substantial declines in stock markets and, thereby, the value of public companies (for example airlines, travel and insurance), and closure of stock and bond markets for several days due to damage near those locations.

The Dow Jones Industrial Average (DJIA) and NASDAQ Composite Index declined by 7.13 percent and 6.83 percent, respectively, on the day the market reopened (17 September 2001). On that day, airline and travel stocks dropped significantly in value, falling between 30 and 60 percent. In the five days after trading resumed, the DJIA declined by 14.3 percent, the largest weekly fall since 1933. During the nearly two-week period after 9/11, the Bank for International Settlements reported global equities lost some $3 trillion – about 12 percent of their value.

In the months subsequent to the 9/11 incidents, US economic growth waned and unemployment rose, while consumer spending and confidence dropped. Commodity prices, such as oil and gold, spiked. The Federal Reserve Board injected liquidity into the money supply and reduced interest rates over subsequent months.

Moreover, the 9/11 attacks resulted in millions of dollars of damage to buildings and infrastructure (for example telecommunications, electricity and subway lines); billions of dollars of lost economic output; some $50 billion in insurance liability; the demise of thousands of talented workers; $5 billion in the government-sponsored Victim Compensation Fund; and billions of dollars in homeland security outlays by government and industry.

New York City spent some $825 million in World Trade Center (WTC)-related costs, including about $350 million in removing debris in the six months following the 9/11 incidents. According to the New York City Partnership, New York City's economy would lose nearly 100 times the overall clean-up costs – about $83 billion. A November 2001 National League of Cities study predicted that the 9/11 attacks would cause municipal revenues to decline by $11.4 billion.

Corporate America suffered severe initial damage to particular sectors, including airlines, tourism, hospitality and insurance. Other sectors that witnessed some declines – in certain regions – were real estate, energy, technology and entertainment. The Washington, DC, area and Manhattan were hit particularly hard as demonstrated by declines in tourism and hospitality revenue.

Another negative ramification of the 9/11 attacks, in addition to the horrific deaths and injuries, was the perception that the United States was no longer immune to catastrophic terror attacks on its soil. Also, by attacking American symbols of economic and military power, American vulnerability to terrorism was exposed.

The impact of 9/11 on the world economy was likewise negative. This was particularly true in Japan and Europe, which were already experiencing recessions prior to the attacks. US neighbors, Mexico and Canada, suffered in the subsequent economic downturn, particularly in the aviation tourism and hospitality sectors.

It is extremely difficult to predict prospective economic and sector consequences in the event of another catastrophic terror attack. Yet, it is probable that immediate financial market shocks will be coupled with declines in the affected sector(s). The severity and breadth of a future catastrophe – whether limited to a city, region or broader in scope – will weigh on the severity of the attacks. With that said, significant improvements in corporate security and government counterterror efforts should lessen the negative implications of future attacks.

Although some sectors were severely damaged, other industries strengthened following the 9/11 incidents. Demand for homeland security products and services expanded almost immediately. In this regard, when the principal US stock markets opened on 17 September 2001, the stock price of some defense, security (for example bomb detection and corporate security) and technology firms (for example providers of videoconferencing) actually rose by over 100 percent. Prospects of huge government expenditure to support the newly declared war on terrorism provided some of the impetus for the rise in prices of stock in the security industry.

On 11 March 2004, multiple bombings on commuter trains in Madrid killed 190 and injured 1500 people. On that day, European stock market benchmarks were hit particularly hard, with the European Dow Jones STOXX 600 Index declining by 2.67 percent. Spain's stock market index fell by 2.18 percent. Likewise, US stock markets were negatively affected, evidenced by decreases in the DJIA (1.64 percent) and NASDAQ Composite (1.03 percent). Travel-related stocks in the United States and Europe declined significantly. International stock markets, as referenced in the Dow Jones World Index, fell by 1.58 percent.

After the 9/11 incidents, there was widespread concern about a possible al Qaeda link to the attacks. Those concerns were confirmed fairly quickly as Spanish and Moroccan law enforcement officials picked up operatives linked to radical Islamic groups. These developments only exacerbated declines and volatility in international stock markets during subsequent weeks.

TRANSACTIONS CANCELLED, DELAYED AND BUSINESS INTERRUPTED

Shortly following the WTC and Pentagon attacks, various companies announced that they would put on hold their previously planned investments. Manpower Inc., the nation's largest supplier of temporary workers, canceled plans to open 40 new offices. Eastman Chemical, a leading supplier of material for plastics and paint, announced that new investments would be postponed. C.R. England Inc., a family-owned trucking company with 2500 tractor trailers, stated that the attacks would discourage the firm from making further investments in the immediate future.

The 9/11 incidents caused some companies to reconsider the appropriateness or timing of certain investments and transactions. Berkshire Hathaway apparently cited a clause in a contract enabling termination of an agreement in the event of 'war or armed conflict', less than a week after the attacks. More specifically, it was reported that Berkshire Hathaway rescinded its offer to purchase up to $500 million of Finova Group's 7.5 percent senior-secured notes. A number of airlines contacted Boeing Co. to request delaying the delivery of several dozen airplanes, valued in total at several billion dollars.

The attacks also derailed very advanced merger negotiations between Keefe, Bruyette & Woods and BNP Paribas in a deal expected to be worth between $300 million and $400 million. It was reported that the parties may resume discussions in the future. Keefe, Bruyette & Woods lost about one-third of its employees during the WTC attacks. Also, the attacks apparently interfered with initial merger discussions between the investment firms of Lehman Brothers Holdings Inc. and Lazard LLC.

A substantial number of conventions and conferences were canceled or rescheduled nationwide as people were concerned about traveling during the weeks following the 9/11 attacks. Leisure travel, including to aviation-dependent locations such as Las Vegas and Miami, declined significantly (for example Miami lost $15 million in revenues daily in the days following the attacks).

Firms delayed construction of high-rise office buildings and condominiums as terror concerns and rising insurance weighed on future developments. New products and long-planned advertising campaigns were put in abeyance, as the public needed time to grieve after the 9/11 incidents. Cross-sector business initiatives were frozen as firms considered what impact the attacks would have on their bottom line.

Commercial airports experienced severe declines in flights and passengers following 9/11. Reduced traffic led to abated aircraft landing fees. Fewer passengers resulted in less income to airport parking-lot operators, stores, restaurants, ground transportation and concessions.

Despite amazing resilience by businesses and the public after 9/11, there was still some apprehension as to whether such attacks would be replicated – or worse – in other parts of the country. There was understandable confusion over whether a state sponsor of terror would assist al Qaeda (or other groups) in providing support for super-terrorism attacks against the United States. Resolve against terror, coupled with a modicum of uncertainty, marked preliminary industry responses to the catastrophic 9/11 incidents.

In the aftermath of the October 2003 massive car bombing of the Red Cross headquarters in Iraq, the organization decided to close its offices in Baghdad and Basra. While that response was likely hoped for by the attackers, it also eliminated the contribution of a leading non-governmental entity. Often, as in this case, an entity that was recently affected by terrorism may temporarily cease operations and evacuate personnel from a high-risk region. If a company should shut down operations following a terror attack, the firm would lose revenue and incur other costs, while the host country would lose jobs and prestige as foreign investment would likely decline.

SUBSEQUENT INDUSTRY RESPONSES

Impact on Sectors

Significant terrorist attacks may negatively impact upon several sectors simultaneously (for example commercial aviation, insurance, hospitality and tourism) during an early period while creating and expanding opportunities in other industries (for example corporate security, defense, biometrics and explosive detection equipment). Product lines may be removed from the market or may be limited in their preference depending on the severity of the attack. Terrorism insurance coverage became scarce and costly after 9/11, though later, offerings in that space expanded. During the initial coverage of 9/11, major television networks did not run any commercials, in honor of the victims.

Terrorist attacks using the instrumentality of one sector (for example public mail carriers) can create negative results on the same sector (for example public mail carriers). Concurrently that same attack can fuel demand in other unrelated sectors (for example pharmaceuticals – Cipro; and electron beam irradiation machine-mail and germ detection equipment).

During the autumn of 2001, a number of anthrax-tainted letters were sent by unknown assailant(s), causing five deaths and over a dozen injuries. The anthrax incidents led to the temporary closure of selected government and private offices. Also, the events injected panic into some segments of the American public relative to the safety of the US mail system.

In light of such threats, the US Postal Service purchased eight electron beam systems (machines to irradiate mail) from industry. The US government planned to purchase several hundred devices, totaling additional government outlays of over $1 billion.

A serious terrorist incident can result in future investments being temporarily delayed or canceled. Likewise, a major attack can shut down segments of an industry for days. This was exhibited when commercial aviation was grounded temporarily and US stock markets were closed for several days after 9/11.

A terrorist incident on one portion of an industry, such as commercial airlines in the transportation industry, can have positive ramifications on other segments of the same industry, such as corporate jets and charter services. The significant downturn in the use of commercial airlines immediately following 9/11 spawned greater interest in the use of trains, buses and rental cars as alternative modes of transportation. Initial declines in airline, tourism and insurance stocks after September were balanced by accelerated demand for homeland-security firm equities.

A severe terrorist incident, even if not directly affecting the target industry, may nevertheless result in the hastened demise of already weak firms. This was witnessed in the autumn of 2001 when Renaissance Cruises and Aladdin Gaming, two large companies in the tourism and hotel industries, filed for Chapter 11 bankruptcy. During November 2001, ANC Rental Corp., owner of the Alamo and National rental car companies, filed for bankruptcy due to declining demand fueled by weak commercial aviation travel in the autumn of 2001.

If terrorists use pathogens such as anthrax to infect the mail system, at the same time that they engage in sniper-like attacks, then two modes of commerce – in-person purchases and online purchases (for example delivery of products via the mail systems) – would be affected. A severe cyber-terror attack against principal e-commerce sites would likewise undermine online purchases.

The consequences of the 9/11 attacks on specific industries, such as insurance and aviation, are being played out more than five years after the incidents. Another effect of terror threats – in this case bioterrorism – is accelerated by investments in biotechnology companies and pharmaceutical firms that have capabilities to countering bioterrorism.

In attacking the tourism sector, numerous businesses are harmed simultaneously such as hotels, restaurants and transportation (for example aviation, car rentals). By attacking the tourism sector of the economy, an important source of revenue is lessened, creating more unemployment and dissatisfaction with the government. Terror attacks can lead to such dissatisfaction with the ruling party as to cause a regime change or a shift in government policies aligned with the terror group's goals (for example in 11 March 2004, terror attacks in Spain contributed to a Socialist Workers' Party victory in national elections).

Attacks against tourist interests have occurred worldwide. For example, in Egypt in 1993, tourists were targeted in multiple attacks, including a bomb which was hurled at a bus carrying 15 South Korean tourists in Cairo, and gunmen fired shots at boats carrying 44 British passengers and 22 French tourists along the Nile during two separate incidents. In Egypt, between 1992 and 1994, there were nearly 130 terrorist attacks. The incidents resulted in the deaths of nine tourists and injuries to about 60. Between 1992 and 1993 the number of tourists visiting Egypt declined by 21.8 percent.

The Irish Republican Army (IRA) has targeted the coastal resort areas of England. The Kurdish Workers' Party (PKK) has been responsible for bombing tourist hotels as well as kidnapping tourists and holding them as pawns in their political negotiations with the Turkish government. Terrorist attacks have discouraged tourism in Corsica. In Spain, the Basque Fatherland and Liberty terrorist group (ETA) claimed responsibility for setting explosive devices at tourist hotels on the Mediterranean coast. The bombings of two Bali nightclubs – resulting in some 200 deaths – in 2002 marked a recent example of terrorist groups targeting tourists.

While the impact of a large-scale terrorist attack can be severe, as witnessed on 9/11, it is also correct to suggest that economies and businesses can withstand substantial pain. The post-9/11 US economy was remarkably resilient despite some initial shocks. Firms nationwide have largely adjusted to the new risk dynamic endemic in the post-9/11 business environment.

Selected Sector: Real Estate

Before the 9/11 attacks, telecommuting was seen as a stagnating trend, as bosses decided that it was too difficult to manage a network of dispersed, remote workers. Employees felt stigmatized if they were not seen around the office. But the 9/11 attacks caused many workers to re-evaluate their priorities, and some companies are exploring this option.

Companies now view home-based employees as a defensive measure should their offices become inaccessible. As American Express Co. offices were damaged during 9/11 attacks, hundreds of employees worked 'virtually', as the company set up temporary locations in New Jersey and Connecticut. Firms located outside New York, such as Charles Schwab Corp. (San Francisco) and ABN AMRO North America (Chicago) acknowledged exploring telecommuting options with great vigor.

The above shift could result in a slight reduction in traditional commercial leasing to smaller-scale commercial developments as well as technologically enhanced residential models. Also, consultants advising on establishing virtual offices and the companies that assist in establishing their telecommunications networks should benefit from this trend.

There has been an initial downturn in larger real estate projects due to higher property insurance as well as reluctance by some lenders. Concurrently, there has been increased interest in smaller development projects, including duplicative offices for sensitive business locations (for example trading facilities and backup operations facilities).

Companies with decentralized real estate set-ups – various units spread out among disparate cities or regions – may become a growing trend among selected firms that seek to reduce the impact of a massive terrorist attack. Some companies have already adopted the decentralized paradigm. A decentralized approach reduces vulnerability should a severe terrorist attack strike one location. Such schemes also raise costs as duplicate facilities and multiple personnel (including persons trained for additional job functions) are necessary.

Some architects and urban planners argue that in light of possible massive terrorist attacks during this century, it is preferable to construct future office developments separated by parks and sports stadiums. Whether such perspectives will be adopted nationwide depend on various factors, such as costs, aesthetic appeal, practicality and the perception that large-scale terror threats are genuine.

The threat of terrorism on US soil adds further challenges to landlords of large-scale retail centers, such as shopping malls. Landlords of such developments must balance the need for great security measures without scaring away customers who might perceive such steps as confirming that shopping malls are imminent terrorist targets.

With that in mind, some shopping centers have undertaken a number of security measures: hired additional security guards; improved safety and security training for property management staff; tightened restrictions on truck deliveries of merchandise and foodstuffs; and broadened parking restrictions. However, searching all shoppers prior to them entering a shopping mall is not envisioned in the United States – at least for now.

RETROSPECTIVE

The American economy's capacity to rebound from the attacks on 11 September was due to various factors. First, rapid, decisive government and industry responses took hold. Second, employees in the public and private sectors displayed courage and dedication, leading in some cases to sacrificing their lives to aid others (for example firefighters and police). Third, consumers contributed to the recovery as they continued to shop, although sales in many spheres declined in the initial weeks after the attacks. Fourth, sector-specific laws were enacted to soften the impact of the attacks. Fifth, intelligence and law enforcement success in rounding up terrorists at home and abroad gave the impression – partially correct – that the US-based component of the war on terrorism was proceeding fairly well. Sixth, the lack of a subsequent large-scale terrorist attack on US soil has aided US economic and business resilience.

CONCLUSION

By its very nature, the terrorist is victorious even in the absence of physical casualties. The threat of force, and its psychological impact, suffices. Also, minimal casualties resulting from an incident can aid the terrorist group in meeting its propaganda objectives. The 9/11 and 3/11 attacks instilled fear in millions of global citizenry.

12 Prospering in the secure economy
Greg Pellegrino and Bill Eggers

Private-sector preparedness is not a luxury; it is a cost of doing business in the post-9/11 world. (The 9/11 Commission Final Report, 22 July 2004)

INTRODUCTION

12 September 2001 – the global economy is forever changed. The new leaders, in both government and the private sector, will increasingly be defined by how well they respond in this period of maximum uncertainty. The organizations that prosper in the face of these new realities will not only proactively invest in compliance, processes and tools to become more secure themselves, but will also discover how to create economic value from relationships, processes and even products that enable security.

The new environment created by heightened security concerns is much different than that experienced during the last major economic revolution – the dot-com period. This new period is defined by greater vulnerability, increased threat awareness, regulatory compliance and rapid response to change. It is an environment not only signified by the global war on terrorism, but also of enhanced visibility – and responsibility – across supply chains and cross-boundary relationships.

Prospering in the secure economy will require three essential capabilities:

- Continual chief executive officer (CEO) and leadership focus.
- Greater collaboration between business and government.
- Enhanced shareholder and constituent value from security.

Organizations that do not translate the current period of increased security compliance requirements and standards into sustained performance will miss an opportunity in this period of rapid change. This chapter shares important insights into the new secure economy and explains what organizations need to do to get started.

We have spent several years working alongside government employees at the US Department of Homeland Security – not to mention advising many other government leaders overseas. The passion, energy and expertise these professionals bring to the challenges of responding to this new environment is inspiring. Their dedication and professionalism has made security one area where the government has become a major source of global best practices.

EXECUTIVE SUMMARY

Since 9/11, global business has had to confront additional terrorist strikes around the world, a steep rise in cyber attacks (at a cost of $12.5 billion in 2003),[1] huge value losses, hefty increases in security spending and insurance premiums, and a spate of new government security regulations and requirements.

With the increased importance of security has come a fundamental shift in the way it is viewed by companies and governments: the concept of security has expanded from primarily protecting assets and people to sustaining business no matter what type of interruption might occur, from a sudden spike in interest rates or the spread of a computer virus, to an act of terrorism.

In short, the economic playing field has changed. We have entered the age of the secure economy, an era defined by five new realities:

1. Rapid change: the global business climate has been nothing if not tumultuous in recent years.
2. New regulatory requirements: on the heels of spending billions of dollars complying with Sarbanes–Oxley regulations, businesses now find themselves confronting a host of new government security requirements.
3. Heightened threats and greater uncertainty: companies remain unclear about what kinds of threats warrant the greatest concern, how they would be affected if particular kinds of attacks occurred, what marketplace conditions would follow particular kinds of attacks, and when the heightened threat will pass.
4. Complex and interdependent risks: for all the advantages of the extended enterprise and its interdependent supply chains, this organizational model also puts firms at greater security risk due to the multiple partners and handoffs involved in production and distribution.
5. Globalization and the 24/7 news cycle: companies now have only minutes – not hours or days – to respond proactively to a security incident before risking possible damage to their brand.

In the face of these conditions, ensuring the safety of goods, people, information and facilities has become an important prerequisite of global commerce. Governments worldwide, and in particular in the United States, are doing their part to try to bring this about. A raft of new government initiatives to secure critical infrastructure, the vast majority of which is owned and operated by the private sector, have been issued in the aftermath of 9/11, with more in the pipeline. New security requirements imposed on shippers, ports, truckers, airlines, food producers, retailers, financial institutions and other industries are forcing fundamental changes in business operations. These changes will cost businesses tens of billions of dollars as companies reconfigure their business processes, purchase security technologies, hire new people, install new equipment, and harden their physical and information technology infrastructures.

BEYOND COMPLIANCE: THE BUSINESS CASE FOR ENHANCING SECURITY

For many firms, the most immediately compelling reason for investing additional resources in security will be to comply with the new government requirements. The prospect of hefty fines and the inevitable bad publicity that will ensue will be enough to convince many CEOs and boards to step up their security efforts. New industry security standards promulgated in energy, food, shipping and other sectors will put additional compliance pressure on firms.

But if the business case for greater security is simply about compliance, the effort will ultimately fall short. Regulations and standards will be treated as only a burden, rather than a stimulus toward greater action. Many firms unwittingly do the bare minimum, treating security as just an add-on cost that should be minimized to the extent possible, while others will ignore the new requirements altogether. The inevitable result: persistent security gaps in the global supply chain and critical infrastructure.

Fortunately, achieving greater security need not involve only costs, and little in the way of benefits. Corporate investments in secure commerce can go hand in hand with real, measurable business benefits:

- Cost reduction: security investments can be used to drive more efficiency into the supply chain and thereby lower costs and raise productivity. For example, in one major public–private supply chain initiative, cost savings of between $378 and $462 per container per shipment were realized from employing a mix of information technology (IT) tools to secure and streamline shipping.
- Enhanced revenues: in addition to providing important security benefits, enabling technologies like RFID (radio frequency identification system) tags can enable timelier and automatic information flows, thereby helping companies increase revenues by slashing the amount of time their goods are not out on the shelves.
- Better risk management: proactive security policies can help firms become more resilient by better managing the risks of a terrorist attack or other security incident.
- Brand protection: security investments, especially in the areas of incident prevention and crisis response, can help to preserve and protect a brand, the most valuable asset for many companies.
- Market share preservation: with various government and industry initiatives inducing retailers and manufacturers to require a higher level of security assurance from their suppliers, verifiable security practices will become obligatory for competing in the secure global marketplace.

THRIVING IN TODAY'S SECURITY-CONSCIOUS ENVIRONMENT

Prospering in the secure economy requires leading organizations to master the following five challenges:

- Managing risks and uncertainty: to cope with the growing risks and uncertainties of today's turbulent world, companies must understand industry-specific threats, assess vulnerabilities, and mitigate those with the greatest potential for disruption.
- Enhancing crisis response management: companies today must be prepared to deal with a crisis immediately after it occurs. A poor response can do permanent damage to a brand.
- Integrating security strategy across the enterprise: many companies take a Balkanized approach to security, and by doing so weaken the effectiveness of the overall security function. What is needed instead is a layered, integrated security model under the direction of an enterprise-wide chief security officer (CSO).
- Extending supply chain protection end-to-end: firms that thrive in today's networked economy will have security and sustainability built into their supply chains and greater security compatibility with their partners.
- Maximizing shareholder value: forward-looking companies can finesse their security investments to achieve competitive advantage in three ways: by enhancing their brand, by securing first-mover advantage, or by gaining a foothold in a new market.

THE ROLE OF GOVERNMENT

Governments, too, have a vital part to play in working with the private sector to secure critical networks, ranging from the transportation system to the food supply. To facilitate the transition to the secure economy, the public sector should:

- Spearhead greater information sharing between the public and private sectors. Public–private information sharing on threats and vulnerabilities has emerged as a critical element of country homeland security strategies.
- Provide incentives for companies to invest in security. Companies with exemplary security policies should be given certain advantages by government agencies, such as fewer inspections, liability protection, tax incentives, reduced reporting requirements or lower compliance costs.
- Promote global cooperation on standards. A nightmare scenario for business would be to be forced to comply with a hodgepodge of disconnected and incompatible country-specific security requirements as their goods move across the supply chain. Global standards (in shipping container and energy pipeline security, for instance) could keep this from happening.

THE ROAD AHEAD

The secure economy is here to stay. While the threats and risks may never go away, by working together to bolster security, private firms and governments can make it a lot less likely that those who would do harm succeed.

FROM THE WAR ROOM TO THE BOARDROOM

August 2003 – a pipe bomb explodes at the Emeryville, CA corporate headquarters of biotech company Chiron, delivered by animal rights activists waging a prolonged campaign of intimidation against the company.

Half a world away, in November of the same year, the British-owned HSBC Bank in Istanbul, Turkey, is reduced to a smoldering mass of charred wreckage by a terrorist attack. The death toll: 27. Later that winter, in April 2004, Osama bin Laden urges his followers to take their global jihad to large multinationals, particularly Jewish-owned companies and American firms working in Iraq. 'It is the warlords, the bloodsuckers, who are steering the world policy from behind a curtain', he proclaims. Several months later, al Qaeda hijacks a California company's website to show a video of Paul Johnson, an American contractor held hostage in Iraq. The next day, the aviation engineer is beheaded.

Across the globe, security has moved from the war room to the boardroom. National security is no longer the province of governments alone. Whether they like it or not, private companies man the front lines in the battle against global terrorism. They own and operate the bulk of the power plants, nuclear energy facilities, power grids and other critical infrastructure in the West – 85 percent of it in the United States. They are generally an easier target than government buildings because of their geographic dispersion. And the ultimate goal of al Qaeda is to destroy a way of life, of which the private sector is a key component.

Though the sustained threat of terrorism is the most visible manifestation of the security threats to global businesses, it is by no means the only one. The 18-year-old student who hacks into a firm's customer database, the disgruntled employee who places cyanide in a drug company's medicine, or the activist organization threatening to punish a company unless it acquiesces to its demands, all represent significant security threats to business.

The secure economy is characterized by a fundamental shift in the way security is viewed by companies and governments: while once mostly signifying the physical protection of assets and people, the concept of security has taken on a broader meaning. It now stands for sustainability and the ability to make rapid adjustments to the business, to enforce compliance, and to absorb unforeseen costs – all essential components of managing a business.

And while terrorism is only one of many security threats to global businesses, it represents the disruptive force driving security to the boardroom level and causing organizations to develop new capabilities, many of which will be relevant to other, more immediate threats. For example, the world's most secure barricades now protect the White House, the American Embassy in Iraq and . . . Walt Disney World. Terrorists who attempt to drive a truck full of explosives into the Magic Kingdom now first have to get past giant, hydraulically powered antiterrorist barricades designed to stop a 20 000-pound truck bomb traveling at 70 mph.[2] Meanwhile in Tennessee, FedEx has created its own police force to safeguard the company's packages, while in Washington, DC, a financial services firm has equipped all of its employees with their own bicycles and gas masks in the event of a biological weapons attack on the nation's capital.

Survey data also demonstrate the growing centrality of security to corporate concerns.

It is named as a top or high priority by 87 percent of business executives.[3] Terrorism itself was cited as the fourth most pressing security concern among US firms, up from number 17 in 2001, according to a Pinkerton survey.[4]

The greater attention to security is beginning to materialize in company budgets. More than half of the companies surveyed by the Yankee Research Group in 2003 said they would increase their security budget over the next three years.[5] Meanwhile, more than 80 percent of transportation executives interviewed by Deloitte in the spring of 2004 said they expected their firm to increase security spending over the next 12 months.[6]

These sentiments represent a dramatic turnaround. As recently as 2002, more than 90 percent of business executives did not see their firms as a potential target of terrorism and not even half said their companies were prepared to handle a wide range of emergencies.[7] Now, more than two-thirds of company executives view terrorism as a significant threat to their organization, according to the RAND Europe institute – and 83 percent believe the threat will rise.[8]

Concern with security may also be linked, to some degree, to corporate governance issues. Boards have a responsibility to assure that management has plans for securing people, facilities, information and business continuity in the event of an incident. More specifically, under section 404 of the Sarbanes–Oxley Act, companies are required to report on the effectiveness of their internal controls, bringing to the surface the need to comply with information security standards.[9]

Meanwhile, companies and governments the world over are discovering just how large an impact the secure economy can have on their bottom line. American businesses, at the time of this writing, have lost more than $30 billion by 2004 due to delays in visas for foreign business travelers caused by tougher screening procedures.[10]

Washington, DC-based Riggs Bank was fined $25 million, a record sum, in 2004 for allegedly violating tough new anti-money laundering laws in its handling of tens of millions of dollars worth of cash transactions in Saudi-controlled accounts that were under investigation for possible terrorism-financing links. Riggs subsequently announced it would give up most of its international banking business. In the Middle East, meanwhile, foreign workers left Saudi Arabia in droves in 2004 as a result of terrorist attacks on Westerners.

Organizations that are lax in their efforts to protect their assets and employees, or organizations that are unresponsive to government or partner security concerns, risk being disaggregated from the marketplace. Alastair Morrison, chairman and CEO of Kroll Security International, explains: 'Security has become a main boardroom focus. Since 9/11 and the Madrid bombings, companies have been asking: What can bring this company down? In the past, it's been a corporate governance issue, but now it's a security issue. Companies are themselves much more accountable and have to become much more farsighted in their approach. They are aware of their own liability.'

Companies must also accept that they will remain unclear about what kinds of threats warrant the greatest concern, how they would be affected if particular kinds of attacks or disasters occurred, what marketplace conditions would follow specific kinds of attacks, and when the heightened threat will pass. It is therefore hard to make assumptions about precisely what the best security investments are. Concrete barriers? Metal detectors? Gas masks? Passwords? RFID tags? Vaccines? What companies need is a strategy that includes a careful appraisal of all the potential dangers. This will enable them to fashion a response that addresses whatever it is that appears to be the most worrisome for their specific profile, thereby avoiding the extremes of focusing on a narrow slice of concerns or trying to prepare a little bit for every conceivable risk.

With the dawn of the secure economy we have reached a key inflection point. If done right – that is, if used as an opportunity to enhance business value – all the time and money spent by governments and businesses on security today could yield much better-prepared public and private organizations tomorrow. Innovation would be spurred as organizations seek inventive ways to achieve both greater security and higher productivity. Greater security and greater prosperity would go hand in hand.

With the wrong decisions and wrong approaches, however, the terrorists could win without firing a shot. The increased emphasis on tightening corporate security vulnerabilities could simply result in overly prescriptive government regulations, higher costs for private companies with little tangible benefits, and grudging and uneven compliance. Governments, unwittingly, could restrict commerce so tightly that the economy slows to a crawl. Delays at borders, ports and airports could cascade through offices and factories, upsetting entire supply chains. The hard-earned gains in global supply-chain efficiencies and trade logistics of recent years – $150 billion worth a year, by some estimates – could be lost.[11] Just-in-time delivery could become merely a distant memory. Distrust between the public and private sectors would retard collaboration.

Such a future is, of course, unacceptable. It is also eminently avoidable. Given the right strategies from business and sensible policies by government, instead of a drag on trade, security can be a means to enable commerce in a more uncertain world.

THE SECURITY REGULATORY ENVIRONMENT

Much of the impetus for the increased emphasis on security is being driven by government. Public sector budgets are swelling with intensified security spending. New high-tech systems are being installed to secure borders, ports, airports and government buildings, intelligence is being beefed up, information sharing improved, and grants to first responders dispersed.

Despite the tens of billions of dollars being spent by governments on strengthening security, however, there are real limits to how much more secure the public sector alone can make us. The reason? Many of the prime terrorist targets and most serious security vulnerabilities reside in facilities owned and operated by the private sector: port terminals and freight containers, airplanes and cruise ships, the food supply and bank systems, electricity grids and water-treatment plants. To reduce vulnerabilities in these and other areas, governments from Canada to Australia have passed a spate of new security-related laws that effectively enlist everyone from brokerage houses to shippers in the global struggle to augment security. In the US, which has particularly emphasized steps to engage the private sector in security, improved collaboration between federal agencies and the private sector is a key goal of the country's homeland security strategy.

Understanding the multitude of new security requirements, directives and partnerships is de rigueur for companies hoping to prosper in the secure economy. In ways both obvious and subtle, they are reshaping international trade.

Consider maritime commerce. One thing that keeps many government security officials awake at night is the prospect of dirty bombs being smuggled into their countries hidden in one of the millions of containers that come through the world's ports each year – few of which are ever inspected. This is almost universally considered to be one of the biggest security vulnerabilities (70 percent of transportation company executives rate shipping containers vulnerable according to a Deloitte survey),[12] prompting dozens of countries – as well as several international organizations – to tighten maritime security. The United States has introduced the 2002 US Maritime Transportation Security Act, the 24-Hour Advanced Manifest Rule, and the Container Security Initiative (CSI), among other major maritime security measures. Globally, the most significant maritime compliance issues revolve around the International Ship and Port Facility Security Code (ISPS), the first multilateral ship and port security standard ever created. The bottom line is that nearly every company engaged in global trade will be affected by new maritime regulations.

Tightened border controls will also affect commerce. Large-scale efforts to tighten security along land border crossings are under way in Europe and the US. The most ambitious initiative is the US-VISIT program, which, at a potential cost of more than $10 billion, aims to create a new high-tech virtual border around the United States. Meanwhile in Europe, the EU has proposed expanding its border information system to include storage, transfer and possible querying of biometric data, particularly photographs and fingerprints.

Rail travel represents another transport target of terrorists, as evidenced by the March 2004 Madrid train bombings. In response, Japan doubled the number of police officers at six major railway stations.[13] Across the Pacific, a US Senate Committee approved a bill in August 2004 that requires the US Department of Homeland Security to perform a national rail vulnerability assessment, recommend security upgrades to the rail system, and allocate grants for the upgrades to be carried out.[14] And in Europe, where rail traffic is 12 times that in America, countries have increased police patrols, bomb detection measures and electronic surveillance.[15]

TRANSFORMATION OF HOMELAND SECURITY STRUCTURES

A number of countries are trying to strengthen their ability to prevent and respond to terrorist attacks by merging the various agencies involved in air, sea, port, border, intelligence and cyber security into one mega-department. These actions are important to business because they mean, in some cases, new missions, new people, new reporting relationships and greater potential private-sector funding for security. These changes represent both new opportunities and new challenges for businesses. The largest such initiative, of course, is in the United States, where approximately 180 000 personnel from 22 different government entities became part of the Department of Homeland Security on 1 March 2003. The department unified the agencies responsible for securing US borders and is implementing a layered security strategy through an increased presence at key foreign ports, improved visa and inspection processes, strengthened seaport security, and improved security technology at airports and border crossings.[16] As Tom Ridge, the Secretary of the department, said at the 2004 Homeland and Global Security Summit about the formation of the department: 'The historical government reorganization that took place, the largest since the Truman presidency, presented the biggest 'change management' challenge of all time – simultaneously a merger, acquisition, divestiture, and start-up on the largest of scales.'[17] Other countries have also done some reorganization in order to address new security threats. Germany's Federal Ministry of the Interior (BMI) was restructured to take the lead on anti-terrorism activities.[18] Canada has also aggressively re-examined its security apparatus. The newly established Department of Public Safety and Emergency Preparedness (PSEP) is responsible for emergency preparedness, crisis management, national security, policing, oversight, crime prevention and border functions.[19] Since 2001, the Canadian government has provided $37 million for the federal–provincial–territorial Joint Emergency Preparedness Program (JEPP).[20]

Food security has also risen in importance on the governmental agenda. In the United States, the 2003 Bioterrorism Act requires companies to give advance notice to US officials of the import of all food products to be consumed by humans or animals before the shipments arrive in the country. Within the EU, Directive 178, Article 18 consolidates 17 existing hygiene directives and is intended to produce consistency and clarity throughout the food production chain from 'farm to fork'.

Other areas of concern are health care, financial services and energy. In the US, hospitals, doctors, insurance companies and other health institutions are required to protect the privacy and security of individuals' health information to comply with the Health Insurance Portability and Accountability Act (HIPAA). The financial services industry has also faced increased security regulations as governments try to shut down the money supply that finances terrorist organizations. Title III of the USA Patriot Act specifically requires the private sector to report money laundering transactions, while the UN Security Council has called on all member states to freeze the assets of those who commit or attempt to commit terrorist acts or facilitate the commission of terrorist acts.

With nuclear energy facilities, oil tankers and pipelines, oil refineries, and national and regional power grids prime targets of terrorists, the energy sector is another high-risk target. But unlike the transport sector, it generally has not seen large new security-related regulatory burdens. Industry officials have successfully staved off calls for new regulations by arguing that existing procedures and planned enhancements are sufficient. This does not mean, however, that the industry has forever escaped new security regulations. A number of reports have warned of inadequate security at nuclear power plants and power grid vulnerability, resulting in a host of bills proposed in various legislatures.

PUBLIC–PRIVATE PARTNERSHIPS TO SECURE THE SUPPLY CHAIN

On any given day, more than 15 million containers are moving across the seas of the world. Millions more are being transported across borders by truck, rail or air. Each could contain a dirty bomb or a biochemical agent that could wreak horrendous damage. But it is simply impossible to inspect each container before it enters a country – doing so would radically slow commerce. Security assurance must therefore begin long before the goods arrive at their port of destination.

For this and other reasons, governments have sought to enlist the private sector in securing the global supply chain through a number of high-profile, public–private part-nerships. While voluntary today, many firms believe the lessons learned from these types of initiatives could to a large extent shape future regulations and requirements, and thus they might feel compelled to participate. Here is a look at some of these initiatives:

- Customs–Trade Partnership Against Terrorism (C-TPAT). C-TPAT offers com-panies various benefits in exchange for signing up for the program and certifying to the US Department of Homeland Security that they have put in place a security plan to cover the full length of their supply chain. As of June 2004, C-TPAT had signed up nearly 3500 certified members, 288 of which had had their security plans validated by the Department of Homeland Security.
- Container Security Initiative (CSI). An effort by the US Customs Service to secure the shipping industry from terrorism and accidents, CSI consists of four core ele-ments: (1) establishing criteria to identify high-risk shipping containers; (2) pre-screening containers before they arrive at American ports; (3) using technology to screen high-risk containers; and (4) driving adoption of the use of smart contain-ers. While a voluntary initiative rather than a mandate, there are strong pressures on governments and private businesses to agree to CSI rules at the risk of losing export business to the US.
- Smart and Secure Tradelanes (SST). SST, a multiphase industry-funded initiative, aims to improve both supply-chain efficiency and security through the develop-ment of a security network that allows a shipping container to be monitored from its point of origin to its point of final delivery.[21]
- Operation Safe Commerce (OSC). OSC is a public–private partnership designed to develop best practices for the safe and efficient movement of containerized cargo. Eighteen proposals, approved by the US Transportation Security Administration (TSA) in June 2003, serve as pilot projects. These cover the three largest container load centers in the US: the Port Authority of New York and New Jersey; the ports of Los Angeles and Long Beach, and the ports of Seattle and Tacoma, to which the TSA has distributed $58 million in funding spread among the three ports.[22]
- Secure Trade in the APEC Region (STAR). Launched in October 2002, STAR is a public–private partnership of Asia-Pacific Economic Cooperation (APEC) countries, major private sector companies, and various international organiza-tions focusing on identifying and examining high-risk shipping containers, secur-ing them while en route, and providing advance information on them to officials before they arrive at a border.[23] STAR will be rolled out in several phases, with implementation of electronic customs reporting and improved baggage screening procedures at airports.[24]

TWO MODELS OF SECURITY COMPLIANCE: PUBLICLY LED OR PRIVATELY LED

The stock market crash of 1929 not only devalued approximately $25 billion of new securities offered in the 1920s, but it also destroyed investor confidence in the capital markets. Subsequently, the 1934 Securities Exchange Act established the Securities and

Exchange Commission (SEC) as the primary regulator of US securities markets, and the SEC sought to restore investor confidence by providing more structure and government oversight of the markets. The financial services sector witnessed a sharp growth of government regulations after the 1929 stock market crash – the 1933 Glass–Steagal Act, the 1933 Securities Act, the 1938 Maloney Act – followed by decades of additional regulations on the financial sector.

The current regulatory environment around security shares some obvious parallels with financial regulations after the 1929 crash. Just as that event ushered in new regulatory controls on the financial sector, so the cataclysmic events of 9/11 and Madrid have brought forth a stream of new security regulations, covering nearly every industry. Some analysts predict that, as with the SEC, these will represent only the first steps toward a sustained regulatory environment.

What makes such a bold prediction hazardous are certain parallels that the current push for greater corporate security shares with total quality management (TQM), a privately led standards movement. Instead of government regulation, TQM standards such as ISO 9000 were driven in part by industry's need for global standards to facilitate international trade. Similarly, the various voluntary, industry-led efforts to improve private-sector security, including the North American Electric Reliability Council (NERC), the Visa Cardholder Information Security Program (CISP), and the Global Food Safety Initiative (GFSI), can in some ways be seen as the next stage of the quality movement, though this time with a greater focus on information integration. Right now, security appears to be moving toward a hybrid of the two models, with significant amounts of regulation in some industries such as transportation, and more industry-driven standards in others such as energy. But all this could change. Companies need to prepare for either or both scenarios.

THE SECURITY TAB

This much government activity, much of it focused on the private sector, is likely to come with a bill attached. The new security measures are no exception. Complying with new government regulations will cost businesses billions of additional dollars and countless work hours. More vulnerable industries like transportation and agriculture will likely see steep compliance costs, but they will not be the only ones affected. Nearly every major industry faces higher costs in responding to the new security environment. The additional burdens hit businesses in many ways: higher insurance premiums, reconfiguring business processes, purchasing new technologies and computer systems, hiring more people and, in some cases, building a new infrastructure.

And these are just the direct costs. Increased wait times at airports, longer holding times for cargo at border crossings and ports, larger inventories, and rising insurance and workers' compensation premiums are just a few of the extensive indirect, security-related costs hitting businesses. Federal Reserve economist Bart Hobjin estimates that every year in the United States approximately 550 million passengers will spend an additional 90 minutes at the airport before boarding their flights. If their time is worth between $10 and $40 per hour, this will add as much as $33 billion annually to private-sector costs according to Hobjin.[25]

Just how big is the overall bill? One widely cited estimate published just months after 9/11 pegged the direct and indirect costs to American businesses at $151 billion annually, including $65 billion for higher supply chain, transportation and inventory storage costs, and $35 billion for higher insurance and liability premiums.[26] And a previous Deloitte Research study estimated private-sector homeland security spending to be between $46 billion and $76 billion in 2003. But these were all early estimates, published before many of the new security regulations were enacted. The actual figure could be much higher or lower. The truth is no one really knows just how much new security imperatives are costing the private sector globally.

One way to get a better sense of the costs of new security regulations is by drilling down and looking at the effects by industry.

Maritime

In the US, various maritime security mandates will impose up to $8 billion in costs on the shipping industry over a ten-year period, and that is considered a very conservative figure.[27] On top of that, shippers will spend another $1.28 billion in up-front costs and $730 million thereafter complying with ISPS – and that does not even include the costs of building new smart shipping containers or retrofitting existing ones.[28] Many shippers have complained vigorously about the new requirements, arguing that it is a low-margin industry with easily substitutable segments of business.

By some estimates, ports face even higher compliance costs, with developing countries confronting particularly large burdens in relation to their gross domestic product (GDP). Jamaica, for example, estimates that complying with new port security regulations will cost the country around $100 million.[29]

Trucking

Because dirty bombs or deadly biological agents can be transported by land, trucking companies face additional expenses from new security regulations. The Required Advance Electronic Presentation of Cargo Information rule devised by the US Department of Homeland Security requires that cargo information be sent to the Bureau of Customs and Border Protection via an electronic data interchange system before being brought into the country. The annual cost to truckers is at least $91 million.[30]

Airlines

In the US, the bill for the bulk of the direct costs to the aviation industry since 9/11 has been picked up by the passengers themselves via a $10 per passenger security screening fee.[31] Airlines have had to contribute an additional $315 million annually to help cover the enormous additional costs of passenger and baggage screening.[32]

These costs, along with longer waiting lines and other inconveniences, also impose an indirect cost on the industry by hindering the ability to raise ticket prices and even discouraging some passengers from flying.[33] Many companies, for example, have chosen to reduce their exposure to the risks associated with air travel by relying more on videoconferencing and less on face-to-face meetings. To help compensate for these indirect costs, the US government distributed $2.3 billion in May 2003 to the airlines in proportion to the amount of security fees they had paid to the TSA since February 2002.[34]

The EU has been less willing to pick up the tab for increased aviation security costs. Despite industry pleas, European airlines have received less than one-third of the $3 billion in subsidies given to American airlines since 9/11.[35]

Rail

The US mass transit industry has spent $1.7 billion complying with mandatory security measures such as using sniffer dogs to screen baggage, terminals and trains for bombs, conducting random inspections for suspicious items, and replacing trash receptacles with bomb-resistant containers.[36] It is estimated that $6 billion more is needed to upgrade radio systems, test for chemical and biological agents, and provide closed circuit televisions, fencing, increased staff and staff training.[37] A bill proposed by US Senator John McCain would authorize $1 billion in taxpayer money to upgrade rail security, including over $600 million to Amtrak.[38]

ECONOMIC IMPACT OF VISA DELAYS

One of the most contentious issues between government security agencies and business revolves around visa issues. In the US almost three-quarters of companies have experienced visa delays or denials; 60 percent said that delays had hurt their company through lost revenue or increased costs.[39] Companies unable to obtain visas for foreign business travelers are conducting business elsewhere. Industry conferences are being relocated abroad. Applications for foreign business school students are dropping. And fewer engineers and scientists are opting to come to America to pursue advanced degrees and work opportunities.

The economic cost has been huge. According to a report from the National Foreign Trade Council, over a two-year period, American businesses lost more than $30.7 billion due to delayed and denied visas for foreign business travelers.[40] One industry particularly hard hit by the more stringent visa delays is conferences. At the China Textile and Apparel trade show in New York in June 2004, a third of the stands were empty. According to Chinese officials, half of the Chinese executives who had applied for visas for this event had been turned down. This is in comparison to an 80 percent pre-9/11 visa acceptance rate. Similarly, the US direct marketing group Amway decided to move its 2004 convention from Los Angeles to Japan because of difficulties in securing visas for its 8000 South Korean participants. This alone cost the US economy an estimated $18 million.[41]

Universities are also feeling the pain. Many foreign students have been deterred from applying to US business and other professional schools because of the cost and wait-time associated with obtaining a visa. In 2004, the number of foreign students taking the Graduate Management Admission Test, required for admission to a US business school, fell 3.9 percent, but for overseas students the decline was a whopping 17.5 percent.[42] The number of scientists and engineers coming to America to work and study has also dropped significantly.

If this trend is not reversed, the long-term economic loss to the US could be severe. Foreign students who would have worked for American companies will seek employment in other developed countries, which will then benefit as America has from their smarts and entrepreneurship. Recognizing the magnitude of the problem, on September 2004, US Department of Homeland Security Director Tom Ridge pledged to streamline the visa process.

Financial Institutions

Strict antiterrorist money laundering provisions designed to curb terrorist financing mean additional expenses for banks and other financial institutions. In America, the anti-money-laundering provisions of the US Patriot Act will cost banks, brokerages and insurance agencies roughly $10.9 billion through 2005 by some estimates.[43] Hit particularly hard by the new regulations are securities firms, which were not previously subject to the stringent reporting requirements that banks have faced for years. Purchasing identity-tracking software, reconfiguring systems, training staff and taking other compliance measures are expected to cost the securities industry nearly $700 million over the first few years.[44] German financial services companies face similar pressures in the wake of the country's tough anti-money laundering provisions passed after 9/11.

Many financial institutions have complained that the considerable costs they have had to bear to comply with the Patriot Act yield few business benefits. In the UK, financial regulators shelved plans to impose a new anti-money laundering rule on British financial institutions after an analysis revealed that compliance would impose too onerous a burden on the industry. The rule, which would have required all regulated financial institutions to perform a special review of their current customers' identities, would have cost the industry as much as $274 million.[45]

CONCLUSION

The emerging secure economy is a lot like the old one, only faster and with more threats of disruption. Advances in information technology, telecommunications and transportation have enabled globalization to the point where no global organization in any sector is immune to events that occur halfway around the world. This new environment is one in which no single organization has the responsibility for success – but nonetheless may still be singled out by failure.

NOTES

1. Hulme, George V. (2004), 'Under Attack', *Information Week*, 5 July, p. 54.
2. (2004), 'Disney Installs High-Security Anti-Terrorist Barricades', 15 May, http://www.local6.com.
3. Opstal, Debra van (2003), 'Private sector stepping up to the plate on security', *Competitiveness Watch*, Council on Competitiveness, 5 November.
4. Moore, Paula (2003), 'Threat of workplace violence remains no. 1 concern among US corporations', *Wichita Business Journal*, 22 August.
5. Hulme, George V. (2003), 'Spending to fend off online attacks to grow', CMP Tech Web, 29 December.

6. Deloitte (2004), 'The unfinished agenda: Transportation security survey', Deloitte Services LP, Aviation and Transport Services Industry, August, p. 4.
7. Evans, Chad (2002), 'The state of private sector security: a year out from 9/11', *Competitiveness Watch*, Council on Competitiveness, 7 October.
8. RAND Corporation and Janusian Security Risk Management Ltd (2004), 'Terrorism and Business Continuity Survey 2004', 9 May, http://www.janusian.com/survey/.
9. Vartanian, Thomas P. and Mark Fajfar (2004), 'Sarbanes–Oxley Act underscores importance of information security', *Community Banker*, 1 June.
10. Of those companies surveyed, three-quarters had been hit with unexpected delays in visa processing or arbitrary visa denials, and two-thirds said that visa delays had hurt their bottom line. See: Alden, Edward (2004), 'Visa delays "cost US business $30bn"', *Financial Times*, 3 June.
11. Preserving these gains should be an important goal for governments and businesses as they work together to enhance security, Riley, Jack (2004), RAND Corporation, NABE teleconference, 4 February.
12. Deloitte, 'The unfinished agenda', p. 4.
13. 'Japan beefs up rail security following threat', *Milwaukee Journal Sentinel*, 19 March.
14. States News Service (2004), 'Sen Snowe advocates swift action on 'Rail Transportation Security Act', News Service, 1 April.
15. Tyler, Patrick E. and Don Van Natt (2004), 'Europe steps up security intelligence officials had expressed fear over rail networks', *International Herald Tribune*, 13 March, p. 1.
16. 'President highlights a more secure America on first anniversary of Department of Homeland Security', http://www.whitehouse.gov/homeland/index.html.
17. Remarks by Secretary Tom Ridge at the Center for Homeland Security's 2004 Homeland and Global Security Summit, 31 March 2004, Washington, DC.
18. In 2002, 60 percent of the total BMI budget of 3.5 billion euros was dedicated to domestic security, and in 2003 additional funds were allocated for the implementation of the Anti-Terror Act. See: Schily, Otto (2003), 'What can and what must Germans and Americans do to fight terrorism?', speech by Otto Schily, Federal Minister of the Interior, 2 February, http://www.eng.bmi.bund.de.
19. 'About the new Department of Public Safety and Emergency Preparednes', http://www.psepc-sppcc.gc.ca.
20. 'Government of Canada announces $8 million to strengthen Canadian emergency preparednes', http://www.psepc.sppcc.gc.ca.
21. (2003), 'Phase One review: network visibility: leveraging security and efficiency in today's global supply chains', A Smart and Secure Tradelanes White Paper, November, p. 1, http://www.chainlinkresearch.com/parallaxview/whitepapers/SST_PhaseOneReport_Synopsis.pdf.
22. Transportation Security Administration website, http://www.tsa.gov/public/display?content=0900051 98000c0be.
23. White House (2002), 'Fact sheet: Secure trade in the APEC region ("STAR")', press release, 26 October, http://www.whitehouse.gov/news/releases/2002/10/20021026-8.html.
24. APEC website, http://www.apecsec.org.sg.
25. Hobijn, Bart (2002), 'What will homeland security cost?', Federal Reserve Bank of New York, November, p. 29.
26. Bernasek, Anna (2002), 'The friction economy', *Fortune*, 3 February, http://www.fortune.com/fortune/investing/articles/0,15114,367800,00.html.
27. (2003), 'Largely unfunded US maritime security requirements have been slammed as a "Tax" on a shipping industry already "taking an enormous financial hit" by the former Chair of the US Federal Maritime Commission', *Shipping Times*, Singapore, 25 July.
28. Shelley, Toby (2004), 'Shipping industry steams for safe haven: the cost of meeting new security standards is high and those affected have a July deadline to meet', *Financial Times*, 15 April, p. 11.
29. Ibid.
30. Department of Homeland Security, Bureau of Customs and Border Protection: Required Advance Electronic Presentation of Cargo Information, GAO-04-319R, GAO Report, 18 December, 2003.
31. Crawley, John, 'US Wants Airlines to Keep Paying Security Costs', Reuters News, 5 November, 2003.
32. Kehaulani Goo, Sara (2004), 'Fuel prices hurt US airlines', *Washington Post*, 29 April, p. A5.
33. Airwise News (2004), US airlines balk at security cost increases', 28 April, http://news.airwise.com/stories/2004/04/1083186259.html.
34. (2003), 'TSA Allocates $2.3 Billion to US Carriers to Offset Security Costs', Transportation Security Administration website, 15 May, http://www.tsa.gov/public display?theme=44&content=0900051 980027028.
35. Dow Jones International News (2004), 'KLM complains of security costs, timeline for US flights', 24 March.
36. Doyle, John M. (2004), 'Rail directive boosts operators' costs but could aid security equipment vendors', *Homeland Security and Defense*, 26 May.

37. Associated Press (2004), 'Feds stepping up security against rail system terror', 21 May.
38. Anderson, Teresa (2004), 'Rail Security', *Security Management*, 1 August, p. A12.
39. Alden, Edward (2004), 'The Americas: visa delays "cost US business $30bn"' *Financial Times*, 3 June, p. 4.
40. Ibid.
41. Alden, Edward (2003), 'US counts the costs of securing its borders', *Financial Times*, 1 July.
42. Murray, Sarah (2004), 'Visa worries deter foreign students', *Financial Times*, 20 June.
43. Wiles, Russ (2003), 'Funds to safeguard against laundering', *Chicago Sun-Times*, 15 September.
44. Loomis, Tamara (2003), 'Anti-terrorism compliance', *Legal Times*, 19 May.
45. Tracey, Patrick (2003), 'UK drops plans to force identity checks on current customers', *BNA's Banking Report*, 28 July.

PART III

DISASTER STORIES WE CAN LEARN FROM

CHAPTER 13   FAILURE TO COMMUNICATE: LESSONS OF
              9/11

Geoff Williams tells the amazing story of Neal Saiff, a telecom executive in New York whose actions on 9/11 were a testament to courage and quick thinking. Saiff's experiences bring home to the reader the very personal nature of the tragedy. He was one of the true heroes of that fateful day. Hundreds of police officers, firefighters and other emergency personnel were killed while rescuing people from the twin towers. Neil Saiff stood out in his remarkable efforts to restore his firm's telecommunications, which was one of the key events that kept world financial markets operating throughout the disaster. Lower Manhattan is the hub of the world financial system; without payments to accompany trade all commerce would have come to a halt. Geoff Williams relates an exciting tale of how the prior planning, expertise and determination of individuals like Neal Saiff played key roles in restoring the continuity of financial processing and communications despite the terrorist attacks.

CHAPTER 14   A NETWORKED MODEL FOR EMERGENCY
              PLANNING AND RESPONSE: THE LESSONS OF
              KATRINA (I)

Bill Eggers, Global Director of Public Sector Research for Deloitte, describes a radically different solution to the age-old problem of inter-agency coordination during disasters. In the present chapter, Bill describes a radically different solution to the age-old problem of inter-agency coordination during disasters. Rather than relying on hierarchical staffs working vertically within their organizations, more successful efforts in recent times have been network models that linked appropriate departments at local, state and federal levels. Needs and capabilities were optimized in pursuit of common objectives. Bill provides excellent examples from Hurricane Katrina that prove the value of this alternative concept and approach.

CHAPTER 15   WAL-MART CASE STUDY: THE LESSONS OF KATRINA (II)

Ken Senser, head of global security at Wal-Mart, furnishes us with a detailed account of one of the world's largest corporations during one of the worst storms in American history. Jason Jackson joined Ken in creating this interesting case study. Ken Senser was a career intelligence professional for the US government. This background in planning and analysis prepared him well to respond to the threat from a disastrous event like Katrina. Wal-Mart is a worldwide retailer, and the organization had the resources needed to support its stores, employees, customers and local communities in the Gulf Coast region. Its business continuity planning and emergency management efforts fit well with the company's constituent-oriented business philosophy. Ken emphasizes the key role of Wal-Mart's dedicated associates, who were empowered by senior management to take charge of the situation on the ground in coordinating the disaster relief effort. The company's enormous and effective disaster response was a testament to the value of prior planning, coordination with government agencies, and a highly effective emergency operations center.

CHAPTER 16   DOING BUSINESS IN NO MAN'S LAND: THE LESSONS OF KATRINA (III)

Geoff Williams helps tell the story of John Brady who is a senior security officer at one of the world's largest oil companies, ConocoPhillips. His chapter discusses his company's crucial plans for reacting to and recovering from major disasters, with Hurricane Katrina as the case in point. This is an industry that has long understood the dangers of hurricanes, due to the concentration of facilities around New Orleans, Houston and other Gulf Coast ports. Oil refineries have had many disastrous fires, both accidental and set by arsonists. The Texas City catastrophe of 1947 lingers in the minds of those in this business and in this region of the country. US fuel supplies, part of our critical infrastructure, are subject to reduction or cut-offs at any time.

13 Failure to communicate: lessons of 9/11
Geoff Williams

If you are going through hell, keep going. (Winston Churchill, orator, author and British Prime Minister, 1874–1965)

It's a heartache, nothin' but a heartache. (Bonnie Tyler)

INTRODUCTION

Nothing that happened on 9/11 was as terrifying and tragic as the senseless murders of almost 3000 people. However, after the smoke cleared, and some of the shock wore away, many of those in New York City and across the country were suddenly worried not for their lives, but for their livelihoods. When buildings were crushed into ruin and rubble, offices and all of their contents were also blown into oblivion.

THE BOND WE HAVE WITH A BUSINESS

While things can be replaced, unlike human lives, it was nevertheless more than apparent to some fast-acting people that if they did not try to rebuild their companies immediately, thousands of jobs would be lost. That in turn would affect innumerable workers and their families, not to mention many of their customers.

At the time of this writing Lehman Brothers was one of those companies. The international corporation, a bulwark in business since 1850, with headquarters in New York, London and Tokyo; was an epic global investment bank.[1] It served the financial needs of corporations, governments and municipalities, institutional clients and affluent individuals, from high-worth entrepreneurs to philanthropists. While nobody wants to see a hot-dog stand go out of business, one can imagine that its customers will persevere and find a new place for lunch.[2] A world bank has more at stake.

To understate it, 9/11 was a frightening time. However, in the midst of the chaos of that Tuesday, executives like Neal Saiff became heroes to colleagues and clients. If a business owner were to go through another disaster, they would do well to follow the lessons laid down by Saiff, who was then the Lehman Brothers Vice-President of Infrastructure Implementations for the Americas.

In 2001, the *International Financing Review*, a leading publication for international capital markets, awarded Lehman Brothers its US Investment Grade Corporate Bond House of the Year Award. It recognized, among other accomplishments, that the company resumed business so quickly after having its world headquarters destroyed.

10 SEPTEMBER 2001

Before the terrorist attacks on New York City, the Lehman Brothers' headquarters were mostly situated in the World Trade Center (WTC) and the adjoining World Financial Center – over 6000 men and women worked here. Across the Hudson River were another almost 3000 employees. Before the attacks, only somebody with a twisted mind or one well-versed in disaster management would ever look at a map and conclude that the business had put itself in a potentially perilous situation – creating a company of sitting ducks.

11 SEPTEMBER 2001

Shortly after the tragedy, a Lehman Brothers employee, Yin Liang, wrote a blog about his experiences that day.[3] He was on the fortieth floor of One World Trade Center, working on the equities e-commerce website. As he described the scene that morning: 'At around 8.46 a.m., when I am still reading and writing emails in front of my computer, I heard a low-pitched "Bom" noise, it's not very loud, then the floors starts moving, it swings back and forth slowly, like floating in the air, then the swing gradually stopped. We are quite alarmed . . .'

In the next tower, many floors below, one woman later described her experiences that day to FoxNews.com:

> I was drinking coffee and speaking to my co-workers at our office located on the 14th floor of Two World Trade Center, the south tower, when the first airplane hit the north tower. We heard two or three explosions, the office kind of shook, and when we looked out the windows we saw what appeared to be burning paper falling down. We immediately started for the stairway . . .[4]
>
> The stairwells were already crowded with people from the upper floors trying to get down the stairs. I was so scared, and I kept telling myself: only a couple of more flights to go. I also thought, I cannot die today, my two small sons need me.
>
> We got to the bottom of the stairs and waited in the lobby right in front of the revolving doors that lead to the plaza. The ground was littered with gray papers. Later on I realized that those burning 'papers' were actually debris and pieces of the airplane.

Little wonder that Hollywood has already produced a couple of movies about 9/11. One of the most common comments one hears is how those horrific hours played out like a disaster movie. It has been said that the evacuation of lower Manhattan across the Hudson River that morning involved more people than the legendary British escape of Dunkirk in 1940, which involved saving the lives of 338 226 citizens.[5] It is believed that the flotilla of private and commercial boats that day moved approximately 1 million people.

Saiff himself had to jump over a railing to scramble onto the last ferry crossing the Hudson River. Moments later, the first tower came toppling down, and the mob of people still waiting to get onto the boat were swept into the river by a tsunami of ash and debris.

The Lehman Brothers global headquarters in Three World Financial Center was ravaged by falling wreckage from the WTC. All in all, the employees of Lehman Brothers were mostly fortunate, in the sense that most of them lived. One person was killed, while the 6500 others were left emotionally scarred, if not physically, wondering if they had jobs and if they would be able to provide for their families.

As Vice-President of Infrastructure, Saiff had his work cut out for him. Virtually nothing of the company was left to salvage. For a brief time, Saiff was, in effect, vice-president of nothing. There was almost no infrastructure – even the website was down. There was virtually nothing virtual.

12 SEPTEMBER 2001 AND BEYOND

The day after the attacks, despite the city being numb and on edge, half-waiting for something else horrific to happen, the leadership at Lehman Brothers was able quickly to relocate its employees to 50 locations over the next 12 weeks, until they could move into a more permanent building. During that period, thousands of employees worked out of their homes, and because the tourism industry had taken such a hit, with visitors canceling vacations and appointments in the city, two Sheraton hotels in New York became something of financial institutions. With their headquarters in shambles, Lehman Brothers set up 1300 of their bankers to work in guest rooms at the Sheraton Manhattan; the other Sheraton had 450 equity research and banking staff members.

Trading operations moved across the Hudson River to the New Jersey building. A trading floor was quickly built and brought online less than 48 hours after the attacks. When the markets reopened on 17 September 2001, Lehman Brothers was selling and trading with the rest of the world. This signified a deep desire to get back to work and, perhaps more importantly, to send a message to potential terrorists that America could get back on its feet quickly in the wake of disaster. It was not exactly business as usual, however. On that day, only half the phone calls – presumably from concerned customers and business partners – were getting through to Lehman Brothers. By 24 September, the estimate was that 90 per cent of the calls were being connected.

Financially, the costs of losing business in the wake of the terrorist attacks was significant. According to *CIO* magazine, that fourth quarter, Lehman's net income fell 67 percent, and the company spent $127 million in costs associated with 9/11. For the first half of the year, the net income was $594 million, compared with $817 million the previous year. One can only imagine the figures, however, if it had taken Lehman Brothers weeks or months to return to some normalcy, instead of days. During that first week, the challenges ahead for Saiff were immense:

- The company had 6000 employees, with no way to contact them. All the phone numbers were somewhere in the mangled headquarters.
- Not only were the employees trying to find each other, not to mention trying to reach family members, but Saiff also wondered how their vendors and customers would locate them.
- Assuming they could get past those issues, they would have to find a way for the 6000 employees to seamlessly and securely connect into the virtual company – their website.
- And then there was the consideration of application recovery. How do you recover hundreds of critical applications and deliver them across an Internet connection?

To borrow from *CIO* magazine, again, the hard lessons of that time were that 'centrally locating systems and personnel can put you out of business; phone lines should not terminate in one location; and people need to gain experience in working remotely'.

THE BLUEPRINT

Every company needs a directory, according to Saiff. Since the attacks he had become something of a public speaker, explaining to other companies how to make their firms more disaster proof. The directory of employees needs to be accessible to everyone on that directory, to maintain it properly.

One of the first things Saiff did was provide a facility from the firm's public web site and extranet for employees to update their contact information. He also provided divisional hotlines through the public site; numbers that would not be made generally public were published on one site, making it easier for displaced employees to get through to various departments. The website also provided alternate work numbers for clients and partners. Also, in order to avoid the phone lines jamming on in-bound calls to the firm's operators, a greeting message first suggested to the public that they use the website as an alternative source of information. Three levels of remote access were furnished to the employees:

- direct dial-in for programmers and system administrators;
- web-based e-mail;
- Tocket, a proprietary software made for Lehman Brothers, which provided secure connection over the public Internet, required no Virtual Private Network (VPN) connection or client-based software to be installed on the desktop, and allowed access to a user's NT environment, their e-mail and other business applications.

IMPORTANT REMINDER

One of the most important lessons Saiff learned in recreating the company's infrastructure was that it is important to have an inventory of your applications and servers, and to know what locations they run from. If you have to rebuild your telecommunications infrastructure, such an inventory would be a major help.

FOR THOSE WHO LIKE NUMBERS

When Lehman Brothers rebuilt its infrastructure, some 2 million feet of copper and 50 000 feet of 48-strand fiber were purchased. Four hundred cabinets were added to a data center, and 600 servers were installed over four days for trading the following Monday.[6]

ISSUES FOR FURTHER THOUGHT

Every business and industry has its unique telecommunication challenges, but certainly on 9/11, Lehman Brothers and thousands of businesses learned that some strategic thinking is not only prudent but universal in scope. In essence, every company should attempt to have a dedicated backup connection to get its business back online promptly, if not seamlessly, if its server is destroyed.

Disaster recovery testing once a year is extremely important. If you do not test your ability to communicate and recover information in the event of a disaster, how do you really know you are ready?

During the hopefully long lull of stability, notification procedures and instructions should be strengthened, and the staff should discuss plans for how they will communicate if an attack occurs in the community or regionally.

CONCLUSION

However, nobody should be mistaken. It is human nature to not want to prepare for a possible disaster. When you are in the heat of business, and profit margins are tight, and deadlines are tighter, it is almost as much of a challenge to get staff to participate in disaster planning as it is actually to plan for a disaster.

NOTES

1. Lehman Brothers, retrieved from Wikipedia.
2. Lehman Brothers website: www.lehman.com.
3. Retrieved from www.911digitalarchive.com, which links to the Lehman Brothers' Yin Liang's account of his escape from the World Trade Center. The actual Yin Liang web page with his story can be found at http://www.miraclebridge.com/wtcescape.html.
4. The FoxNews.com account: http://www.foxnews.com.
5. Dunkirk, number of people saved, according to the BBC: Retrieved from http://news.bbc.co.uk/news.
6. 'Planning for the unplanned: disaster and business continuity', a PowerPoint Presentation given by Neal Saiff on 24 February 2003 at the ABA Operations Conference for Securities, Brokerage and Trust.

14 A networked model for emergency planning and response: the lessons of Katrina (I)

Bill Eggers

A splendid storehouse of integrity and freedom has been bequeathed to us by our forefathers. In this day of confusion, of peril to liberty, our high duty is to see that this storehouse is not robbed of its contents. (President Herbert C. Hoover, American Statesman, 1874–1964)

INTRODUCTION

When Hurricane Andrew crashed through parts of southern Florida in 1992, frightened residents sat in the rubble of their homes for days waiting for food and water, while looters emptied stores. Part of the problem, reported Kate Hale, Director of Emergency Management for Miami-Dade County at the time, was that federal agencies somehow came to believe that local officials did not want the aid they stood ready to provide. 'The state was unable to coordinate effectively with the federal government', she said. And when state officials, arriving in Homestead by helicopter, saw the devastation all around them, they initially committed most of the state's relief resources to that city, which Hale described as 'only a small part of the area of impact'.[1]

In the 14 years since Andrew, Florida has overhauled its emergency-management strategies under the leadership of its governors. It sets new standards for emergency planning and response. 'One of the biggest differences between how Florida and other states handle natural disasters lies in the degree of cooperation between cities, counties and the state', said a story in the *Palm Beach Post* in September 2005. 'In Florida, they are in constant communication with one another as storms advance and during the recovery phase.'[2]

Having honed its emergency management capabilities through numerous hurricanes over the years, Florida can now move quickly when disaster strikes, either inside its own borders or in neighboring states. 'Within hours of Katrina's landfall, Florida began deploying more than 3700 first responders to Mississippi and Louisiana', Governor Jeb Bush wrote in an op-ed piece in the *Washington Post* in September 2005.[3]

Florida's emergency management plan depends on effective coordination among numerous local and state officials, volunteer organizations, public and private health care organizations and utility companies. As governors plan for future disasters, they will find it critical to create similar networks of organizations, each with well-rehearsed tactics that they can deploy as soon as needed.

As Florida demonstrates, emergency management and response is first and foremost about integrating a disparate array of organizations – the Federal Emergency Management Agency (FEMA), first responders, local governments, the Red Cross, nonprofits, private companies – into functioning networks that share information, coordinate activities and synchronize responses to prepare for widespread emergencies and respond to them when they occur. To be sure, one element of the National Response Plan is the mandated Incident Command System, a command-and-control structure. However, without augmenting this with effective network coordination and management, the response to a disaster, such as a public-health epidemic or terrorism incident, will likely not be timely or effective. Organizations with the best of intentions end up duplicating one another's efforts in some areas, while other vital needs fall through the cracks. Lack of knowledge of assigned roles in the network prevent these organizations from performing their duties. Lack of coordination means affected areas have to wait days for FEMA to deliver various goods and services, while officials at FEMA wait for affected states to issue formal requests. Lack of interoperable database systems means organizations cannot effectively track requests for assistance. In short, the lack of a networked approach typically means a slow, uncoordinated, overly rigid, procedure-bound response.

The realization that we are vulnerable to terrorist acts on American soil makes a well-integrated network response more critical today than ever. The emergency management network, no longer focused only on natural disasters, now includes many local, state and federal agencies with investigatory responsibilities. These are loosely tied to the legacy of emergency management agencies through an existing emergency management function or new office of homeland security. Many traditional emergency management personnel, however, lack access to material aimed at prevention and detection simply because they do not meet the 'need-to-know' criteria. Fusing groups that have not worked together in the past creates a tremendous potential for conflict. The situation demands leadership and clearly defined roles.

So what should a state government do to ensure an integrated, networked response? The most important principle to bear in mind is that the role of state government is not necessarily always to stand in the center, shoulder the main burden and call upon partners to supplement its efforts here and there. Instead, state government's role is to coordinate a network of networks.

Public officials need to identify effective emergency response networks that already exist, allow each of them to do the work they do best, and encourage these groups to increase their power by working together. For example, a pandemic flu outbreak would mean coordinating networks across state and local public health and safety services; federal emergency management, health and homeland security agencies; relevant international agencies; and the health care industry, among others. Key resources would include hospitals, clinics, inpatient and outpatient facilities, health care personnel, emergency medical staff, first responders, police, security enforcement, fire departments and the National Guard. Supporting entities to deliver public health and safety services include ambulances, helicopters, vehicles, other transportation, other privately held infrastructure deemed critical, mortuary and funeral services, and veterinary services.

State governments can also identify needs not being met by any existing organization and devise ways to fill those gaps. The networked model of emergency response augments the command-and-control model the United States has traditionally employed to manage disasters. The question for a governor should be: How do I bring together the resources necessary to execute our shared mission as well as possible? Key steps in developing a networked emergency management response include:

- Convening and activating the network.
- Creating the networked governance structure.
- Designing and activating the network.
- Coordinating activities and synchronizing response.
- Realigning the state's organizational structure and governance.

CONVENING AND ACTIVATING THE NETWORK

Creative public officials possess a variety of assets they can deploy to bring together existing emergency management networks and provide for capabilities they do not already possess. A government can bring together parties whose intense yet narrow knowledge will provoke valuable insights when deployed in conjunction with others. Often nonprofit organizations are so overwhelmed with demands for their core services that they lack the time or the resources to find and interact with others even in the same sphere. Using their convening authority as a catalyst, officials can provide a venue for organizations and individuals with similar goals to meet, find common ground and perhaps even find ways to divide labor and share resources, making each more effective and efficient than before.

Arkansas governor Mike Huckabee demonstrated exactly this kind of leadership when the White House asked his state to house survivors after Hurricane Katrina. Huckabee, a former Baptist minister, met with church leaders to arrange for 8000 to 9000 survivors from the New Orleans Superdome to stay at church camps throughout his state.

Without Huckabee's actions, the church network would not have come into existence. While the churches had their own networks within the community, their leaders rarely communicated with one another. Since church leaders serve as community leaders, their influence led to a surge of volunteers to attend to the survivors.[4]

In addition, public officials can add resources, in the form of people or technology, to help activate a network. The Department of Homeland Security created the Office of the Private Sector to reach out to the roughly 25 million businesses in the United States. This office provides the business community with a direct line of communication to the Department of Homeland Security, and it works to build partnerships and relationships with the private sector.[5]

In addition to working with businesses, the Office of the Private Sector worked with nonprofits during the Katrina response.[6] Craig Nemitz of Second Harvest noted the importance of this office in helping his organization obtain warehouse space in Louisiana and housing for volunteers. Second Harvest was able to utilize this resource – without going through FEMA – because it had the contact information for the right person in the Department of Homeland Security.[7]

CREATING THE NETWORKED GOVERNANCE STRUCTURE

Taking a group of organizations with substantial professional differences and tacking them together at the top level can be a recipe for failure. To be sure, leaders of organizations must set the stage for a successful multiparty partnership. They will not succeed, however, unless people throughout their organizations see the benefits of the network.

BOX 14.1   TYPES OF NETWORKS OPERATING IN EMERGENCY RESPONSE

The public sector, private sector and nonprofit organizations that already perform aspects of disaster response in states provide the most valuable resources for building an integrated emergency management network. Few of these entities act alone; many have already formed relationships that allow them to collaborate in times of need.

A first step in building a statewide emergency response network is to take stock of the organizations and networks involved in emergency response. These generally fall into four categories, and it is important to understand where each existing cluster of organizations fits in this scheme. Knowing this, one can conduct a full assessment and inventory of available assets.

Formal, hierarchical networks
Created before an emergency event or disaster happens. Members within the network are legally or financially bound to perform established roles. Within the hierarchical network, official documentation identifies a clear path of authority, delineates decision making, and dictates the roles and responsibilities of network entities. Hierarchical networks generally have detailed procedures that limit the flexibility of the members, as they are bound to operate according to regulation and face enforceable repercussions if they do not. The American Red Cross stands at the center of a hierarchical network. It has a congressional charter and a specific role in the federal government's National Response Plan (NRP).

Contractual networks
Formed from contractual relationships with key suppliers, these networks are critical to emergency response, covering everything from ice shipments to temporary housing to construction. Contracts negotiated in advance for basic supplies and services are needed in most every kind of emergency.

Relational network
Formed through agreements between independent organizations, these are created in advance and designed to facilitate cooperation over the course of multiple emergencies. The agreements may be formal (legally or financially binding) or informal. One example of a formal relational network is the National Voluntary Organizations Active in Disaster (NVOAD), a group of 50 organizations that coordinate a unified response to disasters based on strong partnerships between nonprofit and faith-based organizations. State VOADs help to coordinate nonprofits at the state level.

The Partnership for Disaster Relief is an informal relational network. Formed after the 2004 tsunami in Asia, this group's mission is to bring together the resources and expertise of US businesses to improve recovery efforts for natural disasters. The Business Roundtable, an association of CEOs of major US companies, founded the network and facilitates these partnerships by working with nonprofits and agencies to match them with US companies. During Katrina, the Partnership became a central repository of information and needs, a guide for those wishing to contribute in-kind donations and a media source. Moreover, Roundtable member companies contributed $362 million in funding, services, supplies and equipment to support the Katrina relief effort.

Spontaneous networks
Arise suddenly and are cultivated by the interactions among people and organizations. They typically form out of necessity to solve a specific problem. Immediately after 9/11, for example, numerous individuals who owned boats used them, on their own initiative, to evacuate people from Lower Manhattan.

Witness accounts of those left in New Orleans in the wake of Katrina demonstrated the innovative and immediate response of citizens trying to help each other. These people used their skills and talents to help where possible: maintenance workers used forklift trucks to carry the sick and disabled, engineers started generators and kept them running, and nurses manually ventilated patients when the power failed. 'Stolen' boats and hotwired cars were used to rescue people in need.

Sources: Miller, Ande (2006), 'Roundtable on answering the call: the response of community-based organizations to the 2005 Gulf Coast hurricanes', Testimony before the Committee on Health, Education, Labor, and Pensions, 7 March; NVOAD, 'Organizing protocols for community disaster recovery mechanisms, national volunteer organizations active in disaster', www.nvoad.org/ articles/recovery.php, accessed 20 April 2006; Business Roundtable, www.businessroundtable. org/taskforces; and Bradshaw, L. and L.B. Slonsky (2005), 'Trapped in New Orleans by the flood – and martial law', *Socialist Worker Online*, 9 September 2005, http://www.socialistworker.org/2005-2/556/556_04_RealHeroes.html, accessed 19 April 2006.

The first step is to set up an effective network governance structure. The more points of contact among the players, the more likely trust and communication will flourish. Success depends on quickly identifying and resolving any friction points. Joint governance structures that address strategy, management and organizational activities can frame a successful network by setting out the overall vision and strategy of the network, bringing areas of contention between members of the network to the forefront early on, anticipating problem areas and establishing a way of handling them.

Governance structures must also incorporate procedures for promoting innovation and managing change. Governments need to create at the outset a streamlined way to capture innovative ideas and suggestions from their partners. Since many citizens clearly wish to help in any way they can during an emergency, governments would also do well to leverage that spirit. Individuals accomplish amazing things during an emergency. Governments can provide the leadership and tools to turn independent gestures into organized efforts and accomplish much more.

COORDINATING ACTIVITIES AND SYNCHRONIZING RESPONSES

Along with designing a network structure that enables collaboration, government can provide the infrastructure that allows organizations to share information. Take a city facing a terrorist threat to its water system. The group of individuals charged with responding to such a threat might include FEMA representatives, state environment officials, local hospitals, environmental groups, public utility executives, local law enforcement officers and building inspectors.[8]

Some states and regions have established fusion centers to collaborate on emergency planning and management. While these were initially formed to bring together law enforcement agencies from multiple jurisdictions and layers of governments, there is a trend to include representatives from the private sector as well as personnel responsible for health surveillance, agriculture surveillance and transportation infrastructure.

A basic requirement for any of these networks to function would be some kind of electronic coordination mechanism that allows disparate groups to share information in real time and synchronize their responses.

Pennsylvania's National Electronic Disease Surveillance System (PA-NEDSS) offers one model. In February 2002 Pennsylvania became the first state to introduce a fully integrated disease surveillance system that allows participants to share information quickly so that they can identify, track, predict and contain the spread of disease. More than 130 hospitals, 120 labs, 450 public health staff and 475 physicians connected to the PA-NEDSS. Public health officials can communicate public health alerts and advisories immediately and collect patient case data on a continuing basis over a secure system.

Thanks to the enhanced coordination and information-sharing capabilities, the reporting cycle of each patient case in Pennsylvania dropped from three weeks to fewer than 24 hours, enabling a more rapid and effective response.

During the Katrina response, corporations, countries and individuals wishing to contribute to the relief effort found themselves frustrated because agencies like the Red Cross and FEMA could not handle the thousands of offers and requests they received.[9] The overwhelming public response prompted the Office of the Private Sector of the Department of Homeland Security to activate the National Emergency Resource Registry (NERR), which had been in place for more than a year but had not been used.[10] NERR, an online database characterized as 'eBay for the government', provided a place for companies to register resources available for sale or donation and allowed those involved in the relief effort to register their needs.[11]

While technology is critical, some of the most important work a state performs in creating an emergency management network involves building strong relationships. Successful networks rely, at least partly, on trust. Without trust, network participants shyaway from sharing knowledge, hindering coordination among them. Networks operating with a high level of trust, in contrast, lower the costs associated with interorganizational exchanges.

How can network architects encourage trust-based relationships among partners? For one thing, they must clearly communicate the values and goals of the network at the outset of the relationship. Early-stage trust building and goal alignment is best ensured by making the central goal so clear and compelling that the inherent centrifugal forces will not overwhelm its structure.

REALIGNING THE STATE'S ORGANIZATIONAL STRUCTURE AND GOVERNANCE

Many states rely on emergency management organizational structures established years ago, based upon strict hierarchies and administrative silos. The existing chain of command, the established work flow, the criteria for hiring and the system of rewards may inhibit, rather than encourage, an effective networked response. A government working to create an integrated emergency management network needs to take a long, hard look at its structure, its organizational culture and its information architecture. Once officials understand the current situation, they can determine what changes are needed to encourage better information sharing, collaborative activity and flexibility.

The Transportation Security Administration (TSA) made a transition to a networked organizational model when it established the Office of Transportation Sector Network Management (TSNM). The office is divided into 11 divisions. Ten encompass modes of transportation such as rail and mass transit, and the eleventh works as an integration unit facilitating collaboration across the modes. The TSNM's organizational structure includes staff devoted to stakeholder relations that focus exclusively on external collaboration and partnership with the transportation industry and transportation associations.

To encourage collaboration, the TSNM has structured itself to mirror the current organizational structure of private industry. For example, the aviation industry is split into three passenger modes – commercial airports, commercial airlines and general aviation – plus cargo, because this division best reflects how the commercial arena makes distinctions in this area. By mimicking these divisions, the TSNM hopes to maximize the information flow between government and the private sector. Knowledge is both power and the key to circumventing terrorist attacks, which links directly back to the TSA mission.

The US Coast Guard's performance in the Katrina response provides another good example of an organizational structure that matches the needs of emergency response. During the storm, the Coast Guard rescued 33 000 people, reconstituted waterways, conducted environmental assessments and restored buoys and channel markers.[12]

Critical to the Coast Guard's success was the flexibility in the command structure that allowed those in the field to exercise their own discretion.[13] Captain Frank Paskewich, commanding officer of Sector New Orleans, describes the Coast Guard model as one that has commanding officers setting 'broad-based objectives' for a mission, which frees them from micromanagement since the Coast Guard member on the scene is the one making the judgment calls. Coast Guard members are trained to carry out a mission in the safest way possible, and are given the latitude to do what is needed to fulfill the mission.[14] This type of flexibility helps overcome the bureaucratic hurdles that delay response.

CONCLUSION

The list of emergencies that might challenge a state administration is a formidable one. But a robust emergency management strategy can help avert a great deal of suffering. By coordinating and managing an efficient networked response, establishing structures for effective information sharing, implementing state-of-the-art logistics practices, wisely managing risk and exercising creative leadership, state government can protect its citizens and smooth the path to recovery.

NOTES

1. Interview with Kate Hale, former director of emergency management for Miami-Dade County, 23 February 2006.
2. Kam, Dara and Alan Gomez (2005), 'Lack of plan hurt Katrina-hit states' response', *Palm Beach Post*, 10 September, http://www.palmbeachpost.com/storm/content/state/epaper/2005/09/10/m1a_response_0910. html.
3. Bush, Jeb (2005), 'Think locally on relief', *Washington Post*, 30 September, A19.
4. Dan Hopkins, PhD candidate, Department of Government, Harvard University, interview with Amy Petz, 11 April 2006.
5. Al Martinez-Fonts, Testimony before the House Committee on the Judiciary Subcommittee on Immigration, Border Security and Claims, 18 March 2004.
6. Testimony of Craig Nemitz, Disaster Services Manager, America's Second Harvest, before the Senate Committee on Health, Education, Labor and Pensions, 7 March 2006 (hereafter Nemitz, 2006).
7. Nemitz (2006).
8. Mitchell Waldrop, M. (2003), 'Can sense-making keep us safe?', *Technology Review*, March, p. 45.
9. Bailey, Peter (2005), 'Katrina's aftermath: willing benefactors hit brick wall of bureaucracy', *Miami Herald,* 6 September 2005.
10. Phillips, Zack (2005), 'DHS launches web site for Katrina response', *CQ Homeland Security*, 7 September.
11. Freedberg, Sydney (2005), 'Disaster, Inc', *National Journal*, 17 December.
12. White House (2006), *The Federal Response to Hurricane Katrina: Lessons Learned*, White House Report, February, www.whitehouse.gov/reports/Katrina_lessons_learned [White House Report, 2006], accessed 15 April 2006.
13. Rear Admiral Thad Allen defined the Coast Guard's approach by identifying three critical elements to operations in the Gulf Region: use of resources, use of communications, and use of command and control. He also stressed the importance of planning. Because the Coast Guard prepositioned resources and personnel, it could conduct a flexible and immediate search and rescue. These elements, combined with its adaptability, enabled the Coast Guard to produce a powerful result. See Allen Thad (2005), 'Katrina: it reshaped the Gulf Coast – how will it reshape Washington, DC', remarks at the George Washington University, 2 December.
14. Interview with Captain Frank Paskewich, Commanding Officer of Sector New Orleans, US Coast Guard, 17 April 2006.

15 Wal-Mart case study: the lessons of Katrina (II)
Ken Senser and Jason Jackson

Failing to plan is planning to fail. (Alan Lakein, American author and time management specialist)

INTRODUCTION

Hurricane Katrina was a life- and business-changing event for Wal-Mart Stores, Inc. Interestingly, though, the devastating impact of this storm did not come from its winds or rain. Hurricane Katrina was a national catastrophe because of a series of compounding events that stressed to the point of failure personal, community, business, organizational and governmental plans. For Wal-Mart, Hurricane Katrina was a test of spirit, endurance and process at all levels of the company. But for most, it was a turning point in the 'psyche' of the company – a galvanizing event that reinforced the core values for which the company stands.

Dealing with hurricanes is nothing new at Wal-Mart. While we are not arrogant, we (like many others) went into this hurricane with confidence believing that it would unfold in the same predictable manner as the many before it. Unfortunately, our response ultimately turned from one primarily focused on business recovery to one more closely resembling a relief operation.

This case study describes not only the Wal-Mart experience and lessons learned from Hurricane Katrina, but also the foundational elements that allow us to achieve the best possible outcome when faced with a crisis. Collectively, our nation and the world stand to benefit from examining the crisis leadership and response best practices demonstrated by many different individuals and organizations. No crisis response will ever go perfectly, particularly one to an event the size, scope and complexity of Katrina. But just as one of Wal-Mart's core values describes the need to 'strive for excellence', so any collective response effort short of excellence is simply just not good enough for our communities or our country.

COMPANY PROFILE

Wal-Mart was founded in 1962 and is based in Bentonville, Arkansas. At the time of this writing, our company employed close to 1.4 million associates in the United States at more than 4000 Wal-Mart stores, SAM's Clubs, and distribution centers located in all 50 states. We also operated over 2700 facilities in 14 markets outside the US and employed approximately 400 000 associates in our international and global sourcing operations.[1] Each week, at the time, over 138 million customers chose to shop at Wal-Mart, validating our success as a provider of merchandise at an 'Everyday Low Price'.

Wal-Mart does not just operate stores, clubs and distribution centers; our associates are active in their communities, both personally and on behalf of the company on a number of issues. In this regard, community sustainability is an important part of our corporate DNA. Ensuring continuity of operations and serving as a community resource during times of disaster gives us the opportunity to leverage many of our strengths to serve those who have allowed us to be part of these communities. Basic needs become paramount during crises and we see it as a personal obligation to ensure that those basic items that we often take for granted, such as food, water, diapers, baby formula, prescription drugs and fuel, are available as quickly as possible following a disaster to aid and speed the response and recovery efforts.

BASIC CRISIS MANAGEMENT PHILOSOPHY AND PROTOCOLS

Wal-Mart has spent years evolving our crisis response protocols following serious storms and other natural disasters. For most retailers, getting back into operation as quickly as possible after a serious storm highlights the emphasis placed on serving customers and communities.

After 9/11 we began thinking differently about the risks facing our company. Natural disasters tend to be geographically focused, which generally limit the scope and duration of their destruction. A large-scale terrorist attack, however, could not only create large-scale physical devastation and serious interruptions in the supply chain, but it could also negatively impact upon the psychological outlook of consumers, resulting in long-term changes in buying patterns. The inability to shop, or a major loss of consumer confidence, will have significant negative implications for the global economy.

Understanding these factors, Wal-Mart initiated a program in early 2004 to develop 'Global Readiness'[2] – an ability to handle effectively potential disruptions from all hazards, in any aspect of our business, at any location worldwide. In support of Global Readiness, we established and continue to build processes to prepare our company for potential disruptions, mitigate their impact, respond to them effectively, and fully recover the business to its original operating capability.

Leading a successful crisis response requires a clear strategy in addition to sound tactics. Strategies are built on principles. Those principles that complement the organization's values result in the most effective strategies, and therefore, the best results. At Wal-Mart, during the initial phase of our Global Readiness Program, we recognized that the guiding principles that must shape our crisis response strategy could be represented as follows: (1) the importance of ensuring the safety of our associates and customers; (2) the need to keep our business operating; and (3) the support we provide to our communities. Prior to their adoption, these guiding principles were discussed with our Chief Executive Officer (CEO) and Executive Committee.[3] Debate took place over whether we should prioritize the support provided to our communities ahead of reconstituting our business. Ultimately, we realized that the best way to support communities is by having operating stores and clubs that can supply the basic needs of our customers, taking a significant burden off the shoulders of first responders. Hurricane Katrina validated this thinking.

Wal-Mart's guiding principles complement our company's three basic beliefs: (1)

respect for the individual; (2) serving our customer; and (3) striving for excellence. Any Wal-Mart Associate who is steeped in the company's culture already has a significant head start on how to respond to a crisis – it is the same general approach they take every day when serving their customers and communities.

BUILDING BASICS

From a technical standpoint, we built our crisis response methodology using both process-based and structural elements. From a process standpoint, we identified those hazards that we felt posed the greatest likelihood of disrupting our business and potential impact should a disruption occur. We then developed contingencies for responding to these hazards. On the structural side, we established three levels to oversee the response, to include our Local Incident Management Teams (LIMTs), the Emergency Operations Center, and our executive level. Wal-Mart also established a series of Crisis Management Teams (CMTs) around the globe to bridge the gap between tactical and strategic responsibilities.

Most crises require substantial engagement at the local level. With over 6700 stores, clubs and distribution centers located around the world, the management at every Wal-Mart facility must be prepared to take action, and to do so rapidly and efficiently. This is accomplished using the concept of an LIMT. Local store, club or distribution center management lead the LIMT and it receives functional support from key areas within the business, such as human resources and asset-protection associates. The LIMT adopts the corporate policy framework and response protocols to its specific operating environment. Some of the most important responsibilities of local management, independent of and prior to any crisis, include developing relationships within their communities with elected or appointed officials, emergency responders and other business owners. The importance of having robust and effective networks at the time of a crisis cannot be overstated. As an aside, these same networks similarly play a crucial role in the 'routine' operation of any business. Local management cannot wait until a time of crisis to identify a safe relocation area for their associates or to practice a specific response protocol. The manager's network is instrumental in helping him or her accomplish the things needed to prepare and mitigate a crisis, in addition to assisting with the response and recovery portions of the incident.

The Emergency Operations Center (EOC) serves as the centralized platform for crisis coordination. The EOC functions 24 hours a day, every day of the year. The EOC works both proactively in monitoring the globe for potential business disruptions, initiating mitigating actions to minimize or negate any impact when possible, and reactively by enacting our corporate response and recovery plans and coordinating actions. The EOC focuses on developing the 'big picture' of the event through centralized communications, processes and software applications, and then providing this picture back to the decision makers to ensure that they have the best data set possible from which to make the best decisions. Equally important is driving efficiency through face-to-face communication, which not only keeps players on the 'same page', but also provides a platform for quick decisions to be made.

Most tactical decisions are made rapidly at the working level or with the assistance of more senior business leaders with facilitation by the EOC. Those decisions with substantive impact may be escalated to the business executives from the affected divisions. At the strategic level, Wal-Mart's Executive Committee is kept abreast of the progress of the crisis response in addition to assessments of what is likely to occur as a result of the crisis and the potential impact of the crisis on our business. The Corporate CMT[4] supports the Executive Committee by anticipating, exploring and appropriately framing the strategic issues for the executives so that informed decisions are possible in a short time frame.

KEY FORCE MULTIPLIERS

The three response tiers, with the support of the CMT, form the foundation for a rapid and effective crisis response. Wal-Mart capitalizes on its corporate strengths and benefits from a strong corporate culture during a disaster. Of particular importance is the efficient use of available resources. We move merchandise from point A to point B very efficiently and effectively every day – this is a strength. For our company, additional strengths lie in human talent, merchandise volume and the sophistication of our information systems. Wal-Mart leverages these strengths, and others, to accomplish our crisis management goals and to serve the greater good during a crisis. These serve as 'force multipliers'. Several of the key 'force multipliers' are described here.

Quick Situation Identification

Hurricanes are unique in that they are one of the few disaster types that normally allow for preparation prior to impact. Having an effective monitoring structure to identify potential crises quickly is necessary to ensure the maximum preparation and assessment time.

Scalable Operations

The ability to expand and contract operations appropriately as the event unfolds is also essential to success. Often, time variables emerge suddenly that require immediate attention, expansion of operations, and/or immediate change of direction. The crisis management structure must be devoid of rigidity and allow for maximum flexibility to address any emerging variables properly. Hurricane Katrina, for Wal-Mart, tested this concept to the maximum as the EOC expanded to include five operational annexes and unprecedented field support operations. Key, however, is not the fact that the expansions occurred to meet the needs, but rather the speed at which the expansions occurred.

Flexibility

'Adapt and overcome' is a common mantra in the Wal-Mart EOC. Changing direction 'on the fly' is what allows us to modify our response to the situation at hand. Flexibility in our plans, flexibility in our structure, and flexibility of our associates is paramount to success. When we identify the need for change, the change is completed as soon as possible and we do not wait for the structured corrective action process after the storm to complete this change. An example of this would be the immediate changes in our response protocols between Hurricanes Katrina and Rita. Between the two storms, we identified the need to streamline communication and information flow between the company and government, and also to enhance communication with our associates. To address these needs, we changed processes. We placed two of our managers in the Texas State Emergency Operations Center during Hurricane Rita to improve the effectiveness of resource allocation decisions and to enhance state-level communications. We also enhanced the information provided to associates prior to Hurricane Rita's landfall by anticipating and providing the answers to disaster-related questions before those questions were asked.

Total Company Support

Having a structure in place is simply never enough. It is necessary for all of our associates to utilize the structure effectively to maximize efficiency and success. During Hurricane Katrina, Wal-Mart's CEO, H. Lee Scott, Jr. made it very clear from the beginning of the event that all operations relative to the preparation, response and recovery of the hurricane were to flow through the EOC. This is also evident in the number of departments and divisions that have business unit representatives physically located within the EOC that serve as decision-makers and liaisons for their respective business units.

Efficient Communications

It is often repeated that communication is critical to success, but we strongly believe that efficient communication is absolutely the key to success at a higher level. Timely, accurate flow of data is another essential for success. At the local level, situational awareness is developed and passed quickly to the EOC, which develops the big picture for the business unit representatives who have gathered there. The business unit representatives then make decisions on strategies and tactics based upon the 'big picture' data that have been collected. The business unit representatives are then able to disseminate tactical objectives quickly back to the response teams and field teams for dissemination. While this is reflective of the communications structure, the mode of communication is just as important. During times of crisis, the utilization of voice mail and e-mail become inefficient transmitters of information. For Wal-Mart, face-to-face communication within the EOC, where the tactical decision-makers congregate, is the most efficient method of communication. Communication from and to the field occurs through the standard modes that one would expect (cell phones, satellite phones, analog telephone lines, Voice over Internet Protocol, and so on) based upon the variable presented, but it also comes with many challenges, which will be addressed later in this case study.

As an example of communication flow in the EOC, when an operations vice-president receives a request for five trailers of water and food to support an impacted location, he or she can turn to the emergency merchandise support manager located in the same room and say, 'I need the following merchandise.' The merchandise support manager can immediately say, 'I have it available', and the logistics manager sitting in front of both of them can say, 'I can get it there in six hours.' This example is simplified, but realistically portrays how quickly decisions are made and actions are triggered, which is what creates efficiency for the company.

Following the 2004 hurricane season, Wal-Mart realized the need for expanding this efficient communication process beyond the corporate level. As a pilot program during the 2005 season, we invited members of the American Red Cross (representing the national office) to function in the EOC as partners, which was tremendously successful. In preparation for the 2006 season, we expanded this partnership by incorporating the Salvation Army.

Information Systems

As previously indicated, Wal-Mart's information systems are considered a major corporate asset. For all hurricanes and disasters, we utilize our information systems to tell us what it is that consumers will need both pre- and post-hurricane based upon historical consumer buying patterns. This allows us to get the right merchandise to the right stores at the right time. From a commmunity safety standpoint, it helps the population prepare properly for an impending situation by having flashlights, batteries, food and water in the right quantities, and it also aids a speedy recovery when the right items like plastic tarps, generators and fuel cans are available. Additionally, our Information Systems Division has created a centralized Incident Management Application that is used to coordinate information relative to the event, network teams who quickly reconstitute network and voice communications at the store level, and support critical applications and operations. Modeling and mapping applications are used as regular tools for the EOC to forecast, track and convey information.

Logistics Systems

As a key player in the retail commerce industry, Wal-Mart has many of the resources needed to provide emergency services. At the time of this writing Wal-Mart operates over 110 distribution centers spread throughout the United States. Of these, nine distribution centers allocate square footage for 'disaster merchandise'. In these reserved areas, approximately $4.7 million dollars in 'disaster merchandise' is stockpiled, which includes over 250 000 gallons of drinking water. Further, we maintain strategic relationships with key vendors that aid in handling surge requests during times of crisis.

As part of our processes, merchandise support vendors, government agencies, non-governmental organizations and other private sector entities are only dispatched when requested. We believe that it is important to ensure that resources are being targeted where they are needed, rather than complicating response operations by sending merchandise to places where it is not needed or that do not have the capabilities to handle freight.

In our experience, stored merchandise makes a difference. In 2003, we shipped over 550 trailers of merchandise to assist with disaster incidents and shipped over 1 million gallons of water for Hurricane Isabel relief. In 2004, we shipped over 1300 trailers of merchandise to assist with disaster incidents and shipped over 3 million gallons of water for disaster relief. In support of Hurricanes Katrina and Rita alone, we shipped close to 3000 trailers of merchandise for emergency support.

Understanding the Big Picture

When major crises strike, we find ourselves in a unique position to see the big picture. At the same time that we may be assessing a multi-state disaster, we find ourselves balancing the needs of our associates, our facilities, governmental requests at all levels, community needs, and other private sector entity requests. Additionally, we must ensure that our customers across the nation are still being provided with the goods and services that they need.

Corporate Culture

Our greatest asset is our people. Culture is a difficult aspect to replicate, but it is absolutely one of the greatest strengths of our company. Our managers are encouraged to participate actively in the events impacting their communities, and not just sit on the sidelines. There are countless stories of our associates acting on their own in positive ways to care for their co-workers, customers, friends and communities. The result was numerous acts of courage, kindness and compassion during the aftermath of Hurricane Katrina.

HURRICANE KATRINA PREPARATION AND RESPONSE

Wal-Mart's preparation and response to Hurricane Katrina was a culmination of all the aforementioned components of our crisis response infrastructure combined with thousands of actions taken at a variety of levels within the company. Our efforts began with the early identification of the storm system off the eastern coast of Florida that ultimately became Katrina. On 22 August, we focused on a weather pattern that became Tropical Depression 12 on 23 August. Once we determined that this tropical depression was going to impact Florida as a potential hurricane, we enacted our hurricane plan. Facilities in the potential impact area were identified, communicated with, and emergency merchandise began flowing into stores and clubs to support the anticipated community needs. At the EOC, teams were recalled to support a Florida impact with a likely secondary landfall. Response teams, including generator support, were staged. Price increase blocks were set, dry ice deliveries were completed to mitigate product loss, facilities stayed open as long as possible (taking into account associate safety), and associates finalized preparations at their facilities.

Hurricane Katrina made landfall in Florida on 25 August as a weak Category 1 hurricane and took a southeastern path, which was a best-case scenario for our operations. Of the 15 facilities that closed temporarily due to the storm, all facilities except one reopened within 24 hours to serve their communities.

As the hurricane passed into the Gulf, monitoring and assessment operations continued for the new potential threat. Similar to the first landfall, we began staging response teams and resources to support the second landfall. We received a call from a private meteorologist who informed us of the hurricane track shifting to the west, prior to the National Hurricane Center public release. With this information, we began warning facility management as far west as Louisiana of the shift in track and began shifting our response resources accordingly.

During the next couple of days, the hurricane grew in size and intensity. We began expanding our preparatory activities and called in additional resources. With the warnings issued and preparation efforts under way, a process very similar to what occurred days earlier in Florida now unfolded in Alabama, Mississippi and Louisiana. Pre-landfall merchandise was dispatched, response teams were deployed, generators were staged, and associates were evacuated. Recognizing the increased scope, we modified our Associate Emergency Information Line to handle a call center platform.[5] This 24-hour Associate Call Center would be expanded several times over the next few days to accommodate four, then ten, then 25, then 50, and finally 80 operators, including support staff, to serve our associates during their time of need. It is important to note that these operators were associates representing departments from all over the Wal-Mart Home Office who left their regular duties to assist victims of the storm.

The hurricane slammed ashore again on 29 August, and we watched from the EOC as we lost connectivity with facility after facility. In total, 173 facilities were affected by Hurricane Katrina, but the peak of closures at any given moment was 126 facilities. To put this into perspective, the number of affected facilities represents essentially our entire operations in southern Louisiana, southern Mississippi, southern Alabama and the western portion of the Panhandle of Florida – affecting approximately 34 000 associates and their families, as well as the communities in which they lived.

Immediately after the hurricane passed, Wal-Mart teams sprung into action – searching for lost associates, assessing facilities, reconstituting and restoring operations, coordinating with government officials, and shipping relief supplies across the region. As with our priorities, we viewed our operations in three categories: (1) aiding our Associates; (2) reconstituting operations; and (3) supporting communities and non-Wal-Mart response operations. Our teams responded quickly and facilities began reopening as it was safe and they were able to do so.

The initial hurricane impact proved to be similar to other severe storms experienced in the United States. By the end of 30 August, however, it became clear that this disaster was taking on a different complexion. With the failure of the levees in New Orleans, what is typically a short response and recovery period would become unprecedented in scope and complexity. Wal-Mart's CMT is always kept informed of the progress of our response to hurricanes and other 'routine' natural disasters. However, for a traditional hurricane the CMT does not, usually, convene. With the unique challenges resulting from the levee failures mounting, CEO Scott convened a meeting on the morning of 31 August, so that he could gain a better understanding of the situation. That afternoon, the CMT met for the first time. During this meeting, CEO Scott emphasized that we were facing an extraordinary event and he expected an extraordinary response. His declaration clearly set the tone for what was to follow.

Many of the displaced associates and their families temporarily relocated to other communities. As they did so, we provided them with an initial $250 in cash to help with immediate needs, but also allowed them to apply for up to $1000 in relief funds, based upon their need, through our internal Associate Disaster Relief Fund. This fund provided approximately $13.5 million in cash assistance to more than 19 000 associates affected by Hurricane Katrina.

While store management and our Associate Emergency Information Line operators talked with most of our associates, the EOC kept a close tally on how many were still missing, and we searched shelters for our associates to ensure their safety. Most importantly, we offered employment to any associate displaced by the storm at a store, club or distribution center of their choice. In fact, approximately 2400 associates worked temporarily at other sites during this ordeal, and some transferred permanently. Sadly, we know that five of our associates perished in the storm.

As previously stated, we feel an obligation to reopen our facilities as quickly as possible to support our communities. During Hurricane Katrina, 63 percent of our 173 affected facilities were damaged or suffered some type of loss. Our restoration, energy, systems, security and management teams worked around the clock to recover operations and mitigate further loss. Our pre-staged generators provided power to facilities in areas that did not have power for days and weeks, our security teams worked with law enforcement and the National Guard to ensure safety, and our management teams reopened facilities (often metering operating hours or the customer traffic due to limited associate staffing). Our information systems teams established network and voice connectivity by setting up temporary satellite systems. We utilized mobile and regional command posts to guide local operations and ensure associate and response team accountability. We talked with the Centers for Disease Control and Prevention and state health agencies to develop strategies to best prepare our associates for the potential of a health threat.

Through hard work, good pre-planning, a coordinated response and associates who are dedicated to serve their communities, we were able to recover and reopen 83 percent of our facilities in the Gulf area within six days before we moved into a status quo that required time to repair facilities. Sixty-six percent of our recovery occurred within 48 hours of the storm making landfall. As a demonstration of the lasting impact of this storm and the continuing challenges facing full recovery, there were three Wal-Mart stores and one Sam's Club that had not reopened due to questions of sustainability.[6]

Wal-Mart worked hand in hand with communities, non-governmental organizations, other private sector companies, and governmental officials at all levels on a variety of topics, ranging from provision of supplies to information sharing, communications, energy support, fuel and sheltering. We sheltered police officers and emergency services workers in our stores, supported hospitals and communities, fed people, provided pharmaceuticals, changed tires on emergency response vehicles, and provided vaccinations to both our responders and emergency workers. Further, we provided generator support to power non-Wal-Mart facilities (for example a major fuel depot in Mississippi), hotels, water treatment plants and hospitals. Wal-Mart brought basic needs to communities that had nothing, and often we allowed customers a moment of 'normalcy' as they pushed a shopping cart through an air-conditioned store, even though the landscape around the store had been devastated. In the first three weeks after Hurricane Katrina struck, Wal-Mart delivered approximately 2500 trailers of emergency supplies (for donation and sale) – including trucks of water and supplies that flowed into the New Orleans metro area beginning on Saturday, 3 September for emergency service workers, shelters and hospitals. A total of three temporary mobile pharmacies were provided to support communities, and a 16000 square foot 'tent store' was erected to serve a community where the store had been all but demolished. The list of actions is lengthy.

While there are numerous stories describing the heroic efforts of local Wal-Mart associates, one story stands out and speaks to what makes Wal-Mart what it is – its people.

Co-Manager Jessica Lewis from Waveland, Mississippi stayed in the region with her family as the hurricane passed over. When it was safe, she ventured out and found that her store had been heavily damaged. From the standpoint of the community, Jessica Lewis was Wal-Mart. She chose to act. Jessica and her family gathered non-perishable items and placed them in the parking lot for the people of the community to come and get as they needed – at no charge. She also provided bottled water and other resources to the local emergency services and hospital. Jessica was the lifeline for this community until other help arrived.

These stories of independent action on a local basis speak to the aspect of Wal-Mart's corporate culture and human talent, mentioned earlier, that provide considerable leverage for the company when responding to a crisis. It is people like this that make us a great company and a truly great nation.

While local efforts of responding to directly affected communities were one front that we faced, there was another. It quickly became apparent that the mass evacuation of hundreds of thousands of people was creating a major population shift that would seriously impact other communities. We found ourselves establishing donation stations at major shelter operations, like the Astrodome in Houston and Fort Chaffee in Arkansas. We prepared our facilities and associates in the areas surrounding the immediate impact area for the influx of people who had needs that were outside of the norm. We supported sheltering operations in most states that took in evacuees. In total, Wal-Mart donated over $17 million in cash to relief organizations and more than $3.5 million in merchandise. We were the early leader in donations and set the bar high for the rest of the private sector.

Additionally, Wal-Mart created an online 'locator board' website where people could post pictures and messages. This website, that was accessible from walmart.com, samsclub.com and our gift registry kiosks in all of our stores around the nation, received over 53 000 posts and over 5 million website 'hits'. Our Information Systems Division set up computers that were capable of communicating through the Internet at 150 shelters. Wal-Mart worked with the Federal Emergency Management Agency (FEMA) on the evacuee debit card program to ensure that firearms, alcohol and tobacco products could not be purchased with the cards. We also worked with major cities to provide apartment furnishings for the evacuees who, in many cases, had nothing as they moved out of the shelters. Again, the list of these actions is lengthy, and we may never know of every store or associate who somehow helped their local community in supporting evacuees.

LESSONS LEARNED

At Wal-Mart, we do not use the word 'problem', we prefer to say 'opportunity'. While this may be a play on words, it symbolizes the fact that we must learn from the opportunities that are placed in front of us and always strive to do better. Hurricane Katrina was an immense learning experience for all of us. While it highlighted the tremendous heart of this nation, it also highlighted areas of opportunity. Now is the time that we must capitalize on these opportunities and turn them into successes. Our lessons learned are not solely applicable to Wal-Mart or the private sector, but all sectors, public and private.

Communication

While we believe that we communicated better than ever before with our associates, our teams and external entities, we believe we can do better. We have categorized these into three areas of opportunity, as described here.

Associate communication

As we adapted our processes between Hurricanes Katrina and Rita, we changed the messages that we provided to associates to ensure they had the information they needed to survive a major disaster. However, we recognized that our platform for providing information needed to be more robust so that we could more efficiently and speedily account for associates, determine their individual needs, and act on those needs. We have already deployed an enhanced version of our Associate Emergency Information Line that is more interactive, and integrated this technology with our Incident Management Application to provide a better associate location and tracking capability.

Communication modes

The inability to communicate over the public network after a disaster is a major challenge for all organizations operating in areas where there has been significant damage to the communications infrastructure. This was the case after 9/11, and was also an issue during Hurricane Katrina. We are working with our private sector partners to find an 'all the time' solution but, meanwhile, we continue to apply lessons learned to enhance our tactical plans at recovering communication capabilities as quickly as possible, and when necessary return to archaic forms of communication (for example, using 'runners') as a backup.

Institutionalizing the process

Internally we have found success in our centralized communications process; however, externally this has created a challenge. We found that confusion was created by numerous governmental, non-governmental and private sector organizations when contacting our company during the crisis through their regular business counterparts – for example, a state health department representative contacting one of our Pharmacy Division managers whom he knows personally. This delays crisis-related communication as they may be accustomed to leaving a voice mail or an e-mail that may not be checked regularly. It is important for Wal-Mart to centralize this external communication process to streamline the way in which we communicate. The EOC can route callers to the appropriate representative located in the EOC. This allows us to take immediate action and also further define our 'big picture' based upon incoming information. To remedy this, we are reaching out to stakeholders and response partners, to include state and federal government agencies, to spread this message.

Expectations and Understanding

Both internally and externally, we believe that understanding the capabilities and expectations of another team, department, division, or entity will aid us in better developing our own strategic plans. This bilateral communication must be open, honest and relative. Just as it is important for government to know what Wal-Mart's capabilities and limitations are in terms of providing resources during a crisis, so it is necessary for us – in terms of solid plan development – to know how FEMA is going to respond, what state agencies will expect of us, and whether or not the local Sheriff's Office will allow us to restore facilities if there is a county-wide curfew in effect. For Wal-Mart, this equates to the old adage of building a house on a rock rather than sand.

An example

We did not communicate well with local law enforcement agencies the fact that our company utilizes third-party carriers to deliver products to affected areas. As a result, we saw our private fleet trucks (with Wal-Mart logos) sailing past check points and often with police escorts, while our unmarked third-party carriers were held up for extended periods of time until they could prove that they were transporting goods for Wal-Mart. This created inefficiencies that we now know must be mitigated through proper communication with officials prior to a storm or some other disaster.

Other pre-disaster discussions

These should revolve around enacting limited, temporary, disaster-related legislation providing relief from certain license requirements or operating restrictions. As an example, there may be a need to move firearms to a safer area from a store in the impact zone. Having pre-approvals for disaster periods from the Bureau of Alcohol, Tobacco and Firearms to transport firearms for this purpose would be helpful. Another example might be related to securing an agreement before a disaster from the Environmental Protection Agency to ease mandates for special 'clean fuels' to ensure motorists can get fuel during extremely high-demand periods that result from pre-disaster evacuations.

Finance

As a result of the previous two learning points, this third point is close to being resolved. However, we faced a major opportunity during Hurricane Katrina in determining how governmental organizations were going to pay for supplies. In the early days of the storm, we received frantic requests from governmental organizations for supplies and we allowed them to access our closed facilities and take what they needed – as a donation. However, later in the response process our managers were often approached by federal, state and local officials who told our managers that FEMA would pay for the goods they required. As we began getting to grips with the billing process, we were informed at varying levels that the person who made the purchase was not a 'purchasing agent' or did not complete the proper paperwork. While this may be an over simplification of the issue, the fact is that we found a need to work with governmental and non-governmental agencies pre-disaster to come to agreement on proper acquisition and billing processes to best suit both entities.

Learning from Those That Know

At Wal-Mart, we realize that we do not know everything, and we do not pretend that we do. We realize that there are a number of best practices being enacted by others and we seek out those who have a better process in a particular area so that we can learn from them. We seek these best practices from government agencies, non-governmental organizations and other private sector companies at a local, state, national and global level. There is no telling from where the best ideas will emerge – Hurricane Katrina reconfirmed to us that the key is to continue learning, benchmarking and seeking out new and innovative ways to approach crisis response.

At the same time that we know we can learn, we also know that we can teach. For example, when FEMA or another agency places an order of 100 trailers of water, we often question if the person placing the order really knows what 100 trailers of merchandise looks like or has the resources available to off-load 100 trailers in an efficient and timely manner. Usually the answer to this is that the person making the order was given a dollar amount to spend and they do not comprehend the size of this order or what it means. In this regard, we believe that we are in a strong position to educate government purchasing and logistics managers.

Partnering for Success

Finally, we know that we cannot do it all. Any company would be foolish to think that it was able to support itself during a crisis without public and private sector partnerships, just the same as it would be for any government agency to think that it could succeed without partnering with the private sector. With this realization, we know that we will have to develop an understanding of each others' capabilities and limitations, expectations and requirements and build crisis plans that will lead to success together. For example, we believe that through Wal-Mart's Every Day Low Prices, we can make the government's dollar go further in purchasing supplies, which means that there will be more supplies available for more people.

We honestly believe that we can be one of the industry leaders in refining how we, as a nation, respond to disasters and how we leverage each other's strengths to serve those affected in a timely, efficient and comprehensive manner.

CONCLUSION

As with all of our business processes, Wal-Mart seeks excellence and strives constantly to improve and make more efficient our disaster mitigation, preparation, response and recovery processes. We will continue to focus on our priorities: our Associates, reconstituting operations, and our support for the communities in which we live and work. On a daily basis, Wal-Mart strives to improve the lives of our customers and to better our communities. A crisis only reinforces this commitment.

In life there are certain absolutes. One of those absolutes is the fact that we will face another major crisis in the future. Whether this is a natural disaster or a man-made disaster, a significant pandemic or a terrorist event, we will all be required to respond again in the future. Whether we are successful or unsuccessful in the future depends wholly upon whether we continue to learn from the opportunities that present themselves and whether we choose to partner proactively with each other. Both the public sector and the private sector are filled with talented leaders who can build these partnerships and elevate our country to an unprecedented level of disaster preparedness.

NOTES

1. At the time of this writing Wal-Mart has retail stores in the US (to include Puerto Rico), Canada, Mexico, Guatemala, Honduras, El Salvador, Nicaragua, Costa Rica, Brazil, Argentina, China, Japan, the United Kingdom, Germany and South Korea. Wal-Mart will soon sell its operations in South Korea and Germany and plans to exit those markets.
2. 'Global Readiness' was coined by two associates in our Global Security Division, Eric White and Larry Lundeen.
3. Wal-Mart's Executive Committee is composed of the leaders of the key business and support divisions.
4. Wal-Mart's Corporate CMT is Chaired by the SVP for Global Security, Aviation, and Travel, and has senior representation from its People, Legal, Corporate Relations, and Operations divisions. Ad hoc members participate, depending on the nature of the crisis, to bring subject-matter expertise to the discussion.
5. The Associate Emergency Information Line is a 1-800 line for associates to call for specific crisis-related information.
6. Closed facilities were located in New Orleans, LA and Pass Christian, MS.

16 Doing business in no man's land: the lessons of Katrina (III)
Geoff Williams

If we had all the information to make a decision, it would no longer be a decision but a foregone conclusion. (Anonymous)

INTRODUCTION

Almost a month after Hurricane Katrina clobbered the Gulf Coast with winds up to 145 mph, and usurped much of the infrastructure in its thriving oil industry, John Brady's hindsight kicked in. It was the moment he heard Michael Brown, the abruptly dumped head of the Federal Emergency Management Agency (FEMA), say: 'My biggest mistake was not realizing by Saturday that Louisiana was dysfunctional.'

Brady, the chairman of the ASIS International, Oil, Gas and Chemical Industry Council, felt an ache in the pit of his stomach. If Brown was correct, that Louisiana's government was dysfunctional, that was disheartening enough, but it was further discouraging to hear people at the top echelons of government blaming other entities for the catastrophic response in meeting the needs of the region after such a harrowing experience. He could only hope that the government would learn from its mistakes.

Brady already knew that his industry had learned something. They couldn't afford not to evolve their strategies and thinking after Katrina. Planning for emergencies was, after all, his job – he also served as a security adviser for ConocoPhillips – and arguably without people like Brady at the helm, the oil industry would probably have been much more badly bruised and battered by Katrina than it was.

DISASTROUS RESULTS

At the time there were over 4000 oil-producing sites in the Gulf of Mexico. According to the US Minerals Management Service, a unit of the Interior Department, as the hurricane ripped through the coastline, workers had been evacuated from approximately three-quarters of the Gulf's rigs and platforms. By the time it was all over, at least eight refineries, with a combined capacity of 1.8 million barrels a day, had been shut down. An estimated 58 oil platforms and drilling rigs – and the average rig can cost $90 million to $550 million to build – had been damaged or displaced, and 30 of the rigs were reported completely lost. (Ironically, as bad as things were, the oil industry took an even bigger hit less than a month later, in Florida, when Hurricane Rita hit.)

In the aftermath of Hurricane Katrina, naturally, individual oil companies evaluated their damage and the situation that lay before them. As Brady recalled, there were crisis management support teams and an emergency operations center already in place for ConocoPhillips, and presumably for any serious oil drilling company, and the initial main concerns were locating employees, making sure that personnel and facilities were secure, keeping oil spills in check and other environmental disasters from occurring, and supplying the proper support personnel to restore the oil rigs and platforms.

It was a messy process. Some facilities had remained open with skeleton crews; others were abandoned. The morning after, when industry trade magazines asked about their status, Chevron had to admit that they knew next to nothing, for instance, about the status of their main additive plant in New Orleans; ConocoPhillips, meanwhile, had no knowledge about a primary terminal that made Group III base oils for them.

It was not as if these oil companies were suddenly reduced to rubble – ConocoPhillips immediately pledged $3 million to relief efforts for the Gulf Coast – but all the money in the world could not change the fact that the telephones and power were not working in New Orleans, and that the entire region was suddenly a very mysterious and dangerous place.

Along with sending qualified and capable people into what looked like an apocalyptic environment, oil firms like ConocoPhillips had to make sure that their employees embarking on these adventures took along the proper communications, and once they arrived, would have proper lodging and provisions. Easier said than done; to get to their oil rigs, the oil companies needed fuel, something in short supply in the chaos that followed Hurricane Katrina.

RECOMMENDATIONS

Brady recommends that any company with a complex and diverse infrastructure should be thinking about several issues in security:

- Understand how your company can help the community in a disaster.
- Conversely, plan ahead and know what public sector resources will be available to help facilitate your company's recovery.
- Establish secure places where you can store supplies.
- Plan for a place to be your center for logistics security.
- Have a plan to locate and account for all of your employees.
- Have a plan in place to rescue stranded company employees and family.
- Know where you are going to house the people you rescue.

But just as important as understanding the issues is having the allies to back your company up, and when one looks at the organizations that Brady was working with for ConocoPhillips, one begins to understand what an awesome responsibility and task this is. Brady had liaisons with FEMA, the Department of Homeland Security, the Department of Energy, the Corps of Engineers, the US Coast Guard, the US Maritime Administration, the Louisiana State EOC, the Louisiana State Police, the Louisiana National Guard, right down to the local government, with contacts at the Plaquemines Parish Sheriff's Department and the Plaquemines Parish EOC.

Having those alliances are important, but in a disaster such as Hurricane Katrina, one quickly realizes the limitations of relationships if you cannot reach them. The telephones were obviously out, and even radio communications were unavailable. Anyone who had satellite phones in the days after Katrina felt as if they were touching the face of God. 'They were critical', said Brady of the satellite phones. And so too were fuel for generators and vehicles, emergency supplies for employees, and food, water, shelter, sanitary facilities and safety.

Oil refineries needed to be secured against looters and ransackers.

Brady said that ConocoPhillips had had a disaster plan in place for a long time, but that if anyone learned anything, it was that just because you have a plan, it doesn't mean the other guy does. The state government, as everyone knows now, did not have proper land routes at first, which could bring in supplies of water, food, sanitation, environmental remediation and other materials to various sites through the Gulf Coast region. The land route convoy system simply developed 'on the fly', as everyone from local authorities to the National Guard attempted to minimize poaching of agency materials, extensive looting and general lawlessness.

Not that nothing went right. Brady recalled that employees established beachheads at various facilities, and those who had skeleton crews remaining behind, their on-site accommodations had been relatively self-sufficient, with ample water for sustenance, sewage working properly and enough satellite phones to go around. People may have not been comfortable, but their needs were generally being met. Their incident command structure served the response needs despite the scale of event, most of the plant personnel were accounted for in a timely manner and, something that everyone is proud of at ConocoPhillips, the company was even able to rescue some of its staff at their homes, using the company's resources.

But more should be done, in preparation for the next major weather disaster, whenever that is. Company satellite phones are great, and more should be purchased, but a longer-term solution would be to begin implementing cell towers for refineries, and instead of relying on tankers to lead convoys to sites, refineries should be retrofitted to fuel tankers on the spot. Infrastructure needs to be improved, and employees with experience in everything from communications to flying helicopters and operating generators – their experience should be exploited more. Synergies that can be utilized with the public sector should be identified, and wireless communication channels need to be strengthened.

CONCLUSION

In short, that the oil industry was not wiped off the map is arguably because of all the thought that preceded Hurricane Katrina. But with extreme weather on the rise, according to numerous predictions from scientists, more planning and pondering is not just a smart idea for all industries; it may be life saving.

Conclusions

The National Strategy for Homeland Security, published months after 9/11, addressed only terrorism as a concern – natural disasters were not even mentioned. But after the consequences of Hurricane Katrina, the Secretary of Homeland Security began to speak of securing our homeland in a broader scope. And by 2007, mention of natural disasters, from storms to earthquakes to bird flu, had become the first concern mentioned in his speeches. Such events figured in the '15 National Planning Scenarios' used to shape plans and capabilities at the federal level. Indeed, response to natural disaster became the most popular form of homeland security exercise at state and local levels. Concern over terrorism remained the driver for many federal grants to big cities. But when it comes to state and local leaders spending their own money, response to natural disasters has become their top focus.

The language used to discuss homeland security at the federal level has changed as well. Shortly after 9/11, security activities (and funding) were built around four terms: Prevention, Protection, Response and Recovery. But this placed heavy emphasis on two areas not traditionally addressed by emergency responders and emergency managers who had grown up focused on the power of nature. Prevention of natural disasters is all but impossible. (How do you prevent a hurricane?) And Protection focused on critical infrastructure unrelated to the traditional emphasis on saving lives.

Before emergency-management experts came under the homeland security umbrella, their idea of Prevention and Protection was accomplished by Mitigation – changes to the built (or man-made) environment before an event took place. But Mitigation barely appeared in the lexicon of the most senior homeland security leaders (and funders) until years after 9/11. And the use of these five terms as the framework for conceptualizing homeland security organization and activity remains a great example of the uneasy marriage between security experts and emergency managers today.

This underlying confusion of terms, demands and guidelines is translated into the advice most often repeated by government leaders to business: Be Prepared.

But prepared for what exactly? Prepared for the low-probability, high-consequence attacks of terrorists armed with nuclear, chemical, biological or cyber weapons? Certainly, the information revolution is giving disaffected individuals and small groups access to big weapons never before possessed by non-governmental actors. But what exactly are the implications for business? Can they no longer depend upon government for the 'common defense' of their people and assets? Must they turn to their own resources to plan for business continuity to an extent never before experienced by private industry? If so, how much is enough? How can responsible business leaders avoid the trap of paying for free riders? How can they watch irresponsible competitors 'run naked' without taking protective measures for their businesses? Especially when irresponsible competitors are rewarded by cost savings and even increased market share. The government encourages this moral hazard when they make everyone whole after disasters, by failing to discriminate between businesses who invested in preparedness and those who ignored the possible consequences of disaster.

Or should business 'be prepared' for the high-probability, low-consequence attacks mounted by criminal outsiders, untrustworthy insiders and the occasional natural disaster. The truth is that more businesses (and more citizens) have been affected by these dangers in the past, than by the machinations of the occasional terrorist, foreign or domestic.

Of even greater concern is the possibility that this entire intellectual construct is at odds with business reality. Perhaps the high probability of some challenges, like cyber attack, make for high consequence, just because the loss is going to be repeated over and over again. Perhaps the low probability of other challenges is so low as to make preparedness (or mitigation, or prevention, or protection) unwise expenditure. Big cities and ports may be legitimate targets for a nuclear attack by terrorists. But the probability of such attack in smaller cities in the heartland approaches zero – raising the question of whether money spent on preparedness for these events is well invested after all.

The upshot of such thinking – and of the concerns and experiences related in this book – is that perhaps the entire framework for thinking about the challenges of homeland security to businesses, based as it is on experience, is simply mismatched with the new challenges of business continuity and homeland security in the information age. The simple truth is that much of the language and thinking of homeland security is drawn from national security, with its emphasis on defense and deterrence. National security is by definition concerned with preservation or restoration of the status quo. And any business that pursues this goal in the rapidly changing information age has lost the race before it has begun.

Business is not about the stability of political structure. It is about meeting the needs of life. And increasingly in modern life, this demands change. Successful businesses today are focused on meeting the changing needs of customers. This requires change and adaptation of the core business – and the business mentality.

Everyone understands and agrees with this in theory. But applying this strategic truism is very, very hard. The suggestion that people fear change is a cliché, and wrong. What people fear is the loss of control and failure, and for good reason. Successful business leaders in the past lived by the first rule of mountain climbing: 'don't let go of one handhold until you have a firm grip on the next'.

This is good, reassuring advice. But the information age is moving too fast for this. The goal of business must forever be progress and creating wealth – not seeking the comforting warmth of false security. Success in modern business is about riding the wave at exactly the right spot – neither so far back as to be left behind, nor so far forward as to be crushed in the unexpected collapse of a powerful momentum. Successful adaptation to the dangers and opportunities of homeland security will require exactly this sort of adventurous, entrepreneurial thinking. Not paralyzed by fear. Not beggared by unnecessary layers of protection. Not encumbered by expectations of the past. But prepared in both depth and adaptability if the worst happens.

Homeland security for business is not about protection, but about readiness for change – continuous change that supports the fundamental business goal of profitable return on investment. But the right change – correctly conceptualized and executed – is what some have called the 'Goldilocks Change': not so fast that it exposes the company to excessive costs. Not too slow, which can cost even more for those unprepared for catastrophe. The challenge is finding the right level of preparedness.

These truths are reinforced by the chapters on disaster and forward-thinking provided by the business leaders who authored contributions to this book. They sketch the enormous gap in thinking between government security experts and disaster managers, and the business leaders whose eyes must remain fixed on the promise of the future, and not just the dangers of the moment.

Getting this change right requires five qualities:

● Awareness and understanding of the direction and degree of change.
● Imagination – to craft solutions.
● Intellectual agility to implement them.
● Judgment – that provides balance and timing.
● And Resolve – born of understanding the challenges outlined in this book and the opportunities open to those who can navigate this new world.

These five qualities are not unique to meeting the challenges of homeland security, but they provide a pretty good summary of what business leaders need to do. Here then is the sum of the matter: homeland security may be expressed in new terms, but it is not an unfathomable swirl of danger before which the business community must lie prostrate awaiting government guidance and salvation. Instead, it is simply the current generation's test of business leadership.

Good leaders will survive this challenge and prosper. Others will not. Learning the lessons of this book will determine which camp you fall into – and the future of your business.

Appendix to chapter 9: caveats and conclusions

In April 2009, a unique influenza virus invoked a course of disease that spread from Mexico to the United States, thereafter swiftly advancing across the globe. On 11 June, the World Health Organization declared the novel A/H1N1 the first pandemic of the twenty-first century and raised its alert to Level 6.[1] By the end of the summer, it was projected that there would be a 3–5 percent negative impact on the global GDP, especially affecting the tourism, hospitality and retail sectors.[2]

This was not the pandemic for which the world had been waiting or preparing for. Unlike the much-anticipated H5N1 'bird flu', the H1N1 'swine flu' was characterized by effective person-to-person transmission (H5N1 has thus far remained avian-to-human spread),[3] disproportionately affected young children and pregnant women,[4] and only resulted in a case fatality rate between 0.3–1.8 percent (unlike the case fatality rate for H5N1 which stands at 59 percent).[5]

Irrespective of origin or alphanumeric code, the threat to 'business as usual' was soon recognized. Both large and small businesses took rapid steps to protect their workforce and assure continuity of operations, gleaning information from testimony[6] and sector- and industry-wide guidance documents and fact sheets generated by government and non-government agencies.[7] Newly hung posters reminded workers to cough into their sleeve, and desk-top and wall-mounted antiseptic hand-wash devices were installed in conference rooms and hallways.[8]

The potential disruption to business was ominous. The Harvard School of Public Health found that only one-third of the national businesses surveyed felt they could sustain their operations if impacted by a 50 percent workforce loss for two weeks. Fearing the possibility of grave economic loss, human resource directors engaged strategies allowing sick workers to telecommute to avoid infecting the well workforce and to help sustain business operations. Affecting small businesses more than large operations, the spectrum of policies under scrutiny included providing paid leave for family care, lifting the necessity for illness validation through physician 'sick slips', and extending the allowable duration of sick leave.[9] Overtime for workers picking up the slack, the potential for missed contract deadlines and the need to preferentially target leave policies for some workers over others (for example , pregnant woman) presented additional legal, financial and operational challenges for business owners and personnel directors.[10]

The US government and its pharmaceutical industry partners raced to develop and test candidate vaccines. By October, supplies of vaccine in weekly incremental loads were carefully allotted across the nation following the Advisory Committee on Immunization Practices (ACIP) guidelines' priority groups: children and young adults; household contacts of children; pregnant women; healthcare personnel and emergency medical services personnel; and adults with certain medication conditions.[11] Recognizing both the importance of business continuity to the US economy and the benefit of harnessing worksite locations to maximize vaccine coverage to targeted and at risk populations, vaccine doses were strategically released by governmental public health agencies to the private sector. Although some news articles alleged instances of corporate vaccine misuse by non-adherence to priority-group guidelines – subsequently invoking congressional ire[12,13] – the hue and cry diminished as vaccine supply quickly caught up with demand by mid-December.

In retrospect, the H1N1 pandemic provided the business community with an unparalled opportunity to test the resiliency of their workforce and the agility of their operations. Lessons learned from the 2009 H1N1 pandemic should be captured, studied and exploited to promulgate future practices and policies that will assure the business community's ability to remain competitive within their industry, and the United States' ability to remain competitive in the world. All possible steps to embrace new technologies, strategies and incentives should be applied proactively to prepare for atypical, unannounced, disruptive and potentially long-duration events as a result of potentially near-term and plausibly diverse spectra of natural disasters, disease outbreaks and deliberate acts of terrorism.

NOTES

1. 'World now at the start of 2009 influenza pandemic', Statement to the press by WHO director Dr Margaret Chan, 11 June 2009, http://www.who.int/mediacentre/news/statements/2009/h1n1_pandemic_phase6_20090611/en/index.ht.
2. Lobo, Lucius, 'Managing the business impact of H1N1', 31 August 2009, http://networkcomputing.in/PageContent.aspx?pageId=news-031aug009-managing-the-bu..........
3. Current WHO phase of pandemic alert, currently available at: http://www.who.int/csr/disease/avian_influenza/phase/en/index.html.
4. Centers for Disease Control and Prevention, H1N1 Flu (Swine Flu): Resources for Pregnant Women, http://www.cdc.gov/h1n1flu/pregnancy/.
5. Flu.gov, H5N1 (Bird Flu), http://www.flu.gov/individualfamily/about/h5n1/index.html#affected.
6. Schuchat, Anne, MD, 'Preparing small businesses for the challenges of 2009-H1N1 influenza', testimony before the Committee on Small Business, United State House of Representatives, 9 September 2009.
7. See as examples; Helbush, Alan, 'Where to start: prepare your business for the "H1N1" flu', 26 October 2009, http://www.wtsci.com/2009/10/prepare-your-business-for-the%E2%80%9Ch1n1%E2%80...; Business Wire, 'Aetna Supports physicians, pharmacists, members in H1N1 flu response', http://www.businesswire.com/portal/site/home/permalink/?ndmViewId=news_view&news......; Centers for Disease Control and Prevention, 'Preparing for the flu (Including 2009 H1N1 Flu): a communication tookit for businesses and employers'.
8. Flu.gov., 'Guidance for businesses and employers to plan and respond to the 2009–2010 influenza season', http://www.flu.gov/professional/business/guidance.html.
9. Harvard School of Public Health, 'Four-fifths of businesses foresee severe problems maintaining operations if significant H1N1 flu outbreak', Press Release 9 September 2009, http://www.hsph.harvard.edu/news/press-releases/2009-releases/businesses-problems-main...... See also full report, Blendon, Robert J., Gillian K. SteelFisher, John M. Benson, Kathleen J. Weldon, Melissa J. Herrmann, 'Business preparedness: novel influenza A (H1N1)', Harvard Opinion Research Program, Harvard School of Public Health, 16 July–12 August 2009.
10. Pinckney, Barbara, 'Businesses develop worst-case plans to prepare for H1N1 threat'. *The Business Review*, 20 October 2009, http://albany.bizjournals.com/albany/stories/2009/11/02/story2.html?t=printable.
11. 'Use of influenza A(H1N1) 2009 monovalent vaccine: recommendations of the Advisory Committee on Immunization Practices (ACIP)', 2009, MMWR, 28 August, 2009/58(RR10); 1–8.
12. Young, Alison, 'Corporate employers got scarce flu vaccine', *USA Today*, 8 December 2009.
13. Deprez, Esme E., 'New York businesses get H1N1 vaccine', *Business Week*, 2 November 2009

Index